RASTAFARI

RASTAFARI

For the Healing of the Nations

by DENNIS FORSYTHE

ONE DROP BOOKS
New York

First published in Jamaica by Zaika Publications, copyright © 1983

Copyright © 1999 One Drop Books

All rights reserved. No part of this book may be reproduced or utilized in any form or by any means, electronic or mechanical, including photocopying, recording, or by any information storage or retrieval system, without permission in writing from the Publisher. Inquiries should be addressed to One Drop Books, Post Office Box 20392, New York, New York 10017-0004 or www.onedropbooks.com.

Printed in the United States of America

First U.S. Edition

2nd Printing

3 4 5 6 7 8 9 10

Book design by Interrobang Design Studio

CONTENTS

ACKNOWLEDGMENTS   vii

NEW INTRODUCTION BY THE AUTHOR   ix

CHAPTER ONE: *The Mystery of Rastafari*   1

CHAPTER TWO: *Rastafari—Ancient Mystic Foundations*   11

CHAPTER THREE: *The Jamaican Rebirth of Jah Rastafari*   45

CHAPTER FOUR: *Major Rastafarian Concepts*   91

CHAPTER FIVE: *The Great Ganja Controversy*   131

CHAPTER SIX: *On the Ganja Trail: Enter My Story*   151

CHAPTER SEVEN: *Rastas and the Chakras*   191

CHAPTER EIGHT: *West Indian Culture Through Rasta Eyes*   223

ACKNOWLEDGMENTS

Beautiful things are
Happening in my Mind
Their beauty will reveal
Itself in its own time.
Will you believe it?
I know my own Mind.
Move, if you feel yours
In your own time.

Life is a journey along the road of consciousness. In my journey I give thanks to the guidance, help and inspiration received from many individuals scattered far and wide. There is Dr. Ralph Gomes and Dr. Maurice St. Pierre from Guyana; Michael Hutchinson from Barbados; Barbara Makeda Lee and Nelton Forsythe from Jamaica; Pascal Pradier from France; Dolores Cheeks, Professor Donald Von Eschen, Leon Jacobs and Carol Segal from Montreal. Also from England, my Uncle "Soul" was also a "messenger". My daughter, Abena, was also a source of light in my unfolding consciousness and love. I give thanks to all the many individual souls who have crossed my path and taught me the deeper realities that I now know but were not able to know then. *One Heart, One Love, One Universal Spirit, One Creation.*

—DENNIS FORSYTHE
FEBRUARY 1983
KINGSTON, JAMAICA

INTRODUCTION

This book, *Rastafari: For the Healing of the Nation*, was first published in 1983 in Jamaica and was made possible through the kind financial assistance of my brother Nelton Forsythe. It was conceived and written as my gift to Jamaica on its 21st year of "independence." It was a gift from my heart and intellect, as to the meaning and significance of Rastafari.

The 1970s and 1980s were veritable years of crisis, demoralization, and ideological confusions in Jamaica, which mirrored a general crisis in the world order. In these circumstances and in this island, the birthplace of Marcus Garvey, Robert Nesta Marley and the movement of Rastafari, the returning prodigal that I was discovered the Rastaman's vibrations within himself. I came to appreciate and understand the Rastaman's meaning of "Babylon" and saw its likeness to "Hell" in this reggae paradise of Jamaica. I saw and tested many of the Rastaman's ideas and found them to be based on sound universal truths. Particularly, their emphasis on *Revelations 22:2* was explored and highlighted in my book:

> And I John saw the New Jerusalem...and He showed me a river...On either side of the river was the tree of life...and the leaves of the tree were for the healing of the Nations.

Using the prism of my own African being as well as scientific techniques learned from my formal training as a sociologist, I delved into the mystery of Rastafari and unmasked it's simplicity, for those with eyes that can see, and for students who want to learn. Rastafari came to me in the form of an overpowering spirit or passion for truth which challenged some of the basic assumptions and beliefs of the majority. I experienced and showed Rastafari as a holistic movement that propelled me towards spiritual consciousness and healthy "livity." I even sketched the pathway which I followed up to the time of writing that book. Since then, I was forced by the dialectics of this consciousness to withdraw more and more into the framework of Rastafarian concepts and definitions as the surest way of coming to terms and dealing with the realities in which I was entangled. I was impelled into becoming more of the book, so that the words therein have truly become my flesh.

I discovered that Rastafari was a mystic religion resurrected here in the West carrying on and embodying in itself the great African spiritual tradition in the lineage of Osiris, Ra, Christ, and the ancient prophets. However, it is more than a religion; it is a counter-culture offering an opposing Africanist definition and vision of life, and is not to be confused with "dreadlocks," "reggae," or "dance hall" cultural expressions. It offers a philosophy and a critical social theory of the present local and world order which appear more relevant and persuasive to many than the then-prevailing but crumbling popular theories of Marxism or Liberalism.

In symbolic terms, the Rastafari movement counterpoised the "Lion" as alternative hero symbol to the traditional Anancy hero. This theory was explored and explained for the first time in this book through the inspiration and insights gained from the movement.

It has been most gratifying to see that some of the ideas that were first articulated in this book and in my columns in the *Daily Gleaner* newspaper during the period were readily adopted and applied by many of the leading local journalists. For instance, the concept of "Anancism" as a specific characteristic of our local culture readily found favor among these writers:

Mr. Morris Cargill wrote:
    If we are notably dedicated to Anancy Principles, we

shall fall into Anancy practices or fail to protest effectively against them. The PNP did not create Anancy. Anancy created the PNP and will create all our governments if we are not careful. (April 4, 1979)

Dawn Rich noted:
> It is no accident that the country's only genuinely accepted hero is Brer Anancy, the arch-type anti-hero. (October 25, 1979)

Evon Blake, before he died, noted:
> This pauper island in which we live. Some of us call it Jamaica. Others, thanks to Michael Manley, call it Hell. The older and wiser ones call it, more appropriately, Anancy Island. (November 11, 1980)

Aggrey Brown wrote of "Anancy Principle elevated to the level of political dogma." (November 5, 1979)

Gloria Escoffery wrote of "women falling for the traditional-Anansi wiles of the male." (April 25, 1981)

Oliver Jones, businessman, noted that:
> Confusion and Anancyism find fertile ground where principles are held aloft or bypassed depending on the situation or who or what is involved. (April 22, 1979)

Reverend Erne Gordon, leading churchman, noted that Anancyism is also in the church:

> Selfishness is sanctioned and sacralised to the point where a type of Anancy theology becomes endemic. (*Caribbean Contact*, June 1984)

A recent columnist in the Jamaica *Gleaner* and a university lecturer, Geoff Brown summarized and applied this theory recently in an article called "The Legacy of Anancyism" in which he stated:

> The silent hero of this nation is Anancy. Everyone knows it: few proclaim it. That is in itself the very nature of Anancyism. For Anancy must never manifest in its appearance what it is in fact carrying out in its behavior. The tricks of deception which lead the victim into self-dejecting traps constitute the essence of Anancy syndrome. (*Jamaica Weekly Gleaner* (N.A.), July 21-27, 1995)

The influence of Rastafari has evidently grown much over the years internationally, though it remains as elusive as ever today. I was fortunate to be in Jamaica in these crisis years. I was inspired to write the essays forming this book so that the larger society could benefit from this knowledge.

Though I have left the field of academia for a career in law as a practicing attorney, I still hold firm to the view that Rastafari provides one genuine African source from which the intellectual, cultural and emotional guidelines for an alternative and independent Third World prospective and model of development can grow and develop.

For giving me unprecedented scope for the venting of my ideas initially, I must express my thanks to Mr. Hector Wynter and the *Jamaica Daily Gleaner* newspaper. I also thank Steven Stempel of One Drop Books, New York, for having the courage and commitment to republish this book at this time, and to Michael Lorne of Headstart Books, Kingston, for having encouraged and envisioned this event. Lastly, a special thanks to Mildred Bohan of Denver, Colorado, whose feedback over the years was like the balm of Isis to me, for which I am eternally thankful.

—DENNIS FORSYTHE
OCTOBER 1995
KINGSTON, JAMAICA

RASTAFARI

Chapter 1
THE MYSTERY OF RASTAFARI

He who comes from Above is above everyone, while one who originates from the Earth belongs to the Earth and speaks from an earthly point.

(John 3:31)

...the gateway complex between cultures implies a new Catholic unpredictable threshold which places a far greater emphasis on the integrity of the individual imagination. And it is here that we see, beyond a shadow of doubt, the necessity for the uncommitted artist of conscience whose evolution out of the FOLK as poet, novelist, painter etc. is a symbol of inner integrity.

(Wilson Harris, *Caribbean Quarterly*, June 1970)

Rastafari such as Count Ossie, Douglas Mack and the more recent Coptic Brethren, as well as the articulate intellectual Rastafari such as Dennis Forsythe are proof that "locks" are not a criteria that imparts the ability to understand the deep concepts of this theology. Within the theology, Bob Marley, Peter Tosh and a host of lesser stars are the Psalmists for an ever increasing Black Christian awareness which includes all Garveyites and believers in black liberation.

(Makeda Lee, *Sunday Gleaner Magazine*, 1980)

WHOEVER FEELS IT KNOWS IT
...AND I FEEL IT, AND I KNOW IT.

The songs, chants, and experiences springing from that divine union of Robert and Rita Marley, more than anything else, mirrors the tempo and the pulse of the musically oriented cultural movement which the Marleys aptly named "The Movement of Jah People" and of which they are leading lights or guiding stars. They have felt it, they know it, and they have sung about it...of Jah Rastafari.

All universal truths must indeed manifest themselves in particular places and through particular individuals. They have to come down to earth, so to speak, and take on flesh. This book is about one such manifestation occurring in the Movement of Jah People, in the Marleys, in Rastafari, in "I and I." The evolution of the Rastaman (Congo-man, Bongo-man, Nyah-man) is one of the most significant of developments in the present and future history of Jamaica, the Caribbean and in the world as a whole. In fact, I see this most clearly, and this book is written to explain how I see this process taking place, as it occurs.

Robert Marley, who was the "Tuff Gong" or "King-man" in the proclaiming of "Jah Rastafari Selassie I" as God and King, died of cancer on May 11, 1981, at the age of 36. He left behind him a powerful message and a rising movement, as well as the rich example and experience of himself and of his own spiritual breakthrough, from which we can all draw energy, as he intended. From the bottomless pit of despair, from Trench Town ghetto, Bob and his family came in from the cold and like real giants elevated their music, message, country and God to the center stage of the Third World. He has become accordingly acknowledged by thousands all over the world as a musical messenger from a God that they saw fit to call by this "name, sounding wicked, strange and thunderous to the Heathen—JAH RASTAFARI," They simplified and transmitted the message and reality of JAH-GOD to the poor youths of today who would otherwise be without guidance and effective models with whom they can identify with and look up to.

At Bob Marley's funeral oration the Prime Minister of Jamaica, the Honorable Mr. Edward Seaga, was honest and perceptive enough in acknowledging that Bob was, by virtue of his monumental achievements, "no ordinary man." Those who were close to this kingman in the years that he rose up and matured in wisdom, knowledge and understanding admitted to the "Christ-like" heights and significance of the man, a *prophet* who was not really accepted in his own country, a revolutionary who was also a peacemaker, the little ax sharpened to cut down the big tree of Babylon. Thus commenting on Marley's level and quality of spiritual attainment, the illuminous Barbara Makeda Lee acknowledged:

> Bob attracted, not by a display of sexuality or sensuality, but by being a warrior for the cause of Justice and rights of the still poor children of slaves. This gave him an aura more powerful than that which is flesh-based, for it created perfect love between Bob and the person in tune with those divine vibrations…He lived,

sang and died to show us the truths of Garvey, Selassie and Christ in an African way, for all the peaceful black warriors of today, and for all mankind.

Bob's music, his lifestyle and his philosophy have greatly contributed to the increasing wave of interest not only in Jamaica ("Jahmaica") but also in his *vision* of Jah Rastafari, with its hinterland of spiritual music and love; it is in this larger universal context that Bob Marley is prophetically most significant.

In all spheres of Caribbean life today Rastafari has made its physical, cultural and spiritual presence evident. From an obscure "cult" surfacing in the 1930s, this movement now represents a bubbling, simmering force wherever large West Indian communities have emerged, as in North America and Britain. And in the Caribbean, the Movement has begun to foster a genuine fraternity where the Caribbean Federation, CARIFTA and CARICOM have failed. "Today throughout the Caribbean," writes Jabulani Tafari, "in the Spanish, French, English and Dutch-speaking islands, the spiritual, social and cultural common denominator, especially among an increasing number of youth, is Rastafari."

In the music field, it is Rastafarian "ridims" and sounds which now provide the ascendant vibrations for our era, and particularly for the young—at heart. Many of the best productions of Jamaica's National Dance Theatre Company also draw from this source.

On the more international plane, Rastafarians have taken upon themselves the role of spiritual leaders and cultural pace setters, as a light to the world. It is now being said that the general world interest in "psychic phenomena," health, dieting, physical culture, spiritualism, etc. shows the beginning of a powerful wave which will sweep humanity upwards to the peak of a new Renaissance of a kind the world has never known before. Rastafarians are leaders in this Spiritual World Revolution, often without people in Jamaica being aware of this fact. Can't you feel it? Can't you see it?

What is it? What is it about this Movement or about the atmosphere which causes some 100,000 Jamaicans and an increasingly large section of the world community to be attracted to it and to look on with amazed curiosity as the Movement unfolds?

I write this book to report on a personal discovery, that while Rasta has been called many names, I have discovered it to be a mystery phenomenon, and I now view Rastafari from this perspective. The overall experience which I have undergone since my acknowledgment, contact, study and identification with Rastafari is best defined as "Mystic Revelations." The whole experience should be regarded as a mystical journey and a modern manifestation of the ancient mystery religion tradition. This is how the Rastaman thinks of his experience—in mystical terms—and this has been reinforced by my personal experiences. There has to be a mystery element to the movement—some inner elusive "secrets" (some secret enjoyment, other than the overt mechanical act of smoking), known only to the Rastafarian insiders, which attract and magnetize them, giving them faith and confidence in their sufferation and apartness. It is clear to all by this stage that the Brethren have proven themselves and that they can no longer be abused, harassed and victimized as in earlier days.

One of the earliest Rastafarian groups representing the spiritual voice of the Movement, particularly in the era just preceding Bob Marley and the Wailers, was Count Ossie and the Mystic Revelations of Jah Rastafari, whose Groundations albums did much to uplift and push the Rasta spirit forward. In their name (Mystic Revelations) the spirit or meaning of Rastafari truly expresses itself. Bob Marley defined himself as a "natural Mystic blowing through the air," and Peter Tosh sung of himself in two beautiful albums as the African "Bush Doctor," and as the "Mystic Man," come to prescribe a cure for the ills of Babylon. Jimmy Cliff adds his soulful voice to the increasing chorus: "The Bongoman has come, he has come."

Rastafari follows in the footsteps of the ancient mystery tradition which climaxed some 2000 years ago in the birth and life of Christ. This mystery tradition was in fact a universal tradition among the ancients. The organized churches have taken out this heritage and have denied much of the mystical and transcendental dimension of the here and now. When Bob Marley sings of "wanting to reach the highest regions of Mount Zion High where I and I shall reign forever," he was questing after the same Highness (Oneness) and transcendence which Oriental mystics and philosophers have termed the "seventh level" of consciousness. At this level you see mystic things which others are blind to—through Rasta "Far Eye." When this "heights" is achieved here on earth, there is great mystic jubilation and the giving of prayerful thanks as in this ancient Egyptian hymn, written by an African before Christ:

> My impurity is driven away, and the sin which was in me is overcome...
> I go on my way to where I wash my head in the sea of the righteous.
> I arrive at this land of the glorified, and enter through the splendid portal.
> Thou, who standest before me, stretch out to me thy hands;
> It is I, I am become one of thee; Daily am I together with my Father Atum.

There is a basic sense of "triumph-through-sufferation" in the lyrics of Bob and Rita Marley. Such is what hymns and psalms were and are made of—thankfulness, humility, and strength, based upon certain fundamental realizations. Sometimes these realizations occur as sudden flashes of inspiration and insights. Sometimes as prolonged ecstatic states. The realizations come only after long sufferation, and invariably not all of us can find the hidden door. But when this door is unlocked and this level of consciousness is reached one can accept Truths from Right, Left or Center. One can at this level put things—including Marx and the Bible—within the overall scheme of things.

The special issue of *Caribbean Quarterly* Magazine published in December 1980, which was completely devoted to Rasta's 50th Anniversary, seems to accept this mystic interpretation of Rasta. In this issue, I. Jabulani Tafari stated the Rasta vision in no uncertain terms. First, he stated: "The Rastaman is the mystic man, the man of the past, living in the present and stepping into the future. The mystic Rastaman is the same 'Blackheart' man, who, after growing, gathering and learning has become the wise wonder of the whole wide world." Then Tafari followed this definition by stating the prophetic core of the Rastaman's vision, a vision in which Jamaica and Rastafari have some great historic-prophetic destiny in world history, a destiny which is rapidly unfolding in front of us today. Tafari was most explicit and clear in the expression of this theory or vision, which I now see, through my own intellectual understanding and self-growth. He declared:

> Africans in Jamaica and abroad as well as at home in Africa itself, need and are seeking another Prophet like Garvey, and they wonder if and where they can find another man like him today to stand up and fight for their rights. The good news I and I bear, glad tidings of great joy to the Black World in the Diaspora and on the Continent, is that another Biblical Prophet has indeed arisen from amongst the Rastafari brethren...a man like

unto the "Black Moses"—Marcus, and like unto the Hebrew Moses, who crossed the Red Sea. When he calls, obey him and when he beckons, trod on."

Just as it was 2000 years ago in the case of the mystic Christ, so it is repeated today. People are still perplexed about mysticism and about Rastafari. After 2000 years people still do not understand the meaning of Christian mysticism. It is hardly likely that they will find it easy to understand Rastafarian mysticism today. Society as a whole continues to confuse mysticism with madness, but these mental states are worlds apart, for the mystic knows from whence he comes and where he goes. The madman knows neither, nor does the person who cannot make the distinction between the two. The problem, of course, is not unique to us, for as one notable scholar wrote, "There are Christian mystics, and Christians who denounce mysticism as beginning in mist, centering in "I," and ending in schism."

In spite of the increasing growth of Rastafari, the Movement continues to be misunderstood, particularly here in Jamaica, in the land of its birth. People all over are uncertain about the "real" or the "true" meaning of Rastafari, particularly as there is a general tendency to identify Rastas only by outward symbols which are easily acquired or bought. In spite of all that has been written, spoken and sung about Rastas, reggae music and Bob Marley, people the world over are still asking: What does it mean to be a Rastafarian? What is the nature of the Rastafarian experience? What is the significance of Haile Selassie for the Movement? How can Haile Selassie be God? Even many of the self-designated Brethren themselves are often most confused as to who they are and where they are going and are helter-skelter in their conception of His Imperial Majesty, Selassie I. But they are searching.

While there is no shortage of published material about the movement, most of these accounts do not really take us to the pulsating heartland of the movement, to its inner core of meaning. Yet it is at this level of inner comprehension that Rastafari is meaningful. Most have not drawn from the experiences of the sincere Rastafarian Brethren who are too busy living to be interviewed and questioned by minds that would often not comprehend the visions that swell deep within. The more recent and penetrating works by Leonard Barrett, Joseph Owen and Barbara Makeda Lee have done much to correct the situation and to put the movement within the larger perspective of a world religion and within its own more meaningful framework.

The biographical (or individual) side of the Jah Rastafari story must now be used in testimony, as an important vehicle through which the spirit of the movement can make itself known to the world. The insider's account of Jah Rastafari has been told only in the form of song, dance, parables and symbols. But other methods must now be used. The biographical method used in this study is a necessary complement in the unfolding story of Rastafari. It is written as a response to those who are asking Rastas some serious questions, as they are curious or troubled about the Rasta phenomenon. People indeed are entitled to know, in plain enough terms, on what basis and by what "reasonings" and through what process one has to pass through in order to identify with Jah Rastafari. Who is or what is Jah Rastafari? What is the real significance of the various Rastafarian elements like their locks and chants and drumming? What is the deeper meaning and message of the movement other than what appears on the surface as excessive symbolism?

Instead of asking these profound questions to any so called Rastaman walking on the street, these questions must be directed to those Rastafarians who have reached the level where they can now tell their story. People who ask the above questions about Rastas need to hear my story. My words and my truths are all that I have to give, and I give them honestly, for the Healing of the Nation.

Chapter 2
RASTAFARI: ANCIENT MYSTIC FOUNDATIONS

Old pirates, yes they rob I
Sold I to the merchant ship
Minutes after they took I
from the bottomless pit.

But my hand was made strong
By the hand of the Almighty
We forward in this generation triumphantly...

Emancipate yourself from mental slavery
None but ourselves can free our minds
Have no fear for atomic energy
Cause none of them can stop the time
How long shall they kill our prophets
While we stand aside and look.

Won't you help me sing these songs of freedom
Cause all I ever had, were redemption songs.
(From Marley's "Redemption Song")

CHRIST AS MYSTIC

Notable Bible scholar, A. Spencer Lewis, sees mystery as a central undercurrent in the Christian tradition. He defined the word "mystery" (as used in the Bible) as referring to the secret revelations about the great truths which are revealed only to those few illumined wise men or prophets who have been initiated and purged to receive such inspired truths. The Bible and the authentic Christian tradition, according to this thesis, is firmly grounded in the "Mystery Tradition"— known also as the Gnostic or Coptic (Egyptian, African) Tradition.

Spencer Lewis argues that Christ possessed some rare secret, divine or spiritual knowledge that enabled him to perform miracles and to convey this secret knowledge and power to others.

Christ, for him, personified ancient wisdom in its totality and perfection. This stock of secret knowledge included the mysteries of life and death; the nature, cause and cure of diseases; the secret to love or hate; the spiritual and magical power of words and invocations; the secret of spiritual rebirth and of immortality; the raising of the dead; in short, the esoteric and transcendental knowledge pertaining to unlocking the Kingdom of God in man.

According to Lewis (based on evidence from the Bible itself), Christ was a divine Master who taught the multitudes (the "outer circle" or masses) in one manner, and an "inner circle" (estimated as 120, including the famed 12 disciples) whom he trained to undertake and perform the subtleties of his mystery, which, he said, came from the Father. This smaller inner circle included a number of women, a fact not stressed by the conventional Church. This inner circle was led step by step through the higher secret mysteries and teachings to a degree of development and unfoldment where they could carry on the work that Jesus had started and which he transmitted to his disciples.

The inner circle were the "lamb-men" (shepherds) who also had to be lion-like in order to guard themselves and their flocks from wild lions. The masses or multitude were not expected to master the higher mysteries; they were merely expected to recognize "truth," follow the light, have faith by following the teachings, example and rituals of Christ. This would, however, be enough to land them within the Kingdom. For this outer circle it is noteworthy that symbols were merely teaching aids used to arouse their sleepy consciousness, but for the initiates the symbols and parables took on deeper and more concrete meanings. They became one with their symbols. His famed disciples indeed became petite Christ—miniature replicas of the Lamb.

The conventional Bible itself, from my own independent readings, makes frequent references to its mystery foundations, leading one to agree that Christ was the father of mysticism.

When Christ was asked by his disciples why he spoke in parables, he said:

> "It is granted you to know the secrets of the Kingdom of heaven, but it is not granted them. I speak to them

in parables because they look and see nothing; they listen and neither hear nor understand... Many prophets and upright men have longed to see what you see and did not, and to hear what you are hearing and did not." (Matthew 10:13)

And in the Gospel of John, Christ spoke again to his disciples: "I no longer call you slaves, for a slave does not know what his master is doing, but I have called you friends because I have acquainted you with everything I heard from my Father." (John 15:15)

At many other points the Bible makes frequent references to its mystery connection. Examples running the full course of the Bible include:

"...It is given unto you to know the mysteries."
"Unto you it is given to know the mysteries..."
"...We speak the wisdom of God in a mystery..."
"We are the stewards of the mysteries of God, and understanding all the mysteries, and being of the fellowship of the mysteries, we make known the mysteries of the gospel and the mystery which has been hid from the ages..."

"Holding the mystery of faith in pureness..."
"And I saw a woman sit on a scarlet coloured beast, full of the names of blasphemy, and having seven heads and ten horns, and upon her forehead was a name written: *Mystery*. Babylon the Great. The Mother of the Harlots and abominance of the earth has fallen."

The Gnostic gospels also emphasize secrecy, solitude and mystery as much—and even more than—the orthodox texts. In *The Gospel According to Thomas*, Christ said: "I tell my mysteries to those who are worthy of my mysteries... What your right hand will do, let not your left hand know what it does."

Christ usually referred to himself in mystical terms. To Nicodemus, Christ likened himself to the mystical movements of the wind: "The wind bloweth where it listeth, and thou hearest the sound thereof, but canst not tell where it cometh and whither it goeth; so is everyone that is born of the spirit." Christ at one point reminded John of his secret (divine) knowledge: "Do not fear," he said to John, "I am the first and the last and the living one. I experienced death and behold I am alive forever and ever, and I possess the keys of death and of its realm. Therefore write what you have seen, both what is now and what will occur hereafter." And in the Book of Revelations, Christ described himself mystically as the one "who holds the seven stars in his right hand and walks among the seven golden lampstead," and as "he who has the seven spirits of God" (Revelations 13:1). Elsewhere Christ referred to himself as "God-son," and "the son of man," "the son of light," etc. And to his disciples he gave "the power to become the Sons of God." At his trial the Jews said against him: "We would not stone you for a good act, but blasphemy, because you, a human being, make yourself God," to which Jesus replied: "Is it not written in your law, 'I said you are gods?' If it calls them gods, to whom the word of God came... I am God's son... being sent from the Father, and being at one with the Father." (John 10:34-36)

Thus Christ was the supreme mystic. He was at once complete in God-head and complete in manhood, truly God and truly man, at one essence with his Father as regards his God-head, and at the same time at one essence with us mortals as regards his manhood. *He was the perfect bridge between God and man.* And he saw himself as such.

So it is apparent that the original teachings of Christ contained many genuine secrets of mysterious laws and principles more than were known to the pagans. *These secrets were suppressed by the early Roman Catholic Church fathers.* The early Roman Catholic Church used Latin as the exclusive and official language of the Western Church. It was inconceivable that the Bible could be read in any other tongue at the time. Thus from the 5th to the 15th centuries in the West the only translations of the Bible that were done were by a few spirited dissenters and free-spirited thinkers who were mercilessly persecuted when caught. The availability of the Bible in the popular tongue was regarded as inimical to the unity and authority of the Roman Catholic Church. John Wycliffe's text was the first in English (1320-84).

From the First General Council of Christendom at Nicaea in 325 A.D. to the last Council in Constantinople in 869 A.D., Christian principles, rules and teachings were subject to many deletions and changes. From that time onwards, all who possessed or were teachers of the secret wisdom of the mystery traditions were mercilessly persecuted and put to death. The Roman Spanish Inquisition chopped off the heads of those found guilty of this "heresy"—all in the name of Christ; and indeed it was, but more as the fulfillment of his prophecy of the "ten-horned monster" depicted in the Book of Revelations. Henceforth the secret knowledge became dispersed and exclusive, and eventually threatened with extinction. The occult sciences were studied in secret. They were guarded and kept alive over the years by such people as the Free Masons, the Rosicrusians, the Alchemists, the Troubadours, Knights of the Grail and the Round Table, and by many individual gurus scattered to the four corners of the earth.

THE GNOSTIC TEXTS DISCOVERED

In December 1945, some 52 sacred texts were discovered near Nag Hammadi in Upper Egypt, at the site of the earliest monastery in Christendom, after being literally buried in a jar for over 1600 years. These Gnostic Texts originate from the earliest centuries of the Christian era, and carried such titles as "The Apocryphon (Secret Book) of John," "The Gospel of Thomas," "The Gospel of Philip," "The Gospel of Truth," "The Gospel of the Egyptians," and "Thunder, Perfect Mind."

Apparently these buried texts were deemed "heretical" and "subversive" by the early Roman Catholic Church fathers. Bishop Irenaeus expressed this dislike in five volumes (c. 180) entitled "The Destruction and Overthrow of Falsely So-Called Knowledge." Possession of these books was made a criminal offense by these early totalitarian Church fathers, but in upper Egypt (Africa) a monk must have hidden these 52 banned books in the jar, where they remained buried until 1945.

Most of these texts claim to offer traditions about Jesus Christ that were secret and hidden even from the official Catholic Church.

These "heretical" or Gnostic Christians claimed to have had a differing interpretation of the meaning, message and significance of Jesus Christ. *The Gospel of Thomas* declares itself to be "the secret words which the living Jesus spoke and which the twin, Thomas, wrote down." He, along with the other Gnostic authors, claimed to have had insights into the mysterious and *secret knowledge ("Gnosis") which Christ exemplified and which centered on mastering the mystery of knowing the Self.*

According to the Gnostic teacher Theodotus (c. 140-160), a Gnostic is one who has come to understand "who we were, and what we have become; where we were… whither we are hastening; from what we are being released; what is birth, and what is rebirth." Another Gnostic teacher, Monoimus, entreated his listeners to "Abandon the search for God and the creation and other matters of a similar sort. Look for him by taking yourself as the starting point. Learn who it is within you who makes everything his own and says, 'My

God, by mind, my thought, my soul, my body.' Learn the sources of sorrow, joy, love, hate… If you carefully investigate these matters you will find Him in yourself." (Quoted by Elaine Pagels, *The Gnostic Gospels* p. XIX).

When analyzed, the central theme which runs throughout these suppressed texts is the resurfaced Rastafarian theme that *knowledge of self is an absolute prerequisite of knowing God and experiencing spiritual rebirth.*

In *The Gospel According to Thomas*, Christ said: "The Kingdom is within you and it is without you. If you know yourselves then you will be known, and you will know that you are the sons of the living Father. But if you do not know yourselves, then you are in poverty." Christ further stated to Thomas: "When you bring forth that which is within yourselves, that which you do not have within you, will kill you… Whoever finds himself, of him the world is not worthy… Whoever knows the ALL, but fails to know himself, lacks everything."

In the Thomas text Christ advocated a gentle form of natural yoga or "movement with repose," and he equated the ultimate state of repose (peace of mind) with images of light: "We have come from the light… He will manifest himself in the image of the light of the Father, and his image is concealed by his light… The man of light illumines the entire world… whoever is near to me is near the fire, and whoever is far from me is far from the Kingdom."

The Gnostic tradition thus had a much closer affinity to the central thrust of Christ, much more than the Roman Catholic Church fathers were willing to admit. For the texts in both traditions bear a striking similarity underneath. The Gnostic emphasis on self-knowledge as the first commandment finds support even in the "authorized" (King James) Bible. To the Pharisees, Christ said: "Even if I do testify concerning myself, my testimony is valid for I know from where I come and where I go" (John 8:31). "You will know the truth," he said, "and the truth will set you free" (John 8:31).

At another point Christ castigated the Pharisees in no uncertain terms: "Blind Pharisees, first clean the inside of the cup and plate so that its outside may be clean as well... For you resemble whitewashed tombs which appear beautiful on the outside, but inside they are full of dead men's bones and every impurity. So you seem to be men outwardly upright, but inside you are full of hypocrisy an lawlessness"
(Matthew 23:27).

The end result of knowing the self is the ultimate realization that man is divine, that "I am divine, therefore I am God." *Mystics search after direct union with God, to wrench from Him the secret of immortality, and many claimed to have achieved this spiritual power, with its associated gift of prophecy and power to heal and create miracles.* They craved for immediate apprehension of and communion with God, without any go-between. They acknowledge their inner experiences. Becoming at one with God meant that the mystic (or "Gnostic," or "heretic," or "pantheist," or "millenarian") is himself lifted up to divine adoration. But while the Catholic Church removed the "becoming-one-with-God" until the time after death, the mystics see this as taking place here and now, or at least starting here. Mystics feel themselves transformed, reunited, and even identical with God.

Norman Cohn in *The Pursuit of the Millennium* has described in detail one Gnostic "free spirit" movement which developed in thirteenth century Europe, particularly in France. The *Amaurians*, as one group in this movement, claimed that "each one of them was Christ and Holy Spirit and were convinced that what Christian theology regards as the unique miracle of the Incarnation was now being repeated in each one of them." In fact, they claimed to be the "first Spiritualists," those whom the great Spirit used for its fleshy incarnation in this life. Through them the Holy Spirit, it was believed, would speak to the world and under their guidance the world would enter the supreme epoch in which every man would be and know himself to be divine, so that the soul of each could escape from its sensual bonds and from its awareness of itself and sink motionless and unconscious into the *One*. Several of these free spirits were quoted in Cohn's book. One adept said:

> The spirit of Freedom or the Free Spirit is attained when one is wholly transformed into God. This union is so complete that neither the Virgin Mary nor the Angels are able to distinguish between God and Man. In it one is restored to one's original state, before one flowed out of the deity... One can be, according to one's wish, Father or Son or Holy Spirit.

Another stated:
> It is the same with me as with Christ in every way and without exception. Just like him I am eternal life and wisdom, born of the Father in my divine nature, just like him, too, I am born in time and after the way of human beings; and so I am one with him, God and Man... When his body is elevated at the altar during the sacrament, it is I who am lifted up; where his body is borne I am borne; for I am one flesh and blood with him, a single person who none can divide.

The Roman Catholic Church could not afford such bypassing of its authority. The saw themselves as the "official" representatives of Christ, the *Holy See*, infallible in their truths. So ecclesiastical disapproval of chiliasm or gnosticism became firm, and early in the fifth century St. Augustine propounded, in *The City of God*, the doctrine which became the accepted Church position. According to

St. Augustine, The Book of Revelation was to be understood only as a spiritual allegory, and the millennium accepted as having begun with the birth of Christianity and now fully realized in the Roman Catholic Church. Thus, in 431 AD., the Council of Ephesus condemned belief in the millennium as a superstitious addition to the faith. The Book of Revelation was thus officially devalued.

Thus one can almost feel the moral indignation of the 13th Roman Catholic Abbot of St. Victor, near Paris, as he raged against Amaurians:

> The supreme madness and the most impudent falsehood is that such men should not fear nor blush to say that they are God. Oh, what boundless folly, what abominable presumption that an adulterer, a male concubine, one weighted down with infamy, a vessel of iniquity, should be called God.

This Free Spirit Brotherhood did not hesitate to say: "God is all that is..." or "God is in every stone and in each limb of the human body as sure as in the Eucharist bread..." or "Every created thing is divine."

For the Amaurians, heaven and hell were merely states of the divine soul. To have the Holy Spirit incarnated in oneself and to receive the revelation which that brought was how they conceived of the resurrection to heaven. A man who had knowledge of the God within himself carried his own heaven about with him. One had only to recognize one's own divinity and one became resurrected as a spiritual, a denizen of heaven on earth. To be ignorant of one's divinity was for them the greatest moral sin.

On this quest for "becoming one with God," the noted psychoanalyst Carl Jung wrote:

> To bear a God within one's self signifies a great deal; it is a guarantee of happiness, of power, indeed even of omnipotence, as far as these attributes belong to the deity. To bear a God within one's self signifies just as much as to be God—one's self.
>
> (Dr. C.G. Jung, *The Psychology of the Unconscious*, p. 96)

THE MYSTERY TRADITION IN ANCIENT AFRICA

Our Western education has caused us to frown on the Mystery tradition and has created a great divide between us and it. Black nationalists, Marxists and others who seriously quest after Africa for their roots and for their culture (in the search of finding themselves) must sooner or later come to terms with the Mystery Tradition. They must come to terms with the works of Christ and with the other teachers of righteousness, as these prophets constitute the highest traditions of our past.

Neither Christ nor the prophetic tradition which has gone on for thousands of years can be easily pushed aside as mere mythical folk superstitions. On the contrary, *they are solid historical happenings. Christ lived(s) and our historical social sciences cannot ignore the historical meanings of this man-God reality.* They have bypassed this reality, teaching us instead that it was others—such as Plato, Aristotle, Marx, Einstein, or some other Western "scholar"—who has been the most "educated" man in history. But it was the man-God Christ who answered the fundamental questions of life in ways superior to those of all the other historical personages put together: they are all round and total answers to the fundamental questions of life and of society.

Christ is linked inseparably to African traditions. Many wise men and scholars traveled from all over the world to study under Egyptian priests, including Christ, Plato, Moses and Pythagoras. The caliber and fame of the official priesthood of Egypt was in fact legendary. The mystic or prophetic tradition was a basic feature of African culture, reaching great heights there long before the actual birth of Christ and the coming of the Hebrews. Africans believed in *living oracles* and the *gift of prophecy* long before the era of the Jewish prophets and the embodiment of this element in Christianity.

Other mystics in Africa, long before Christ, were known to have raised the dead, turned water into wine, and created many other kinds of miracles. It is even believed that Christ and John the Baptist were members of the Egyptian *Essene Sect*, whose similarity to Christianity has been recently revealed in the Dead Sea Scrolls. Christ was unique because he *perfected* this spiritual prophetic tradition to the point where he had a Divine University in his head. He undertook a divine mission which no other God-man had attempted before—*to save all of mankind*—by revealing to them the secrets or the way to immortality, of the all-important spirit in man. Christ's work also transferred the possibility of attainment of this Kingdom status from the few to the many, and he simplified the *great truths* for the use of all humanity. He introduced the ultimate act of attainment, the awakening of the love principle in the heart, to all mankind.

"In the beginning was the Word (Truth), and the Word was God and the Word was with God. And the Word became Man and lived for a time among us, and we viewed His glory." In no other place was this deep prophetic statement so much manifested in reality as in ancient Egypt and Ethiopia—the "Land of the Blacks," simultaneously called "Land of the Gods" or the "Land of the Spirits."

Egypt and Ethiopia were recognized from ancient times as the "Cradle of Civilization," particularly the high level of religious civilization which it attained.

The story of civilization coming down the Nile from the South—from the Land of the Blacks—has been heralded from as far back in the annals of Western history as the seventh century B.C., and these commentaries have been reprinted and amplified by many European historians even into the twentieth century. But the closer we get to the mid-ninteenth century, the more many of these writers were inclined to deny that these folks were Negroes or Black Africans. Lady Flora Shaw Lugard, a distinguished journalist and wife of the British High Commissioner and Commander-in-Chief of Northern Nigeria (1900-1906), noted, however:

> The fame of the Ethiopians was widespread in ancient history. Herodotus describes them as, "the tallest, the most beautiful and long-lived of the human race," and before Herodotus, Homer, in even more flattering language described them as "the most just of men; the favorites of the gods." The annals of all the great early nations of Asia Minor are full of them. The Mosaic records allude to them frequently; but, while they are described as the most powerful, the most just and most beautiful of the human race, they are constantly spoken of as black, and there seems to be no other conclusion to be drawn, than that at that remote period of history the leading race of the Western world was a black race.
> *(A Tropical Dependency)*

Also Count and Peer of France, Constantin F. Chasseboeuf—also known as Count Volney—made this comment after visiting Egypt between 1783 and 1785:

> ...once I had visited the Sphinx, its appearance gave me the key to the enigma. While looking at this distinctively Negro head in all of its traits, I remembered

that remarkable passage of Herodotus where he says: "Personally, I believe that the Colchians are an Egyptian colony because, like the latter, they are black-skinned and kinky-haired;" which means that the ancient Egyptians were Negroes in the true sense of the word, of the same kind as all the indigenous inhabitants of Africa...[and] to think that this race of black men, today our slaves and the object of our contempt, is the same one to whom we owe our arts, our sciences, and even the usage of speech...

(C.F. Volney, *Voyage to Egypt and Syria*)

And the Scottish Episcopalian prelate, the Right Reverend Michael Russell, Bishop of Glasgow and Galloway, penned:

There is no country in the world more interesting to the antiquarian and scholar than that which was known to the ancients as "Ethiopia above Egypt," the Nubia and Abyssinia of the present day. It was universally regarded by the poets and philosophers of Greece as the cradle of those arts, which at a later period covered the kingdom of the Pharaohs with so many wonderful monuments, and also of those religious rites which, after being slightly modified by the priests of Thebes, were adopted by the ancestors of Homer and Virgil as the basis of their mythology...

It is universally admitted that, if we except the ancient inhabitants of Egypt, there is no aboriginal people of Africa who have so many claims to our attention as the Ethiopians, a nation which from the remotest times to the present, have been regarded as one of the most celebrated...

> In the earliest traditions of nearly all the civilized tribes of the East, the name of this remarkable section of mankind is to be found, and when the faint glimmering of fable gives way to the clearer light of history the lustre of their character is still undiminished. They continue the object of curiosity and admiration and we discover that the most cautious and intelligent writers of Greece hesitated not to place them in the first ranks of knowledge and refinement. The praise bestowed upon them by Homer is familiar to the youngest reader. He describes them not only as the most distant of the human race, but also as the most righteous and best beloved of the gods... In the ILIAD...[it is written] "Ethiopia's blameless race."
> *(Nubia and Abyssinia* 1840)

Far from being opiate to stupefy the masses, religion was their spiritual food, reflecting the extent of their inner understanding, control and at peaceness with the world around them and in them. Ancient man was in communication with this visible world outside, but the felt world of unseen forces within himself was discovered from these early times to be intricately interwoven with the external. Their high level of spiritual attainment went hand in hand with their known technological wonders such as their pyramids, tombs, temples and the sphinx that were built to last forever, and involving a mode of knowledge and a level of understanding which is still a mystery to our modern Western "scientist."

This was made evident by Peter Tomkin's book, *Secrets of the Great Pyramid* (1971). This Harvard historian made the following revolutionary observations, based on many years of studying the Great Pyramid. It is quoted at length because of its importance:

Till recently there was no proof that the inhabitants of five thousand years ago were capable of the precise astronomical calculations and mathematical solutions required to locate, orient and build the pyramid where it stands.

It was also attributed to chance that the foundations were also perfectly oriented to true north, that its structure incorporated a value of pi (the constant by which the diameter of a circle may be multiplied to give its true circumference) accurate to several decimals and in several distinct and unmistakable ways; that its main chamber incorporated the "sacred"... triangles...which were to make Pythagoras famous, and which Plato ... claimed as the building blocks of the cosmos.

Chance was said to be responsible for the fact that the Pyramid's angles and slopes display an advanced understanding of trionometric values, that its shape quite precisely incorporates the fundamental proportions of the "Golden Section," known today by the Greek letter *phi*... and revered...by masters of...modern architecture.

According to modern academicians the first rough use of *pi* in Egypt was not till about 1700 B.C.—at least a millennium before the fifth century B.C.; and the development of trigonometry to Hipparchus in the second century before Christ. That is what the Egyptologists say, and that is what they put in their textbooks. Now the whole subject has had to be reviewed.

Recent studies of ancient Egyptian heiro-glyphics...have established that an advanced science did flourish in the Middle East at least three thousand years before Christ, and that Pythagoras, Eratosthenes, Hipparchus and other Greeks reputed to have originated mathematics on this planet merely picked up fragments of an ancient science evolved by remote and unknown predecessors.

The Great Pyramid, like most of the great temples of antiquity, was designed on the basis of a mermetic geometry known only to a restricted group of initiates, mere traces of which percolated to the Classical and Alexandrian Greeks.

These and other recent discoveries have made it possible to re-analyze the entire history of the Great Pyramid with a whole new set of references: the results are explosive. The common—and indeed authoritative—assumption that the Pyramid was just another tomb built to memorialize some vainglorious Pharaoh is proved to be false.

For a thousand years men from many occupations and many stations have labored to establish the true purpose of the Pyramid… the Pyramid has been shown to be an almanac by means of which the length of the year…could be measured as accurately as with a modern telescope. It has been shown to be a theodolite, or instrument for the surveyor, of great precision and simplicity, virtually indestructible. It is still a compass so finely oriented that modern compasses are adjusted to it, not vice versa.

It has also been established that the Great Pyramid is a carefully located geodetic marker, or fixed landmark, on which the geography of the ancient world was brilliantly constructed; that it served as a celestial observatory from which maps and tables of the stellar hemisphere could be accurately drawn; and that it incorporates it its slides and angles the means for creating a highly sophisticated map projection of the northern hemisphere. It is, in fact, a scale model of the hemisphere, correctly incorporating the geographical degrees of latitude and longitude.

The Pyramid may well be the repository of an ancient and possibly universal system of weights and measures, the model for the most sensible system of linear and temporal measurements available on earth, based on the polar axis of rotation, a system... now confirmed by the mensuration of orbiting satellites.

Whoever built the Great Pyramid, it is now quite clear, knew the circumference of the planet, and the length of the year to several decimals—data which were not rediscovered till the seventeenth century. Its architects may well have known the mean length of the earth's orbit round the sun, the specific density of the planet, the 26,000 year cycle of the equinoxes, the acceleration of gravity and the speed of light.

In certain aspects of knowledge the Egyptians surpassed most of the nations of ancient times. They were famous for their medical knowledge, for their skill in divination and the interpretation of dreams by which they could declare the will of God.

Imhotep of Third Dynasty Egypt has been dubbed the world's "first physician." His reputation as a healer and as a medical practitioner was so great that he was venerated throughout Egypt, and in time the ancient Greeks also deified him and identified him with the God of medicine, Aesculapius. To the Egyptians themselves, this builder of the oldest standing monument in the world (the Step Pyramid) was equated, because of his greatness, with the Sudanese deity, Thoth, God of the Moon, of Mathematics and of Learning. Under the guidance of Imhotep, Egyptian physicians, it has been said, performed brain surgery and treatment of cancer some 4,600 years ago. Crippled pilgrims from all over Europe visited his tomb near the famous medical school he founded.

Egyptians were the first to introduce the names of the twelve gods, and the Greeks later borrowed their names from them; they were the first to assign altars, images and temples to the gods (Herodotus). In almost every aspect of human life, Egypt made the earliest advance towards civilization and their wisdom became proverbial both in ancient and in modern times:

> The splendour of Egypt was not a mere mushroom growth lasting but a few hundred years. Where Greece and Rome can count their supremacy by the century Egypt counts hers by the millennium.

The well-known pioneer of Egyptian studies, Dr. Margaret Murray, in *The Splendour that was Egypt* (1963), had this to say of this earliest civilization:

> Egypt was the supreme power in the Mediterranean during the whole of the Bronze Age and a great part of the Iron Age; and as our present culture is directly due to the Mediterranean civilization during the Bronze Age it follows that it has its roots in Ancient Egypt. It is to Egypt that we owe our divisions of time; the 12 months and the 365 days of the year; the 12 hours of the day and 12 hours of the night are due to the work of the Egyptian astronomers. They

invented the earliest clocks and the earliest recorded events... Of the Seven Wonders, the Pyramids of Egypt alone remain almost intact... The temples of Egypt still stand as a witness to that firm belief in God which can be traced back to the most primitive inhabitants of the Nile Valley.

The religious texts from all periods of Ancient Egyptian history contain evidence that they were always occupied in trying to solve the mystery of creation with each clan or nome asserting their God was the creator of heaven and earth. In fact, *monotheism* (belief in a supreme God) first arose in Ancient Egypt and Christianity eventually incorporated a great deal of this tradition.

The belief in one supreme deity and the striking similarity between this early monotheism and Christianity can be seen clearly if we look at this early phenomenon in Africa. *Their highest gods were Ra, Amon, Osiris, Isis and Horus.*

Egyptians developed the first universal religion, centering around the worshipping of the majestic *Sun God, Ra,* whose vitality, energy concentration and nondiscriminatory nature has made it the first universal embodiment of God, a symbol that was real in its universal power. Egyptians were the first to worship the sun. The sun became the visible father of the world, and Africans were children of the sun, blessed with blackness by the Sun God himself and thus protected from his fiery rays. The sun was a natural healer. They saw in the sun all that a man may know of the Creator, the guarantor of justice and long life, health and vitality.

Ra was often represented in the Egyptian monuments seated and holding a cross (as symbol of the four quarters, or elements) attached to a circle. In one old text the qualities of Ra come out in this incantation to him:

> I am the God Autumn, I alone who was;
> I am the God Ra at his first splendour;
> I am the Great God self-created;
> God of Gods to who no other God compares;
> I was yesterday and now tomorrow.

Akhenaten has been dubbed "the first individual in history," as it was he who established monotheism by recanting his devotion to some 2,000 gods and elevating Aten, the Sun God, as Supreme God. He saw Aten, the "Radiating Sun Disk," as the source of life in the universe, dispenser of joy and light to the world. The national motto during his stewardship was: "He who lives on Truth ("Ma at")." This God-King Akhenaten promoted this lofty ideal in the conduct of his office as chief executive through religious emphasis and by public works that stressed this theme.

Thus centuries before the Old Testament prophets, the Egyptians developed monotheism along with a democratic concept of the hereafter—a vision of democracy not in the political sense, but in the assertion of the equality of all men before a supreme God. The possibility of glorious immortality was extended to all. With the notion of a triumphant afterlife, there came a shift of emphasis from rites to right living, from goods to good.

Contemporary precepts at the time advised: "Make thy memorial last through love of thee…" "More acceptable is the character of the upright of heart than the ox (sacrifice) of the evil doer…" "Do to the doer the cause that he do you." How similar are these to those in the Authorized Bible!

Around 2800 B.C. the worshipping of the Sun Ra was made official and thereafter kings took the title of "Son of Ra," believing themselves to be the incarnation of Ra. *The worshipping of Ra was the father idea of all other religions* (Ra has been called "Father of the

Gods") so that later on Ra was called other names like the great God Edfu, or his female equivalent—the Cat Moon Goddess, Bast—but the image of this one almighty God remained identical.

The high spiritual qualities attained by way of this earliest root religion is attested to in this prayer to Ra, taken from the Ptolemaic texts of Edfu, and which reveals also the *evocative* and man centered nature of our religion. The gods are invoked or called upon by "nommo" or word-magic, and in ecstatic states people become united with the gods, take these gods unto themselves, are ridden by them and, through proper invocations and drum-beat formulas, the gods are made the instruments of their will:

> Oh you prophets, great and pure priests, guardians of the secret, priests, pure in the Lord, all you who enter in the presence of the administrators of the land …stewards…turn your gaze towards this dwelling in which His Divine Majesty has placed you! When he sails to heaven, he looks here below and he is satisfied as long as you observe the law! Present yourself not in a state of sin! Enter not in a state of impurity! Speak no lies in his dwelling place!

> How happy is he who celebrates Thy Majesty, oh great God, and who never ceases to serve Thy temple! He who extols Thy power, who exalts Thy grandeur, who fills his heart with Thee… He who follows Thy path, comes to Thy watering-place, he who is concerned for Thy Majesty's designs! He who worships Thy spirit with the reverence due the gods, and who says Thy office…He who conducts the service regularly and the service of the holy days without error…

> You who tread the path of Ra in His temple; who watch over His dwelling place (occupied) to conduct His holy days, to present His offerings, without cease; enter in peace, leave in peace, go in happiness! For life is in His hand, peace is in His grasp, all good things are with Him; there is food for the one who remains at His table; there is nourishment for the one who eats of His offerings! There is no misfortune or evil for the one who lives on His benefits; there is no damnation for the one who serves Him; for His care reaches to heaven and His security to the earth; His protection is greater than that of all the gods. (Edfu V, transl. M. Alliot)

Amon was a local god whom Blacks of Thebaid worshipped from prehistoric times as supreme. Amon's power was like that of the wind, and his votaries called him *King of Kings* and thought of him as that mysterious and unknown power that brought about conception in men and animals.

An article of faith arose around Amon accounting for the divinity of the Egyptian rulers by relating how Amon consulted with twelve other deities to decide who should be the human mother of his child. The Pharaoh's wife was selected, and when Amon (later Amon-Ra) became the Supreme God of the entire State, Egyptian kings were considered earthly incarnations of God. Little by little all the attributes of the old gods of Egypt were ascribed to him, and the title and powers which Western nations give to their gods were given to the concept of the god Amon.

The holy family of native Egyptian theology comprised the gods *Osiris* and *Horus* (father and son), and the goddess *Isis*, the wife-mother—a "holy trinity" approximating the Father, Son and Holy Ghost of Christianity. The god Osiris comes down to us as having undoubted negroid features. Osiris and Isis were the grandchildren of Amon. They married, gave birth to Horus and together they ruled the world wisely and well. Osiris represented—in one aspect—an ancestor-god, spreading like Amon-Ra, first from being the central religious figure of a small community (in Meroe) until he was finally adopted all over Egypt as the ancestor-god par excellence of the whole nation.

The Egyptian *Book of the Dead*, discovered in the tomb of King Tutankhamon, reveals rituals of the Osiris religion existing during the First Dynasty (c. 3400 B.C.). These rituals aimed at preparing the "Ka" (ethereal double) of the King in real life. The God Osiris is shown as a God who could make man inherit "everlasting and eternal life" and who alone had the power to "cause men and women to be one again." He was shown as the one Supreme Being, the "great benificent King," "loving life and hating death." Under the ascendancy of this God-Osiris, people had the one supreme goal of perfecting their character in earthly life in preparation for his journey through the nether world or astral planes, and his gradual progress through the subtler planes to paradise or to the heaven world, helped on by the various workers and representatives of the spiritual hierarchy.

It was thus in this religion of Osiris that the idea of a future life took clearest definitions, long before the Hebrews entered history and Abraham was born. They gave Osiris the attributes of a nature akin to their own, although like other ancestors he was worshipped as a spirit-being, a spirit above the mortals but more sympathetic towards them and more approachable than the distant and eternally unknowable sun-god or wind-god or nature-gods.

The differing interpretations of the death of Osiris is most fascinating. In fact, there are two versions. The version less known claims that Isis was actually mother of the Sun God Ra, and that it was she who destroyed her Sun God by treachery: by fashioning a snake which was placed in Ra's path and which delivered a poisonous bite from which Ra never recovered and had to eventually retire on the back of the "heavenly cow" (a cow-headed goddess).

The more popular version of this legend shifts the blame for Osiris' death away from Mother (Isis) to Osiris' brother. For it is claimed in this other version that Osiris had a devil brother, Seth (Typhon), who, like Cain in the Authorized Bible, was exceedingly jealous of Osiris' position and stature and plotted to kill Osiris. Eventually he waylaid his brother, cut up his body into 13 pieces and hid these segments of flesh in various parts of Egypt. Isis, the loving wife of the dead king, was distraught, but through her determination and faith—and with the aid of dogs—located and collected the fragments of her husband's body, and by assembling them made it possible for him to be brought back to life. Osiris then became God of the Dead and Judge of Souls. Osiris, who had tried to lead a good life, had been overcome by the forces of evil—a circumstance of life which was so often the lot of mortal men—brought these folk to the conviction that they too might obtain the help, protection and support of such a Father-God. Not only the circumstances of Osiris' death, but also the miracle of his being born again, struck a responsive chord with the Egyptians, for as Osiris had suffered death only to be brought back from the dead—and then made Judge of Religious Souls in the Other World—so too, undoubtedly, might the average Egyptian look forward to a triumphant afterlife.

The way to this afterlife was expressed through the Egyptian word "Ma'at," which means a combination of order, justice and truth that holds the world together and enables man to hold himself together. Ma'at was a concept of harmony and ethical conduct. In the words of Egyptologist Henri Frankfort, "It allows a man to strive after every excellece until there is no fault in his nature—in harmony with the established order."

However, it is of significance that Osiris' resurrection was still not complete. For although Isis found a way of resurrecting Osiris, this resurrection was not finished. The phallus (sex organ) of Osiris had been eaten by the fishes, so that the power of procreation was still missing. This was in part a result of the curse placed upon the family by Helios (bush doctor) who had condemned the incestuous relationships in the family: between Osiris and his own sisters in their death stage. The incestuous tone of the story is reflected in Lord Kitchener's contemporary song about Caribbean family relations today called "Shame and Scandal in the Family." The effect of this curse by Helios was that Osiris' second son, Harpocrates, was born sick—feeble in the limbs at the feet, ugly, crippled, and impotent like the dismembered Osiris.

Thus, resurrection (including phallic resurrection) was the hope of all Egyptians, and they created a series of prayers to Osiris requesting a similar immortality. For instance, Pharaoh Thotmes III, the "Young Bull" (1504-1550 B.C.), delivered this invocation or prayer to Osiris:

> Homage to thee. Oh my divine Father
> Osiris thou hast thy being with thy members
> Thou did'st not rot away... I shall not decay
> I shall not rot. I shall have my being
> I shall live, I shall germinate, I shall wake
> up in peace. My body shall be established, and
> it shall neither fall into ruin nor be destroyed
> off this earth.

Until around the fourth century A.D., Osiris was recognized as God of Immortality all over Egypt, in the Greek islands, in Rome, and even in the forests of Germany. One account by Apulius, a priest, of the initiation of one named Lucius, into the cult of Isis in Rome, showed Lucius being purified by water, then fasting, then being given unspoken instructions, and at the innermost sanctuary he made a cosmic voyage and died to our world to be reborn, transformed. Lucius' testimony: "I approached the limits of the dead; I trod the threshhold of Proserpine and I was carried beyond all the elements; in the middle of the night I saw the sun shine with a brilliant light."

Osiris no doubt preceded Christ in the promising life after death, *but with the coming of Christ Osiris was dwarfed*. Egyptians began to renounce their own ancient religion, and became converts of Christ. When they were made to believe that Christ had the power to raise upon their bodies in a spiritual form, they felt that there was no need to have them mummified, and so the need for the "Book of the Dead" disappeared. *The attributes of Isis were transferred to the Virgin Mary, and those of Horus to the babe Jesus. Both promised resurrection, both had identical moral systems, and the personalities and legends do overlap, showing African origins, as Osiris and Isis were undoubtedly African.*

That this Egyptian mystery of Osiris and later of Christ was the same one universal mystical tradition embodied also in the Eastern religious traditions is attested to by certain common symbolic references shared by all these traditions. One common cue is the common usage of the mystical "number seven," e.g., seven days of the week, the seventh day is holy, the "seven seals" referred to in Revelations, the "seven spirits of God" which revealed themselves as "Seven Torches of Fire Before the Throne." In the Eastern esoteric tradition, number seven is used to reveal a certain significance, particularly their emphasis on the "seven Chakras" or the seven levels of consciousness.

Iusa or Horus (the Evercoming One) or the Egyptian Jesus was believed to be reborn every 2,000 years, or every time the earth passed into the next sign of the zodiac. During each of these 2,000 year periods, he was believed to embody the quality, lesson and type of the signs of the zodiac. Under the sign of Leo, Iusa or Horus was worshipped as a young lion, and it is likely that the famous Sphinx statue (lion-faced emperor) was raised in his honor. Later on, under Jewish influence, he was reborn as a lamb. And still later on, the early Christians worshipped him as Pisces (the fish), which was the sign of Christ, and which is still engraved upon the Pope's seal ring. Thus God (Christ), according to the moral of this folk cosmology, manifests himself in different forms at different times—lion, lamb, fish, or any other symbolic form.

A special note is required on the priestly caste of holy men found in Egypt at this classic period. Egyptian priests were recognized as a group of "superior men" functioning as official guardians of wisdom in the society. The renown of their wisdom crossed the seas, and numerous passages in Greek and Latin texts speak of the immense wisdom and technical knowledge of these African priests: they could heal the sick, and they knew the medicinal plants, the signs of the sacred animals, the history of the ancient kings, how to foretell the future, and reputedly how to make rain fall. Commenting on the activities and reputation of these priests, one scholar recently remarked that "They represented for the Egyptian people the same type of popular magician, hero of romances and fables, that have become part of our folklore."(Sauneron, *The Priests of Egypt* p. 64)

One early Greek traveler to the banks of the Nile commented thus about its priests:

> Through contemplation, they arrive at respect of the soul and at compassion; through reflection, at knowledge; and through the two, at the practice of the esoteric and dignified customs of former times. For to be always in contact with divine knowledge and inspiration excludes greed, represses the passions and

> stimulates the vitality of the intellect. They practice simplicity in living and in dress, temperance, austerity, justice and non-attachment. Their gait is measured, their gaze steady and modest without wandering to every side...Their laughter is rare and does not go beyond a smile...They say wine is harmful to the veins. (Forphyhus, *On Abstinence*, IV 6-8)

Most well-known among these early African mystics was *Petosiris*, who lived in "Free Egypt" just before the arrival of Alexander the Great around 350-330 B.C. One Egyptologist tells us that this priest was a great personage in his town, bearing such esteemed titles like "High Priest, seeing the Lord" and "Prophet himself of six primary Gods." At Petosiris' death he was buried in the desert of Hermopolis, with the inscription on his tombstone: "One whose soul resides with the Gods. Sage he is, reunited with the Sages." In 1919, Petosiris' tomb was rediscovered, along with a sort of "Collection of Maxims" intended for the living and extolling the favors and advantages found in this life and after death by those who "live in the fear of the Lord and walk in his path." They are quoted in full because they speak for themselves in their contemporary relevance, yet they were written before Christ and not by Him, but by others also in communion with the Father:

> He who walks in thy path, he will not falter: since I have been on earth and until this day, when I have come to the perfect regions, there has been found no fault in me...

> Oh you living...if you listen to my words, if you heed them, you will find their worth. It is good, the path of

the one who is faithful to the Lord; he is blessed whose heart turns toward his path. I will tell you what befell me, I will teach you the will of the Lord, I will make you enter into the knowledge of his spirit.

If I have come here to the city of eternity, it is because I have done good on earth and that my heart has rejoiced in the path of the Lord, from my infancy to this day. Every night the spirit of God was in my soul, and at dawn I did as he willed. I practiced justice, I detested evil. I had no dealing with those who ignored the spirit of the Lord... I did all this thinking that I would come to God after my death, and because I knew that the day would come when the Lord of Justice would make the final division, on the day of judgment...

Oh you living, I will have you know the will of the Lord. I will guide you to the path of life, the good path of those who obey God: happy is he whose heart leads him towards it. He whose heart is firm in the path of the Lord, secure in his existence on earth. He who has in his soul a great fear of the Lord, great is his happiness on earth.

It is useful to walk in the path of the Lord, great are the advantages reserved for him who follows it. He will raise a monument to himself on earth, he who follows in the path of the Lord. He who holds to the path of the Lord, he will pass all his life in joy, richer than all his peers. He grows old in his own city, he is a man respected in name, all his members are young as an infant's. His children are numerous and looked upon as first in the city; his sons succeed him from generation to generation... He comes finally to the city of the dead, joyfully, finely embalmed by Anubis, and the children of his children live on his place... You have walked in the path of your master Thoth; thus, after having received the favours he grants you on earth, he will please you with like favours after death.

(Quoted in Sauneron, *Priests of Egypt*, p 12)

Sometimes bordering on fantasy, these early reports of these ancient African priests took on legendary proportions. The spiritual author of the *Philosopseudes* recounts the adventures of Eucrates, his hero; with Pancrates, a priest and sorcerer in Memphis, Africa. Eucrates reported in story form on what he saw in the "land of spirits":

I was yet young, and I sojourned to Egypt where my father had sent me to complete my studies. One day I decided to go up the Nile to Coptos and to see the statue of Memnon and hear the marvelous things that it renders to the rising sun. I heard it then, not like ordinary mortals, emit an inarticulate sound; but Memnon himself opened his mouth and spoke an oracle in seven verses, which I would recite if it were not inappropriate.

In going back on the river it happened that there was among the passengers a citizen of Memphis, one of the sacred scribes, a man admirable for his knowledge and versed in every doctrine of the Egyptians. They even say that he spent twenty-three years in the subterranean sanctuaries where Isis taught him magic.

It is *Pancrates* of whom you speak, says Arignotos; he is my master, a holy man, clean shaven, dressed in linen, pensive, speaking Greek (but badly), large, flat-nosed, prominent lips, spindly legs…

It is the same man, Eucrates puts in, it's certainly Pancrates… At first, I was unaware who he was; but in seeing him every time the boat dropped anchor, perform miracle on miracle, in particular riding the crocodiles, and swimming with the sea monsters, who bend down before him and caress him with their tails. I recognized that here was a holy man; and little by little, by courteous attention, I became his comrade and we became so intimate that he revealed to me all his secrets. In the end, he invited me to leave my servants at Memphis and follow him alone, telling me that we would have no lack of people to serve us.

Since then, this is how we have been living.

When we arrived at the hostel, my man took the bolt from the door or the broomstick, or the pestle, covered it with clothing and pronouncing over it a magic formula, he made it walk, and everyone took it for a man; and the object went to fetch water, fixed our provisions, accommodated us, served us in everything with courtesy and ran our errands. Finally, when the magician no longer had need of his services, he made the broom a broom, or the pestle a pestle, by pronouncing over it another incantation. Eager as I was to learn his secret, I could not obtain it from him; he was jealous of it, although he put everything else entirely at my disposal. But one day, being in an obscure enough corner, I heard the incantation without his seeing me. It was a word of three syllables. He then went out, after having told the pestle what to do.

Chapter 3
THE JAMAICAN RE-BIRTH OF JAH RASTAFARI

"We have gradually won our way back into the confidence of the Creator, and He shall speak with the voice of Thunder, and shall shake the pillars of a corrupt and unjust world, and once more, restore Ethiopia to her ancient glory."

(Marcus Mosiah Garvey)

"We'll be forever loving Jah…
We found a way to cast away our fears
so old man River don't cry for me
I have got a running stream of love you see…
So no matter what stages or rages they put
    us through, we'll never be blue…
Only a fool lean upon his own misunderstanding
and what has been hidden from the wise and the
prudent shall reveal to the babe and the suckling.

(From Marley's "Forever Loving Jah")

PROPHECY

The pulsating grassroots movement presently identifiable with Jamaica, Reggae music, His Imperial Majesty Selassie I, Bob and Rita Marley, Peter Tosh, Jimmy Cliff, and ganja, surfaced mystically sometime during the 1930's among a segment of oppressed African folk living in Jamaica, precipitated by the crowning of Haile Selassie I as *His Imperial Majesty* and *Emperor of Ethiopia* in 1930. While the crowning of the Emperor became the catalyst of this movement, the deeper and more significant foundation for this movement was the Biblical African folk tradition which was firmly rooted in Jamaica amongst African folks there. Whether Jamaicans attend church or not, they are either religious, superstitious, spiritual, or all three. A good many believe in the Bible deeply and in its associated emphasis on prophecy.

In spite of all its errors of omission and commission, African folks in Jamaica on the whole believe in the Bible not only as a book of truth; they see it fundamentally as being very African in its nature and symbolism in spite of its distortions by our conquerors.

These early Rastafarian folk leaders in Jamaica held the view that the Bible is very much about Africa and very pertinent to present day Africans. Africa was variously called in those ancient times "Egypt," "Ethiopia," "Nubia," "Kush," "Meroe," or "Land of Punt." In fact, Genesis 10:6 and 1 Chron. 1:8 are often cited to show that "Punt" is derived from the name Phut, who was supposedly the youngest son of Ham, the reputed patriarch of the black races.

These Jamaican folk leaders noted that the Bible shows itself as being very African in spite of centuries of attempts to conceal this fact from the slave descendants of those ancient Bible people. For them Egypt was more than a place; it is a people. These early Rastafarians made conscious note of the fact that Ethiopia and its peoples were often spoken of by the ancient prophets in very glowing terms. The Prophet *Isaiah* specifically spoke of the "wealth of Egypt and the merchandise of Ethiopia, and the opulence of the Sabeans," and of her "men of stature" (Isa. 45:14). In another breath Isaiah described the reputation of Africa thus:

> Ah, the land of rustling of the winds which is beyond the rivers of Ethiopia, that sendeth ambassadors by the sea, even in vessels of Papyrus upon the waters, saying: "Go ye swift messengers, to a nation tall and smooth, to a people feared near and far, a nation mighty and conquering, a nation that meeteth out and treadeth down, whose land the rivers divide."   Isa. 18:1 & 2)

The Rastaman also points to the prophet *Jeremiah* who specifically noted the celebrated strength of the males of the Upper Nile, Africans:

> Prepare buckler and shield
> and advance for battle!
> Polish your spears, put on your coat of mail!
> Who is this rising like the Nile,
> like rivers whose waters surge?
> Advance, O horses, and rage, O Chariots!
> Let the Warriors go forth
> Men of Ethiopia and Put who handle the shield,
> Men of Lud, skilled in handling the bow
> That day is the day of the Lord God of Hosts
>   A day of vengeance, to avenge himself in his foe.
>   (Jerem. 46:3-10)

Many Biblical indications were used by the Rastaman to make the Christ story the watershed in African and world history. His reasoning goes like this: "Christ was educated in Egypt, as were Moses, Abraham and Joseph—long before the Hebrews were anything but roving nomads. Some of these prophets were born there. Abraham's second wife—Hagar, who mothered Ismael—was an African, as were Solomon, Jesse and King David; in the fourteenth century B.C. Moses took an Ethiopian wife, and Ethiopia became identified as the Son of Ham. The Acts of the Apostles tells how Philip baptised the Ethiopian official. Egypt was originally the Garden of Eden and it was Black, but over the millenia, through invasions, conquests, intermingling, and commerce with all peoples then known, Egypt was diluted down and became Coptic—a nation of Bronze."

The related Bible belief in the power of prophecy and the principle of reincarnation are part of the fundamentalist folk tradition held dearly by African peasants everywhere. In the African folk tradition existing in Jamaica, this power of clairvoyance is widely acknowledged and is locally referred to as *moving in the spirit, trumpping, sounding, traveling in the spirit, groaning in the spirit, laboring, talking in tongues*. In the Orient this process is referred to as *astral traveling;* in the West it is referred to as *telepathy*.

By *moving in the spirit* it was said that one slave on one plantation could communicate, through the spirit, with another of like mind on another plantation miles away. The Bible illustrates the nature and effects of this process:

> "And suddenly there came a Sound from heaven as of a rushing mighty wind, and it filled all the house where they were sitting. And there appeared unto them cloven tongues like of fire, and it sat upon each of them... And they were filled with the Holy Ghost and began to speak with other tongues, as the spirit gave them utterance." (Acts 2:2-4)

There is also the Bible case of Saul the persecutor who was struck down in a vision for three days, in which time the spirit gave him his new name, Paul, and instructed him to go to Titus. Titus, himself traveling in the spirit, knew Saul was coming to him. There are several other Bible illustrations of this phenomena.

Dreams and visions are still powerfully important to Africans in Jamaica. Some of this has to do with the strong belief in the spirits of our dead ancestors. Folks are quick to assert that "God works in a mysterious way in his wonders to perform." They will tell you that "the testimony of Christ is the spirit of prophecy," and that "God grants the spirit in unlimited measure."

Through divine communication it is believed, and it does appear, that certain exceptional men, inspired or infused by divine spirit, emerge from time to time in history with special insights (from the Creator or from some Force) and manifesting such powers as that of foretelling the future and creating other exceptional deeds. Abraham, Moses, Elijah, John the Baptist, and Christ were some of these earliest and biggest lights to mankind. Christ was the Super-Prophet. Others outside the Christian tradition include Buddha, Confucius, and Mohammed. In modern times Marcus Garvey, Elijah Mohammed, Malcolm X, Martin Luther King and Bob Marley have also been added, through and by similar processes which created the prophets of former times. These prophets have varied in character types, usually from "Lion" (King David), "Lamb" (Job, Christ), and "Anancy" ("False Prophet").

Among African peoples, faith in prophecy abounds and is often referred to by scholars as "African Fundamentalism" or as "African Spiritualism" or "Revivalism." Most African religious groups manifest this tendency, for instance, the "Mial People" (or "Angel Men") of Jamaica, who are said to be "four-eyed" because they can "see" spirits, and are said to dance with the spirits while in a trance and to cut "unknown tongues;" the spirits are also said to come into their drums at a particular point, making their drum hot. The Mial people foresee the world coming to an end, and for this reason they believe they were sent—to forewarn.

The *Crowning of Selassie I as "His Imperial Majesty and Emperor of Ethiopia"* was "staged" for diplomatic reasons, and the regal aura of African ascendancy and dignity was beamed across to the world, reaching down even into the hills and valleys of Jamaica where some African peasants gleaned Biblical and divine prophetic significance from this crowning.

In Ethiopia itself, the Emperor was officially accorded such prophetic titles as "Haile Selassie" (meaning, in Amharic, Power of the Trinity of Jesus Christ), "King of Kings," "Lord of Lords" and "Conquering Lion of the Tribe of Judah."

In Jamaica, a number of folk leaders saw this coronation of Haile Selassie as the fulfillment of Biblical prophecy, as foretold by John the Baptist and other prophets like Garvey, concerning the Messiah (Christ) that would come back to Africans and to mankind in order to redeem them. The smoking of "herbs," which became more popular at the time (during the 1930's), intensified their power of insight and the belief in themselves as being "the" Bible people and as individuals who recognize the higher spiritual dictate which says that "man cannot live by bread alone."

The early Rastafarians were thus simply African folks who felt moved to announce this mystical or prophetic discovery. They announced themselves as modern-day prophets who have deciphered the Biblical mystery of Revelations: they saw themselves as ancient Ethiopians intimately tied in with the secrets of Jah's New Creation or Second Coming. They are its manifestation, and His Imperial Majesty was the Messiah.

Particular verses in the Bible gave them this special insight and faith in themselves and in the Bible: "Out of Egypt I call my son" (Matt. 2:15); "I mention Egypt and Babylon as those who know me. Behold Philistia and Tyre, together with Ethiopia—they say, 'This one was born there'" (Psalm 87); "Princes shall come out of Egypt, Ethiopia shall soon stretch forth her hands unto God" (Psalm 68); "And I saw a strong angel proclaiming...Behold the Lion of the Tribe of Judah, the root of David, King of Kings" (Rev. 5:2).

Jamaican folk leaders like Leonard Howell, Joseph Hibbert, Archibald Dunkley, Paul Earlington, Vernal David, Ferdinand Ricketts, Mortimer Planno, Ras Sam Brown, Prince Edward Emmanuel and Claudius Henry assumed the role of minor prophets come to announce Haile Selassie of Ethiopia as the returned Christ and Africans as now holding the Covenant of Jah, as it was in the very beginning.

It is significant that *Joseph Hibbert* had been a Freemason, a member of the Ancient Order of Ethiopia, and was thus familiar with the ancient mystic tradition. Upon the coronation of Haile Selassie, he returned to Jamaica from Costa Rica and founded the Ethiopian Mystic Masons.

Archibald Dunkley opened a mission in Kingston in 1933 proclaiming Haile Selassie as Jah God, King of Kings and the Conquering Lion of the Tribe of Judah. One of his attractions was his possession of the Book of Macabees, a part of the Bible taken out of the King James version, which inspired the popular song, "Macabee Version" ("Bring back Macabee Version that God gave to black man").

Leonard Howell had fought in the Ashanti wars in 1896 in Ghana, but then went to the United States before returning to Jamaica where, in 1934, he founded the Ethiopian Salvation Society. Howell brought back with him from the United States a copy of an icon, which he said was a picture of the Black Christ. By then people had come to know what Selassie looked like. For many this icon was identical to Haile Selassie.

Howell (or "Gangunguru," as he was called) established an early community of Rastafarians at Pinnacle in the early 1940's and became noted for a number of reasons. Howell preached the radical doctrine of Selassie's divinity, cultivated ganja (or "gunja"), allowed his hair and those of his followers to grow on their heads like the hairy locks of the lion's mane, and encouraged polygamy, with Howell himself reputed to have 13 wives.

Eventually Howell was committed to a mental asylum when he started to identify himself with Christ. At his height he was cut down. He was much ahead of his time.

Rev. Claudius Henry, who has since become leader of one of the oldest Rastafarian communities on the island of Jamaica, was also central in the early preaching of His Imperial Majesty as the "King of Kings." In a sermon quoted by the sociologist Barry Chevannes, Rev. Henry describes here how European princes went to Addis Ababa in 1930 to pay homage to H.I.M. and how the event marked the return of the legendary Sceptre (symbol of power and grace) to Ethiopia. The Reverend informed us:

> It is said, or it was public in those days, that Edward (of England) who abdicated the throne went also with his gift for His Imperial Majesty. He was late (and made apology) and he gave to His Imperial Majesty a sceptre. This sceptre was taken from Ethiopia while Hezakiah was king over Israel. It was sent to Britain and it was not given back to them until the coronation of His Imperial Majesty. And when the sceptre was handed to him by Edward from his father, King George, it is said that he was the first to open it. But by then he was already

crowned King of Kings and Lord of Lords, and when the sceptre was handed to him and he opened it, it was said that it was written "King of Kings and Lord of Lords," and "Ethiopia shall stretch forth her hands unto God."

These early folk leaders bestowed on Selassie all the titles and attributes which the Book of Revelations and the ancient prophets attributed to the returning Christ: *Most High, Triumphant High, Jahovah, First Ancient King of Creation, King Alpha and Queen Omega, The-Beginning-Without-End, Protectorate of all Human's Internal, Ruler of the Universe, King of Kings, Lord of Lords, Conquering Lion, Light of the Most High, Prince of Peace, the True and Living God, Christus Negus, Hosannah.*

The 1968 statement by the Ethiopian Orthodox Church made the deification of His Imperial Majesty unequivocally clear. It declared:

> Every Rastafarian recognizes HIM—Haile Selassie I of Ethiopia to be the returned Messiah, the only mediator between God and man representing Christ... We base these beliefs on the interpretation of the scriptures, and can quote many passages in the Bible which endorse these beliefs and the concept of the Divinity of HIM. He is the 225th rebirth of Solomon... He is the Black Christ of this era.

Ordinarily *Ras* in Ethiopia meant a provincial prince, with land and wealth. Now, by identifying with the Emperor and by calling themselves by his name (Rastafarians), these early Jamaican Brethren—like those of today—not only proclaimed intentionally their union with their Ethiopian Emperor and King, and thus with

Christ. In turn, His Imperial Majesty, like Christ, gave the crown and the glory to the Father—Jah.

ETHIOPIANISM: THE IMPERIAL SELASSIE I TRADITION IN RASTA FOLKLORE AND IN ETHIOPIAN HISTORY

Why should events and the history of Ethiopia and the crowning of the Emperor be of such prophetic significance to African folks so many thousands of miles away in Jamaica and elsewhere? What aspects of the Emperor and of Ethiopian history brought about this mystical marriage between Haile Selassie and Jah people?

There are several important factors which go towards explaining the close emotional and spiritual bond between downtrodden Africans in the West and Haile Selassie.

Ethiopia was known as and was felt to constitute the heartland of ancient black pride, dignity and independence. Ethiopian civilization was the only one from the era of the Roman Empire that survived into modern times with unbroken political continuity, or with substantial resemblance to its classical state. Of all the countries in Africa, Ethiopia had a coherence that other African countries lacked.

Secondly, the Ethiopian Christian folk tradition pointed to Haile Selassie as descended from the lineage of King David, and this was even written officially into the first written Constitution of Ethiopia (1955): "The Imperial dignity shall remain perpetually attached to the time which descends without interruption from the Queen of Sheba and King Solomon of Jerusalem."

Haile Selassie was thus regarded as son of a dynasty that can be traced back to around the tenth century B.C. (when Queen Sheba visited King Solomon) with at least as much confidence as Elizabeth II's roots being able to be traced back to Edward the Confessor in the eleventh century A.D.

The *Kebra Negast* ("The Glory of Kings") is an Ethiopian epic dating from the thirteenth century, which school children in Ethiopia had to learn along with the ABC's of the Amharic alphabet. In this epic, the story is told of how the ancient and beautiful Queen of Sheba (Makeda) traveled to Jerusalem to meet with the great King Solomon, and begat him his first son, Ibn Hakim, whose "whole body and its members and bearing of his shoulders resembled those of King Solomon his father." Sheba, hitherto worshipper of the sun (Ra), was converted to monotheism by King Solomon. Abraham (father of the Jews) has taken an Ethiopian wife; now Sheba the Ethiopian queen had returned to take herself a Jewish husband—a pattern which persists to this day. King Solomon, Ethiopians maintain, then sent priests and wise men to advise his son in Ethiopia and sent also a replica of the Sacred Ark, and so established Judaism there.

From this Solomonic dynasty King Menelik I, King of Ethiopia, was born. There took place during the nineteenth century under Menelik the reassembling of the Solomonic attributes whose official title included: "The Conquering Lion of the Tribe of Judah" and "King of Kings."

Rastafarians take great pride in the fact of this great Solomonic lineage. However, the continuity of His Majesty's lineage is often questioned by many who have noted that Menelik I had no son. After his great victory against the Italians at Adowa, Menelik, it is said, passed on his title to his bravest soldier, Ras Makonnen, who became the father of Haile Selassie I. There is also another known "interruption" in the Solomonic dynasty when Zagwe, who made claims to have been descended from Moses, had earlier conquered the Inland plateau during the twelfth century, and this dynasty remained for 133 years until 1270, when the Solomonic line was resumed.

But to the Rastaman, these historical details or historical "unknowns" make no difference to the essence of his conception: "Ethiopia shall stretch forth her hands unto Jah."

A third plus for Ethiopia in the eyes of Rastafarians was the fact of its strong Christian tradition, which meant that many Ethiopians lived according to the dictates of the Old Testament. The first words of the National Anthem of Ethiopia were: "Oh Ethiopia, be happy, By God's power and your Emperor." Selassie himself stated:

> We in Ethiopia have one of the oldest versions of the Bible, but however old the version may be, in whatever language it might be written the Word remains one and the same. It transcends all boundaries of empires and all conception of race. It is eternal.
>
> No doubt you all remember reading in the Acts of the Apostles of how Philip baptised the Ethiopian official. He is the first Ethiopian on record to have followed Christ, and from that day onwards the Word of God has continued to grow in the hearts of Ethiopians. And I might say for myself that from early childhood I was taught to appreciate the Bible and my love for it increases with the passage of time. All through my troubles I have found it a cause of infinite comfort. "Come unto Me, all ye that labour and are heavey laden, and I will give you rest"—who can resist an invitation so full of compassion?
>
> Because of this personal experience in the goodness of the Bible, I was resolved that all my countrymen should also share its great blessing, and that by reading the Bible they should find Truth for themselves. Therefore…I caused a new translation to be made from our ancient language which the old and the young understood and spoke.

> Today man sees all his hopes and aspirations crumbling before him. He is perplexed and knows not whither he is drifting. But he must realize that the Bible is his refuge, and the rallying point for all humanity. In it man will find the solution of his present difficulties and guidance for his future action. Unless he accepts with clear conscience the Bible and its great Message, he cannot hope for salvation. For my part I glory in the Bible.

The aforementioned Kebra Negast reports also that the Ark of the Covenant (the Ten Commandment tablets) was transferred back to Ethiopia from Jerusalem by Solomon's first-born, where it is kept locked within seven caskets in Aksum. It was often displayed in public ceremonies during Selassie's reign. For Rastafarians, this presence of the Ark is symbolic of Jah's blessing being transferred from the Jews to the Ethiopians—and Ethiopians are everywhere.

Ethiopia was a Christian land from earliest times, but later, with the rise of Islam all around, Ethiopia was cut off for centuries from contact with the Christian civilization of Europe. A tenuous link was retained with the central church organization in Alexandria (Egypt) through an official called the Abuna. Even the ancient language of Ethiopia—Geez—was the original language of the Bible, and until recent times Geez was the language of the church and of literature in Ethiopia.

The isolated hilltops or ambas of the northern plateau region of Ethiopia were used often as monasteries.

The presence of some estimated 25,000 *Falashas* (or "Black Jews") in Ethiopia also testifies to Ethiopia's claim of being a Bible people. The title Falashas means strangers or immigrants, and it is believed that these Falashas are the remnants of Jewish prisoners taken by Ethiopian kings over 2,000 years ago. Large numbers were transported to Ethiopia. They regard themselves as one of the "ten lost tribes of Israel." They worship a God of life, righteousness and justice, and believe in a future of universal peace and happiness. They abhor all idol worship. They follow old testament traditions, particularly the Five Books of Moses. They held until recently the view that the Ethiopian Jews were the only remnant of their people in existence, and look forward to the day when a Messiah will come to take them back "home."

The walls of Aksum in Ethiopia were surrounded by figures of lions, made in stone. In that city there is a place called "The Path of Christ," and there is also an altar stone reputedly sent from Mount Zion by the apostles of Christ.

The official church of Ethiopia—the Ethiopian Orthodox Church—integrated itself within its own local culture.

It integrated the animism of the ancients with the belief in One Almighty; it encouraged music as part of its ritual while the Western church tended to censor music. They have also preserved many of the earlier books of the original Christian Church which were considered to be apocryphal by the Catholic Church, such as the Books of Enoch, Jubilees and Ecclesiastics, which have long been translated in Geez. Western Christians have thus tended to mock the Ethiopian Coptic faith largely because they despised its syncretisms and its coming to terms with the divergent elements of culture within Ethiopia.

Ethiopia also "stretched forth its hands to the world" and to Rastafarians by virtue of its *theocratic tradition*. This meant that a ruler was expected first to attain wisdom and spiritual maturity before he can be trusted with political power. Spiritual power was made a precondition for political power. Thus on the death of the former Empress, Selassie as Crown Prince and Regent issued a proclamation acknowledging this theocratic or Christ-like conception of rulership:

> Since it is the long standing custom that when a King, the shepherd of his people, shall die, a King replaces him, I being upon the seat of David to which I was bethroned, will, with God's charity, watch over you by the law and ordinance that has been handed down from my fathers.

Education in the school incorporated this theosophical striving.

Haile Selassie's *personal character* itself contributed to the deification of His Majesty. He had to be a natural prophet. Selassie's father, Ras Makonnen, was justly admired as the greatest military genius Abyssinia had ever known and was greatly respected on all sides for his high intelligence, his uprightness, justice, goodness, and for his spiritual character. Haile Selassie's character was often depicted in Christ-like terms: "His eyes are extraordinary. They stand out with a penetrating intensity which sometimes give the impression that they are living an extistence of their own and looking at them one can understand the feelings of those ministers who are said to tremble before him like a mouse before a cat."

Selassie combined in himself both lion and lamb. In fact, his tamed lions, which he sported at his side, were symbolic of this combination—of the lion turned into the lamb.

His tough military campaign against Mussolini's invasion of Ethiopia enhanced Selassie's image (particularly among New World blacks) as the "Lion of Judah" battling against Mussolini, who was pictured as the "Pig" or the "Great Beast" threatening modern civilization with fascism, and wanting to subjugate this one remaining ancient Christian country. Mussolini declared:

> Our [Italy's] future lies in the East and South, in Asia and Africa... Italy is a nation on the march.

Mussolini celebrated July 7, 1935 as the 2688th birthday of the city of Rome, and he called upon his countrymen to revive their classical warlike Roman skills against Ethiopia. Mussolini spoke of the rebirth of the Roman Empire and the Eagles of his legion became the reincarnated Eagles of Augustus. But he faced a polity and a people older than Rome's:

> Judah is a lion's whelp; from the prey, my son, thou art come up: he stooped down, he crouched as a lion, and as an old lion; who shall rouse him up?
>
> (Genesis 49:9)

Lion symbolism was particularly significant to the Emperor. He was himself born under the sign of Leo on July 23. "Ara," the lion, was the emblem of the tribe of David from which the Emperor descended. Solomon himself used lion emblems to decorate his house and temple. It was the official seal used by Selassie I and his predecessors throughout Ethiopian history. Sven Rubenson, in *The Survival of Ethiopian Independence*, reproduced 12 separate historical pictorial displays of these various lion seals, several of which show a lion holding a Christian cross or a flag of Ethiopia.

A huge lion statue (and the Star of David) guarded the palace of the Emperor, and the inside of his palace featured tame lions. When Selassie sailed on an official tour to Europe in 1924, he brought 6 lions with him as presents for the various heads of Europe. It was also a neat symbolic twist that at the time of their earlier friendship Mussolini had also presented Selassie with two lion cubs.

The lion-image of the Emperor developed during his early militant constitutional reforms and through his tough leadership of this Italian-Ethiopian War with Mussolini (1935-40), which left 275,000 Ethiopians killed and a further 78,000 killed during Mussolini's brief occupation. Bob Marley's *Survival* album in fact carries a picture of the Emperor himself firing a machine gun during the campaign. Garvey, however, an active contemporary, described the Emperor as a "cowardly lion" because of disagreements over his conduct of the war and administration of his country.

No doubt His Imperial Majesty was a man of war, but above all he was a man of peace. As an Ethiopian, the Emperor subscribed to the ancient view which may be simplified thus:

> Warfare was not meant to kill the enemy, but to overcome them with fear if possible, such as that induced by screaming war cries, loud noises and hideously masked faces. Where killing is unavoidable, it must be kept to a minimum. In defeat, some kind of retreat with honour was allowed. Such was the traditional concept of African warfare.

In 1936 Selassie was forced into exile, but proceeded with his battle in the League of Nations. His speech to that assembly was said to be "the most moving moment in the history of the dying League...as the Emperor called forth a new hatred and fear of Fascist aggression." When Selassie returned triumphant to Addis Ababa on May 5, 1941, he issued the famous *Great Mercy Proclamation* which shows the high lamb-like level of his statesmanship:

> Today is a day on which Ethiopia is stretching her hands to God in joy and thankfulness... Therefore let us rejoice with our hearts...in the spirit of Christ. Do not return evil for evil. Do not indulge in attrocities... Take care not to spoil the good name of Ethiopia by acts which are worthy of the enemy.

This strong but merciful posture of the Emperor is celebrated by Bob Marley's "War," which puts to song a speech made by Haile Selassie in California, February 28, 1968. There is much power in these words, and, through the voice of Marley, the Psalmist, they have become immortalized:

> What life has taught me I would like to share
> with those who want to learn...
>
> Until the philosophy which holds one race superior
> and another inferior is finally and permanently
> discredited and abandoned
>
> That until there are no longer first class and
> second class citizens of any nation
> Until the color of a man's skin is of no more
> significance than the color of his eyes
>
> That until these basic human rights are equally
> guaranteed to all, without regard to race
> That until that day, the dream of lasting peace,
> World citizenship and the rule of international
> morality will remain but a fleeting illusion to
> be pursued, but never attained
>
> And until the ignoble and unhappy regime that now hold our
> brothers in Angola, in Mozambique,
> South Africa in subhuman bondage, have been
> toppled, utterly destroyed
> Until that day the African continent will not
> know peace

We Africans will fight, if necessary and we know
we shall win
As we are confident in the victory of good over evil, of good
over evil.

THE IMPORTANCE OF SYMBOLS
Was not all the knowledge of the Egyptians writ in Mystic symbols, Speak not the scriptures oft in parables. Are not the choicest fables of the poets, That were the fountains and first spring of Wisdom, Wrapped in perplexed allegories.
(Ben Jonson)

The foregoing discussions of the mystical roots of Jah Rastafari is based very much on an analysis of its symbols and rituals that are so evident in Rastafarian circles. So it will be helpful for us to reflect on the general importance of symbolisms. "Watch symbols, they become people"—this holds as a law of social life, and an understanding of the Bible tends to support this theory.

A symbol can represent an entire philosophy through condensation and concentration. Symbols plumb depths which the intellect can see only obliquely. Parables and legends present ideals in such a way as to make the hearer long to embody them in his own life, for it is by myths and fables—not logic—that men are moved. The power of symbols lies in their capacity to anchor man within the universe, in the simplest but most effective way. One's interior world is living, moving, experiencing the constant flow of vibrations and sensations. These feelings, insights and fancies are very private and can be communicated only through symbols. They can also become shared by others of like vibrations and feelings. They provide the most effective and practical way of harnessing and using the creative power of the mind. A symbol is in fact the key through which man mentally makes contact with a particular quality which he desires to use. By this means internal transformation is achieved. A man becomes what he sees. "You saw the Spirit, you become the Spirit. You saw Christ, you become Christ... You see yourself, and what you see you shall become... Whoever achieves gnosis becomes no longer a Christian, but a Christ."

By concentrating on the mental picture of a lion, for instance, persons eventually can get beyond and behind the form and will find that their minds are gradually assuming the quality symbolized by that form. The mind actually changes its rate of vibration. So for the inner circle who followed Christ closely, symbols were not mere allegories, but very much models for concrete becoming.

There is an appropriate symbol for every quality or vibration, though its meaning will vary between persons. Thus, while some people picture and feel God as a spirit, others comprehend him roaring like a lion, others hear him in the ghostly stillness that precedes the storm, and others perceive him in the weaving subleties of the spider. "Man created God in his own image," was the dictum of Voltaire. These gods, however, have not always been visualized by man in human form. The ancients thought that man as man could not adequately symbolize or personify the conception of divinity innate within himself.

Every concrete object of perception was recognized as an idea and manifestation of the creator God, and therefore a claimant for man's reverence. Beasts, birds, fish, reptiles, insects, plants, stones and all kinds of monstrous images, have all been seen by converts, poets, artists, children and the ancients as images having attributes of the Infinite. Likewise God was often referred to as God of Sound, or God of Light (Sun, Fire) or of Love.

Thus, at this stage the fundamental equality of all things animate or inanimate was first accepted. But profounder study proved that certain forms presented such many-sided facets that they outshone all lesser lights, and in themselves conveyed to their observer something more of the all-inclusiveness of the Divine—Serpent/ Anancy/Spider/Lion/ Lamb all served as symbols of totality or wholeness and power. These convey the thought of God as All. They symbolize the allness of both good and evil, of light and darkness, of sun and moon, of father, mother, and son.

This attempt to convey the Allness of the Creator led early Africans to portray God in multiform images. There were many trinities of Gods, for example, the dread *Sekmet-Bast-Ra*, who was a man-headed woman with wings springing from her arms, and two vultures growing from her neck and lion's claws that armed her feet. This image conveyed Plurality, Unity and Power. The *Isis Hathor* deity was described as having a dual image: as "kindly is she as Bast, terrible is he as Sekmet." Here, too, the Serpent not only represented evil and darkness (thus slain by the Divine Lion of the Sun), but was also the symbol of the Sun God himself, especially when the solar orb was personified as Ra-Tem, the setting sun entering the darkness. As the spouse of Ra, she personified destruction and chaos.

The *worship of sacred animals* commenced in Egypt before the dawn of history, and survived for many thousands of years in conjunction with later creeds. The Cat of Babostis, the Ram of Thebes, the Bulls of Memphis, the Hawk of Edfu, are the remains of faiths that were ancient when Bast and Amen, and Ptah and Horus, eclipsed them in the cities where they reigned so long. With the fusion of the different races came the intermarriage of their respective ideas, resulting in the extraordinary animal-headed human figures of the gods, which until the time of the Romans were deeply venerated by the Egyptian people, as is proved by the multitude of amulets in the form of sacred animals which they have left behind.

Important though they are, Western scholars like Levy-Bruhl have dismissed such traditional folk symbols and folk thought as "prelogical," though in American television today the same idea is expressed in Walt Disney's productions and such television characters as "Mr. Ed" (the talking horse), "Lucan," "Tarzan" (apeman), "Hulk," "vampires" and "werewolves." They cannot *see* that folklore supplies the master keys to the ancient collective wisdom of a group. However, a countryman of Levy-Bruhl, the well-known sociologist Emile Durkheim, in his quest to understand *The Elementary Forms of the Religious Life*, sees the penetration of these symbols as the only "scientific" way to unravelling their meaning:

> One must know how to go underneath the symbol to the reality which it represents and which gives it its meaning. The most barbarous and the most fantastic rites and the strangest myths translate some human need, some aspects of life, either individual or social. The reasons which the faithful justify them may be, and generally are, erroneous; but the true reasons do not cease to exist, and it is the duty of science to discover them… In reality, then there are no religions which are false." (p. 15)

This has been our guiding assumption throughout the foregoing discussion of Rastafari. For above all, Rastafarians embody and activate African folk consciousness, not only in the content of their beliefs and symbols, but also in the style of their symbolic communication.

To begin with, Rastas, as African folks, have a deep intuition of the unity of the animal, human, and plant worlds, and of their interrelationship to an all-powerful creator. Jamaican folks say that even "Bush have eyes…path have ears." The spirit of the Creator or Supreme God permeates all of his creations, living and dead. Therefore any object may be sacred as each object of nature possessed a natural life or vitality—or an indwelling spirit.

Every living thing, in fact, shows us hidden knowledge through signs and omens. There is, therefore, no big differentiation between things "sacred" and things "profane," as Durkheim postulated. For the folk the world is sacred, at the center of which is a spiritual center or force. Such a spirit or secret force, Africans believed, could be manipulated by man.

The noted anthropologist Lucien Levy-Bruhl, author of *The Soul of the Primitive*, observed that aboriginal peoples in general held on to the mystical beliefs which he termed the "law of participation"—the view that persons and things form part of one another to the point even of identity: A man participates in his social group, in his name, in his totem animal, in his shadow, in such a way and to such an extent that his mentality may be said to be formed by these many mystical links.

The traditional folk believed that the gods and the spirits of their dead ancestors assume the shapes of animals and plants. For this reason, most ancient people deified a particular animal or its image (the totem). Most signs of the different Zodiac systems are based on animal symbolisms. Africa has produced kings known as the "Crocodile Kings," the "Bee Kings," "Bull Kings," "Lion Kings," "Shark Kings," etc. Tribes often named themselves and modeled their behavior on that of their sacred totem, and through certain sacred rituals often worked themselves into taking on the form, spirit, and powers of their individual and tribal totem. *Hindus*, for example, believed that the souls of the dead transmigrate, i.e., enter the body of a living animal, and so they revere all animals, particularly the "sacred cows" which supposedly contain the souls of the noble who have departed. The Arawak Indians worshipped idols of Zemis, which they believed were the dwelling places for the spirits of their dead ancestors. These Zemis took the shape of animals or anything. *Buddhists* believed also that all animals have souls and are reborn to earth in successively higher incarnations. In "The Myth of Er," *Plato* records his astral traveling to the netherworld, where his hero, Er, witnessed how departed souls choose to return to the next life, one as a swan, another as a nightingale, another as a lion; a swan chose to be a man, another an eagle, and so forth.

The ancient Egyptians (Africans) considered most of their common animals sacred, and it is reported that at the time of the Roman occupation of Egypt, the Pharaoh—despite his desire to please the new rulers of his land—could not save a Roman soldier from being stoned to death by an irate mob after the soldier had accidentally killed a cat, an animal deified by Egyptians. (See Roy Pinney's *The Animals in the Bible*.)

Because of its intense religiosity and spiritualism, Africa was once regarded as "land of the gods," and it was reported that "the god of each religious city held in awe a given animal or plant. At birth a child was assigned an animal protector, and it became the duty of the priests of the area to abstain from eating the meat or drinking the milk of this animal. One certain way to war with one's neighbor in those times was to desecrate its sacred animal.

Enslaved Africans in the Caribbean carried with them their folk consciousness, if nothing else. Jamaicans still believe that shopkeepers and butchers steal so much and kill so much that when they die they become the dreaded "Rolling Calf." This is well illustrated by the followers of the Santeria religion in Cuba and Brazil, which centers on the worship of Yoruba deities called Orishas.

The *santero* is a "man of knowledge and power" whose allies are the Orishas of the Yoruba pantheon of deities. They regard animals such as the goat, the elephant and the turtle as good protectors, but regard reptiles, venomous insects, birds of prey and the spider as spiritually obnoxious. The priest (Papa) and priestess (Mama) of Santeria designate themselves the horse of the saints who mount them. When mounted or "possessed" by any one of the many Orishas, the possessed individual takes on all the supernatural characteristics of the Orisha by whom he is believed to be possessed or ridden.

Such persons might collapse in twitching and shaking convulsions, froth at the mouth, speak in strange tongues, dance for hours, eat and drink lustily, and perform oustanding feats of physical strength. Under the influence they are often able to divine the future with stunning accuracy, and to get rid of negative influences on others.

Another illustration is in the West African voodoo religion, practiced to this day in Haiti, in which the "voodoo" is conceived as a great supernatural being taking the form of a snake that knows the past and present and who, through the medium of the high priests and priestesses, foretells the future.

Thus by using such collective animal symbols like lion as a tribal totem, Africans tell how they see themselves and what they aspire to be. This same kind of animal symbolism is embodied in the Bible, thus reinforcing the Rastaman's view of the Bible as being a very African book. The Bible abounds in animal/insect symbolism:

> Whoever loves discipline loves knowledge, but he who hates reproof is like a cow. (Proverbs 12:1)
> Go to the ant, you sluggard, consider her ways, and be wise. (Proverbs 6:6)

In the symbolism of the ancient Biblical prophets, the two major animal symbols used to describe God are lion and lamb. But he was also described by other images: that of the child, the spirit, the sun, and the dove.

The Rastafarian interpretations of John's vision is in fact based on the general African folk belief that man is intimately linked to the world around him and that it is possible to cross the thin divide which separates man from the animal world. Thus even Levy-Bruhl noted this as a general feature of folk societies, noting that for these folks the transit from animal to man and from man to animal is "accomplished in the most natural way, without astonishing or shocking anybody" (p. 36). In fact, this metamorphosis from humans to animals is a central theme in folk epics and in aboriginal folklore as a whole, and is known as lycanthropy to Westerners—the projecting of one's soul into a particular animal with which his human body becomes intimately associated.

In African folk tales—from the Hottentots of Southwest Africa to the Akamba tribe of Kenya, to the Dagamba an Ashanti people of Ghana—we see the folk-willingness to accept the transformation of animals into men or gods, usually through the medium of the dance. Thus in West African countries it was once common to hear of men-tigers, men-lions, men-leopards, men-panthers, ape-men, spider-men, snake-men, etc. Sem priests in ancient Egypt wore the skins of panthers.

Trying to make sense of this phenomenon, Levy-Bruhl tells us that "with the aid of certain drugs and fetishes (and masks) men seem able to transform themselves into animals." Says Levy-Bruhl: "Assuming the skin of an animal is, literally, becoming that animal… He veritably is a leopard, without ceasing to be a man. From that moment he has its instincts: he has the ferocity and the super-human force that he will lose at once, when that covering is taken from him… He is then both one and dual. In every social group the men who have been admitted, by a long and secret initiation, into the world of occult forces has at the same time acquired the power to assume, when he pleases, some other than the human form."

Don Juan, the Yaqui guru discovered and immortalized by Carlos Castaneda in *The Teachings of Don Juan*, testifies to the transformation of humans into animals with the aid of a herbal mixture of peyote and mushroom, which he calls affectionately "the little smoke." Castaneda's apprenticeship with Don Juan consisted of learning the secret knowledge of how to become a crow so that he could move freely and develop bird sight. Says Don Juan to Castaneda, his scribe:

> To me those who think they are above animals live worse than animals... Some people in the street are not people... I learnt to become a crow because these birds are the most effective of all. No other birds bother them, except perhaps larger hungry eagles, but crows fly in groups and defend themselves... Men don't bother crows. A crow is safe.
>
> It is ideal in size and nature. It can go safely into any place without attracting attention. On the other hand it is possible, to become a lion, or a bear, but that is rather dangerous. Such a creature is too large, it takes too much energy to become one. One can become a cricket or a lizard, or even an ant, but that is even more dangerous because large animals prey on small creatures.

When Castaneda began his apprenticeship under Don Juan, drugs, men, perceptions, animals and visions all seemed discreet and incomprehensible. At this stage the young scribe was blind; he could not see (i.e., penetrate) through his whole body—not just with his eyes, ears or mind, but with all of his senses. Thus, at his first meeting with Mescalito, the Great Spirit, Castaneda heard a group of men babbling in a language he did not understand, talking meaninglessly about sharks. But a decade later, at the close of his apprenticeship, he meets a magical deer who talks soothingly to him in a combination of English and Spanish!—a "chicano" deer, he thinks, symbolizing a syncretic culture of spirits, animals and men.

Castaneda has not been the only Western social scientist who has sought to understand this phenomenon. David Loye in his book *The Healing of a Nation* pondered the issue: "Unfortunately, men do not become insects only in fables, dreams, or in stories of Franz Kafka." Then, in Chapter nine of this book, he discusses, conceptually, "how and why they [men] undergo this strange metamorphosis." The experience and effects of black slavery, he went on to argue, "must suggest a diminishing of humanity to a certain hard-shelled, predatory, swarming type of being we associate mainly with insects. Thus an extremely important question for modern Social Science is just how do responsible human beings become such insects? What goes on within our minds that allows us to shut out much of what makes us regress not merely to the animal level but below?" (p. 82).

Tied in with this folk-belief of animals transforming into men, and vice-versa, is the associated notion of giants, super-men and gods. For at the point of transformation, such metamorphosized beings seem to exhibit supernatural strengths and formidable powers.

To the modern mind, the phenomenon of "giants" is relegated to child-fantasy. But even the Bible tells us that "once there were giants in the land," and several cases were illustrated (Samson, Goliath).

Likewise, Don Juan in his *Teaching* makes mention of an ancient time when men performed phenomenal deeds and were admired for their strength and feared and respected for their superior knowledge. Says Don Juan:

> My teachers told me stories of truly phenomenal deeds that were performed long, long ago. But now we, the Indians, do not seek that power any more... Power that acts like a magnet, more potent and dangerous to handle as the root goes deeper into the ground. When one arrives at a depth of four yards—

> and they say some people have—one finds the seat of permanent power, power without end... Little by little we have lost interest... I myself do not seek it; and yet at one time, when I was your age (Castenada's), I too felt its swelling inside of me...
>
> I killed a man with a single blow of my arm. I could toss huge boulders not even twenty men could budge. Once I jumped so high I chopped the top leaves off the highest trees... But they said I was crazy and I frightened the Indians... It was different when there were people...who knew a man could become a mountain lion, or a bird, or that a man could simply fly.
>
> (Teachings of Don Juan p. 66)

The same notion was expressed by the Tibetan mystic, *Tuesday Lobsang Rampa*, in *The Third Eye*:

> Many years ago, according to our legends, all men and women could use the Third Eye. In those days the gods walked upon the earth and mixed with men... Everyone had the ability to travel in the Astral, see by clairvoyance, telepathize and levitate... But mankind had visions of replacing the gods and tried to kill them, forgetting that what man could see the gods could see better. As a punishment, the Third Eye of man was closed... There was Babel... But throughout the ages a few people have been born with the ability to see clairvoyantly. (*The Third Eye* pp. 78, 106)

Thus in both traditional African and esoteric European thought and Eastern traditions, the gods once dwelt with humans as teachers.

Folklore proper must therefore be seen as the ancient sublime and profound wisdom of the gods which have become the natural inheritance of the group. Aboriginal peoples acquired meaning in their lives by deliberately repeating, through song, dance and rituals, the original acts of God or their ancestors. Nothing is real except when it follows such archetypal patterns, doing what the gods did in the very beginning. Even Jesus Christ tells us that he did not come to annul the law of the prophets but to complete them

(Matthew 5:17).

There is great wisdom to this methodology of grounding ourselves firmly on the wisdom of our ancients, particularly for the scattered and dismembered tribes that have lost their way.

ANCIENT PROPHECY REVISITED

We are now able to re-examine the prophetic foundations of the Rastafarian movement, and this will better enable us to understand Rastafari in its spiritual strivings, its unity as well as its divergent tendencies. The major Biblical prophets all spoke in one tongue insofar as they spoke of redemption and the return of Christ after a cycle of changes.

These prophets revealed their visions in symbolic language, largely in animal symbolism. This was the ancient form of symbolic language, universally understood. Around 550 B.C., *Daniel's* vision pictured the coming of Christ after a change of empires, symbolized by a change in animal types which not even Walt Disney would dream of reproducing because of the colorful nature of this epic unfolding:

> The four winds of the heaven strove upon the great sea. And four great beasts came up from the sea. The first like a lion had eagle's wings, and it was lifted up from the earth, and made to stand upon the feet as a

> man, and a man's heart was given to it. And behold another beast, like a Bear...which devoured much flesh... And a third Beast, like a Leopard, with four wings upon its back like a fowl and also four heads; the fourth beast was terrible, exceedingly strong, with great iron teeth, and ten horns... from which sprung up up another little horn which had the eyes of man, and a mouth speaking great things.   (Daniel 7:2-8)

The prophet Ezekiel visioned Christ's return in terms of a similar symbolic drama between four-winged and multi-eyed creatures, one looking like a man, another like a lion, another like an ox and the other as an eagle (Ezekiel 1:10). Also the Book of Revelations, authored around 93 A.D. in response to the Roman persecution of Jews and Christians, contained a similar picture. It was authored by John the Divine, of the inner circle of Christ. While "being in the Spirit," John heard "a voice as loud as thunder" and he saw the "Scroll" or pathway into the future present of now.

> Around the throne on each side there were four beings full of eyes in front and behind; the first being was like a lion. The second being, like an ox; the third with a man-like face and the fourth, like a flying eagle. Each of the four living beings had six wings, and each living being was full of eyes around and within...

The prophet *Daniel* made it clear who these animals are: "These great beasts, which are four kings, which shall arise out of the earth" (Daniel 7:17). The lion represented the then ruling Babylonian regime.

In 539 B.C., Persia (the Bear) did overthrow Babylon to become ruling power. Greece (the Leopard) in 331 B.C. wrested power away from Persia; and the fourth beast (Rome) took over world leadership from Greece around 168 B.C. Such is the settled opinion of Bible scholars.

In the revelations of both Daniel and John, Rome and its priesthood of "false prophets" were envisioned as a terrible "ten horned beast" exercising power over all kingdoms, tongues and nations and making "war with the saints," and also as the "great harlot."

These four universal empires were envisioned to come into being from the time of the ancient prophets until the coming of Jesus Christ—and so it did.

The same cycle was then prophecied by John for the Second Coming of a Redeemer, which is yet to take place. Or rather, is now being fulfilled in the Jah Rastafari movement, among others, says the Mystic Revelation of Jah Rastafari.

Rastafarians have combined elements of Bible knowledge with their own folk theories, fragments of history, and herbal illuminations as a means of deriving relevance and applicability of Bible insights and Bible knowledge. *If prophets of old journeyed into the future—our present—why should not prophets of today be able to journey back into the past, to derive a greater understanding of what was said about us then, about us now?*

The level and depth of a particular Rastaman's understanding is to be measured by the form and level of his application of the wisdom contained in ancient prophecy. All Rastafarians, at one stage or other, focus on that part of John's prophecy which identifies the Lion of Judah as the redemption spirit:

> I also saw in the right hand of Him who was seated on the throne a scroll with writing inside and outside, sealed with seven seals. And no one, either in Heaven or Earth or under the Earth, was able to open the scroll or to look inside…
>
> So I cried bitterly because none was found worthy to open the scroll or to look inside it. And one of the

elders said to me, "Do not weep... The Lion out of the Tribe of Judah, the offspring of David has conquered, so as to open the scroll, and its seven seals..."

The "orthodox" tendency among Rastafarians (the dominant tendency) is to identify Haile Selassie as the Lion, the seed of King David, the Returned Christ, ordained by Jah to break our slave chains, giving us victory once again. Some take this literally, others symbolically.

But a deeper yet more abstract reading of John's prophecy has emerged among Rastafarians, particularly since the 1970's, one which has scattered the god-head to Selassie I brethrenship as a whole, not restricting it to the Emperor alone; and making themselves out not only as the elect of God, but also the I-lect, by stressing the self-selective aspect of redemption: "Only we ourselves can free our minds."

This latter-day tendency begins with a closer and deeper penetration and understanding of the particulars of these prophets. For instance, early Rastafarians over emphasized one aspect of the imagery and overlooked other aspects which present-day Rastafarians have reintegrated in order to derive overall and deeper meanings and truths. For instance, the Lamb figured much more significantly in the original visionary preconception of John, but is largely overlooked by the orthodox interpreters:

And I saw standing mid-air between the throne and the four living beings and among the elders, a Lamb as it had been sacrificed. It had seven horns and seven eyes, which are the seven spirits of God dispatched over the whole earth. He came and took the scroll from the right hand of HIM who was seated on the throne; and he took the scroll from the four living

> beings and the 24 elders fell down before the Lamb...
> And they sang a new song saying: "You are worthy to take the scroll and to open its seals, because you were sacrificed and have bought them for God with your blood" ... And all those gathered around spoke saying: "Worthy is the Lamb that was slain to receive Power and Wealth, and Wisdom and Strength, and Honor, and Glory and Blessing... Then I looked and saw the Lamb standing on Mount Zion and with him 144,000 who had his name and his father's name inscribed on their foreheads...

At first glance it does appear that the prophecy points to the Lion as the central figure in the drama, but on second examination the role shifts from Lion to Lamb, or on the transformation of the Lion, as the above quotation indicates.

The distinction between lion and lamb indeed becomes blurred as both images run into each other—the lion becomes the lamb. *It would seem that the very essence of this mystery is the switch from lion to lamb, or the synthesis of the two. The roaring God-lion of the Old Testament is transformed by the New Testament into the gentle Lamb destined to rule and inherit the earth.*

God as lion took up the suffering path of the cross, and became the lamb of Calvary, so that his example could be a lesson to all mankind, forever. The lamb symbolized spiritual over physical or material power: it takes real strength, faith and self-confidence to turn the other cheek, to bear the cross, and to love people even when they hurt you. And only someone with real spiritual power could have accomplished this.

That such transformations are possible is a basic belief of the mystic tradition: "Behold I make all things new," promised Christ. That such a transformation is possible is suggested to us by other parts of John's vision. For instance, reference is made to some plant that should be used in the healing process. Healing and transformation in essence mean the same thing.

> It is also written:
> The city [of Jerusalem] has no need for the sun or the moon to shine on it, because God's glory illumes it and the Lamb is its Light. By its light the nations will walk and to it the Kings of the earth will bring their splendor. (Revelations 21:23-24)

Here the lamb is equated with light from the sun (God), yet it was known by the ancients that it was the lion which was the Zodiac sign of greatest heat, and in astrology the lion sign represented the sun. In spite of this known fact, John's prophecy emphasizes the lamb as being the chosen manifestation of God, the Sun.

On penentrations it does appear that Jah the Father saw the lamb as best able to undertake the leadership task at hand, so He transformed Himself and his lion Son into a lamb-man. But beneath the lamb the lion-spirit of the Father remained: "And I John saw heaven opened up and behold the white horse and he that sat upon him was called Faithful and True, and in righteousness he doth judge and make war... And the armies which were in heaven followed him... And out of his mouth goeth a sharp sword, that with it he should smite the nations." The sharp sword is the Truth—that will set us free—the right word-formula.

Africans, familiar with prophetic symbolisms since ancient times, have not only sought to penetrate these symbols but they have also simplified and applied them to their day-to-day lives. It does appear that both African and Rastafarian folk used the term "Anancy" as the folk expression referring to all of the "false" kings and prophets that preceded the coming of Christ. The Biblical image of these world persecutors of Christ and their false priests is similar to the African folk image of Anancy—the spider-man. In the Book of Revelations "wolf in sheep's clothing" is used to depict this general type—the false prophets, counterfeit apostles, fallen angels... Christ himself warns: "Be wary of the false prophets who come to you in the guise of sheep while at heart they are voracious wolves." (Matthew 7:15)

In the Bible this general character type (Anancy) took the form of any type of animal who took on the form or features of other animals: "After this I beheld, and lo, another like a leopard, which had upon the back of it four wings of a fowl; the beast had also four heads; and dominion was given to it." (Daniel 7:6) This same devilish creature reappears in the Bible as the fiery serpent. The Bible tells of how fiery serpents were sent down upon the people to destroy them (Numbers 21:6). Isaiah the prophet makes mention of this type also:

> The burden of the beasts of the South: into the land of trouble and anguish, from whence come the young and old lion, the viper and fiery flying serpent, they will carry their riches upon the shoulders of young asses, and their treasures upon the bunches of camels, to a people that shall not profit them. (Isaiah 30:6)

Many Christians attempting to fathom the meaning of John's revelations seem to have left out this character type ("Anancy, the false prophet") who was competing with Lion and Lamb for leadership of humanity. Most interestingly, the Jehovah Witness magazine, *Awake*, on July 22, 1982 carried the feature article: "From a Lion to a Lamb." But for Rastafarians the full dialectical development is "From Viper [Anancy] to Lion to Lamb." The personality of the modern man (like that of the ancients) can be analyzed in terms of these competing images—images that reflect our jungle reality, but also the way out for those that are lost.

In African folklore Anancy or Spiderman was indeed the major competitor of both Lion and Lamb. Rastafarians have, in the process of self-examination become far more concious of Anancism as an overpowering force in its own right and have added him to the pantheon of spirits that compete in the world

Who is Anancy? Folklore attests to the fact that Anancy is an international character, having symbolic significance not only in Africa, but also in also to the Greeks, Romans, American Indians and the Celts. They involve stories with spider images, hanging goddesses, tricksters, magic, entanglement in trees, magic threads, spinning wheels, disguises, riddles and defiance of gods.In most of these stories the Spider is portrayed as a "fallen angel"-partly divine and partly satanic.

The Spider, inspite of its small size, is one of nature's most effective beasts of prey. Their eight eyes give them excellent vision, while six legs make them highly acrobatic. They have the title of nature's most effective weavers and spinners. It uses self-made threads in the most inventive ways. It climbs, descends, and builds traps of the most imaginative kind. Baby spiders migrate to new territories by using their threads as aircraft and riding the wind for miles.

Like the sun, the spider pours forth its thread from itself and takes it back again. The web of the spider, beautiful and harmless-looking, is in reality a snare for unsuspecting prey. Only five out of 10,000 known species are deadly to humans.

Because of these qualities, the spider has long been an international mystic symbol. Because of its very mystical associations this symbol has been suppressed. In fact James Vogh in The Thirteenth Zodiac has put forward the thesis that "When Christian Rome purged old religions, one of the Zodiac signs was discarded. Arachne, the Spider, the house of the psychic and intuitive element in human nature, is the lost thirteenth sign." Since 400 BC knowledge of this thirteenth sign has been suppressed as dangerous. Thirteen is still regarded as jinxed. This is based on the thirteen lunations of the moon at 28 days each.

From anthropological evidence it is clear that many different cultures used the symbolism of the spider. At Nazca, Peru, the giant figure of a spider (some 50 yards long) was gouged into the stony plain to represent one of a number of planetary constellations (Erich von Daniken, Return to the Stars,1970, p 117). The belief that the spider has the power to bring good or evil fortune is ancient. It was popular with the Romans who had a mascot in the form of a precious stone on which a spider was engraved. Among the Celts, the lunar goddess of the Druids was Adrianhod, the "Lady of the Silver Wheel." The Greeks later called this moon goddess Ariadne. She was pictured as the spider drawing up the tides by an invisible thread. The Greek legend of Arachne was that she was once a woman who was a skilled weaver of tapestries. Athene, the powerful Goddess of War, challenged Arachne's skill out of jealousy. Arachne won and Athene was so angry that she turned her into a spider. Upon this transformation, Arachne hanged herself. In the tale of Ariadne, she was King Mino's daughter who helped Theseus to kill the Minotaur. This she did by giving Theseus a magic ball of thread which he used to find his way in and out of the monsters lair. She also hanged herself when Theseus failed to marry her.

In almost every age and place the spider is portrayed as a shaman whose magic does away with death. He was even said to be the Muse, the mother of all living, the ancient power of fright and lust. One Sumerian incantation says "White wool, black wool, a double thread, the spindle of spinning, a wonderous thread, a thread that does away with the curse." There is no doubt that the Greeks and Romans sung and danced the rope-dance in the figure of a maze. The Italians used to dance the Tarantula so that its spirit could lend its quickness and power of movement to victims of paralysis. The swastika symbol was derived from the figure of the spider by early American Indians.

Odin, like other manifestations of the spider, was a priest and shaman. He was able to journey in the furthest heaven or to the land of the dead so that he may visit the gods, His constant companion was his horse, which had eight legs, and from which he seldom dismounted.

The spider was attributed with the mystical power of traversing the realms and of cheating death and defying the powers. In short, he is the survivor. The Ashanti tell how the spider visited the Kingdom of Death and escaped to bring messages to the living. A Jamaican legend tells of how Anancy rescued himself and his children from death by climbing nimbly to a roof beam.

Spider was also known to help humanity. In the Limba myth when the twin heroes Kota and Yemi wished to visit a land in the sky to find wives, it was the spider who ran his thread to the sky for the twins to climb. The Blackfoot Indians of America tell how a maiden married the Morning Star and went to live among his people in the sky. One day, looking through a hole in the sky, she saw her tribe and grew homesick. It was the spiderman who let her down to earth by a thread and her people beheld her coming to earth like a shooting star. In an African story, the spider brings a dead princess down from the sky on a thread and restores her to life. "Wherever this child went she had peace and blessing, by grace of the spider."

In African folklore, Spiderman or Anancy is like the fallen angel (Judas) who uses residue of his former power to survive through tricksterism and con-artistry. The Ashanti say Kwaku Anansa is the best known rascal in West Africa. Even Nyame, the sky god, admits that he is the cleverest of the animals. For the Limba of Sierra Leone, the most common character in their tales is the spider, represented as a cunning trickster who gets the better of the bigger animals.

Because of his cunning Anancy is made resonsible for the way things are in the world. In Jamaican/African folklore Anancy is responsible for the fragmentation of the original secret wisdom. We are told that our ancient secret knowledge was once amassed by Anancy in a calabash for his own profit. He then climbed a tree where he intended to hide the wisdom calabash. As he climbed the tree, with the calabash hugged to his chest, he heard a little boy laughing at him from the foot of the tree. "Why do you not hang the calabash on your back? It will make your climb less tiring!" So angry was Anancy for overlooking this piece of commonsense that he threw down the calabash. Thus wisdom was scattered by the wind to the ends of the earth. "Is Anancy mek it."

The wisdom of the spider was said to be greater than that of all the world put together. He professed to have magic powers of Obeah. In a Dagamba tale, Anancy was said to be a shrewd man who claimed to have greater power than the chief. The chief attempted, but failed, to kill Anancy. Anancy then caused the death of the chief's son and turned himself into a spider. In effect, the cleverest man became the cleverest creature living in the house of man.

Anancy's greatest asset is his ability to change himself outwardly for tactical purposes. Anancy became a kind of lovable rascal, personifying the genius of our race to survive under Babylonian conditions. He was often elevated to the status of divine, as he was conceived as having supernatural powers. It was even believed by the Hausas that the slender threads of the spider became little solar rays and that the sun became the spider which in artful ways ensnared the souls of mortals. The Bogos of West Africa represented the sun as a thievish witch in the middle of a spiders web. Often Anancy is represented as the God Exuba Elegba, God of Chaos. Sometimes he is named Papa Legba.

Anancy became the central cutural focus for the African folk. Adults associated most of their traditions with him while children loved him as one day they would need the wit cunning and other qualities of the spider in a world not unlike that of the spider. Not even other animals will betray Anancy. So popular and dominant was the Anancy character that a search for a explanation of his popularity was itself sought by the Hausas. They came up with the fable that Anancy obtained popularity from a magician.

In African folklore the two omnipresent animals are Brer Anancy and Brer Lion. In the symbolic world of animals was a conflict between those two most popular ideas or images. These two animals were always in conflict. In one Hausa story it was a Lion who trampled a blacksmith to pieces and these pieces later became a spider. Another story tells how the Lion, not Anancy, was king before the arrival of man. In one Jamaican story Brer Tiger was originally king of the forest with many things named after him - Tiger lilies, Tiger moths, etc. He was acknowledged by all the other animals (including Brer Anancy) as being the strongest and Brer Anancy as the weakest. Brer Dog explained: "When Tiger whispers the trees listen. When Tiger is angry and cries out the trees tremble. But when Anancy whispers noone listens. When he shouts everyone laughs." In order to have the stories of the forest named Anancy stories rather than Tiger stories, Brer Anancy accepted the challenge set by Brer Tiger to catch Mr. Snake alive. This Anancy did by using flattery to entice and trap Mr. Snake. Having the stories named after him, the others could laugh at Brer Anancy no longer.

In another tale, The Spider and the Lion, we find these two animals in conflict with the spider getting the better of the Lion by means of his cunning and psychological skill. In this story it was the lion who started the trouble by eating the fish of the spider Anancy. The spider then used his brains in getting the lion to tie himself to a big tree. The evil-headed spider then punished the lion with a hot iron until he was near dead. The lion was saved and in hot pusuit of Anancy he was again tricked by Anancy. In the end when Anancy dropped his disguise and appeared, Lion was seized with fear and was chased away by Anancy with the warning: "Tomorrow, if I hear you are following me you will see! If you do not obey me in this bush you will see trouble... You are pardoned, you who despise people. Get up, you hypocrite." In another Hausa tale the Lion had to get the help of an old woman on the only occasion in which he comes off best in a contest with Anancy. In many instances then, the Lion was outwitted by the goat, the hyena, the buffoon, the hippopotamus, the elephant, and many times by Anancy.

PROPHECY RE-INTERPRETED

John's revelations climaxes the Bible story of the earth transforming itself into heaven, after going through a cycle, symbolized by signs. Rastafarians have simplified the categories in the drama by reducing them to three types: Anancy, Lion and Lamb. African folks have worked it out that these are symbolic of the three major human-animal types competing in the ring for survival. The ancient Egyipan Zodiac chart of the human body (used by its healers) gives us a clear cue as to the relative importance of these three animal types within the overall scheme of the human body. For in this system we find that the Lamb is pictured as symbolizing the mind (higher self), the Lion is in the middle, symbolizing the heart - a powerful physical emotive force, and an eight legged insect (like a spider) represents the lower station of eros or libidinal energy.

One basic question tackled by Christ, John the Baptist, the Prophets, Plato and the ancients alike was the same: Which animal should be in control of our Being? The answer was that since each of the animals belongs to the overall system, each one must find its proper place. The Lamb represents the mind and this station or animal should control the others. The heart should be "Lion-hearted" and the insect represents the lower physical self.

It is clear that the Spider symbolised the qualities of the flesh and of the lower self as depicted by Christianity. In this sense the meaning of Isaiah comes to light: "The Wolf also shall dwell with the Lamb and the Leopard shall lie down with the kid; and the calf and the young Lion and the fatling together and a little child shall lead them." (Isaiah 11:6).

Anancy symbolizes the devilish Power of Eros which will do anything to find physical expression and outlet. Since Anancy feels mainly with the lower physical self, he cannot really feel for others, which comes only when one uses the Higher Self (Big I) of the mind through which one can empathize and feel for others. Fixated at the lower physical level of physical-eros-survival, Anancy is trapped in this kind of animal selfishness. Christ stated through Galatians that: "The deeds of the flesh are evident such as immorality, impurity, sensuality, idolatry, magic arts, animosities, strife, jealousy, bad temper, selfishness and carousings." The Lamb, however, symbolizes spiritual qualities like "love, joy, peace, forbearance, kindness, generosity, fidelity, gentleness and self control." (Galatians 5:19-22). A Christian was one who subjugated (not crucified) the flesh with its passions, desires, deceits, weaknesses and lack of self control.

The most influential Greek scholar Plato was educated in Egypt. In his famous *Republic* the triad of Anancy, Lion and Lamb can clearly be seen. Each one is assigned a particular level in the hierarchy of society and of the personality from bottom up. Instead of calling them Anancy, Lion and Lamb he called the Workers (governed by appetite and materialism,) Guardians (governed by spirit) and Philosopher Kings (governed by Divine Reason.) Plato did not envisage a static class structure as he has been accused, but one that allowed for forward and upward movements. From Anancy to Warrior-Guardians to top ranking Philosopher Kings who are the rightful rulers by virtue of their enlightening discoveries away from darkness and illusion.

Direct evidence of the similarity of Plato's usage of animal symbolism to the Rastafarian folk interpretation rendered here, may be found in Plato's *Dialogue*. Plato here asks us to imagine a many-headed monster who is joined to a lion and then to a man, so that all three become one in outward form. Plato asks: "Is not the noble that which subjects the beast to the man, or rather to the God in man; and the ignoble that which subjects the man to the beast? And is not a man.who subordinates the spirited animal to the unruly monster and for the sake of money habituates him in the days of his youth to be trampled in the mire and from being a lion to becoming a monkey?"(In Chinese monkey is equivalent of Anancy and Chinese symbols were often used by Greek scholars).

Plato also raved against the decline and fall of Ancient Greece. He saw this as the result of the reversal of the natural order. Disorder comes about when Anancy becomes king, because then the physical is elevated about the spiritual and the Philosopher Kings lose their rightful position in such an order. Chaos then becomes certain.

The power of John's Mystery and of its secrets resides in a clear perception on the part of the Rastaman that the system has made us all into Anancy. We face the challenge of redeeming ourselves by reincarnating ourselves forward to the stage of Lion and then on to Lamb. What is important to this interpretation is movement forward. John's vision is thus seen as dealing with the movement from Babylon to Zion. This movement is also interpreted as a movement of personality types—from wolves in sheeps clothing (Anancy) to Lion to Lamb. For the Rastaman of today this evolution in the personality is itself underscored by the term "the Seven Seals" mentioned in the prophecy and which Rastafarians equate to the Seven Chakras stressed by Eastern mystics. These are the gates which must be opened up and developed if the individual is to evolve to the fullest.

In folk terms Rastas often explain these seven body points as our two eyes, two ears, two nostrils and one mouth. Until these seven sense organs are opened up people remain underdeveloped, having eyes that do not see, ears that do not hear, living deads:

"I have given you as...a light to the nations, to open the eyes that are blind, to bring out he prisoners from the dungeon, from the prison those who sit in darkness" (Isaiah 42:7)

Each Rastaman relies heavily upon his own interpretation, but this fits within the overall pattern. One Rastaman explains his interpretation which he calls "the Five H". One H is for the Head which is to be made holy by correct spiritual and Bible teachings. The second H is for Hand which is to be made handy and skillful in the usage of tools. The third H is for Heart which is to be made happy. The fourth H is for Hip which, as the physical crossroad of the body must be made healthy through movement exercises that will ensure rhythm and maximum body movements. The fifth H is for Heel and this for Brother Mac must be made hardy and firm to ensure balance and speed and footing.

While early Rastafarians sought and emphasized the physical movement from Babylon to Zion, others of today seek to embody the mystical transformation in personality types which for them constitutes the surest way of getting out of Babylon and into Zion. The movement of Jah People has become a train from Babylon to Zion, from one way of life to another, from one kind of person to another. The animals represent the different stations. They begin as Anancies, fallen angels, who discover a way of moving on to become a Lion, also a survivor like Anancy. The Dread warrior Lion eventually transforms himself into the Lamb, but only after being a Lion. For Rastafarians the tamed lion sported by Haile Selassie was symbolic of the transformation from Lion to Lamb, as well as the Life and meanings of the Lion trinity-Haile Selassie, Marcus Garvey and Bob Marley.

Chapter 4
MAJOR RASTAFARIAN CONCEPTS

But, if oxen (and horses) and lions had hands, or could draw with hands and create works of art like those made by Men, horses would draw pictures of gods like horses and oxen of gods like oxen, and they would make the bodies of their gods in accordance with the form that each species itself possesses. Aethiopians have gods with snub noses and black hair.

(Xenophanes of Colophon, c 530 B.C.)

By their *concepts* we can know them. Over the years Rastafarians have shown their collective growth and unity as a significant social movement by evolving their own distinct vocabulary and concepts which express their particular vibrations. These concepts are the general names and terms used by Rastafarians to emphasize those general factors and forces that are significant in their life experiences. While our Third World intellectuals and politicians have been overzealous in the adoption of foreign and alien concepts, Rastafarians insist on creating and developing concepts much more fitting to their experienced realities. The concepts and ideas which they share as a group give us an overall picture of the past, present and future as they conceive them to be. When put together, these spontaneous folk creations add up to a distinct social theory of Jamaican society and of our times, one that is spiritual in its orientation. And because they are created from the folk bowel of their felt experiences, they will insist that these are "scientific" as they reflect the realities of their lives; they are created and reinforced by the day-to-day experiences of one section of poor African folks living at the base of a historically entrenched race-class pyramid, where they are trapped.

The intellect of the Rastaman is highly productive of reflections and meditations on his life and condition. His concepts are evidence of this re-evaluation that is taking place in his conscious mind. The concepts are many, but those that have caught on most deeply are the following, which we will explain: "Jah-Jah," "I and I," "Reincarnation," "Livity," "Babylon," "Baldhead," "Zion," "Herbal Meditations" (Initations). These concepts reveal Rastafarian folks to be very adaptable intellectually, as these concepts are very much concerned with the universal issues facing all of humanity, but are given fresh life and meanings.

JAH-JAH

The Rastaman is most conscious of the presence of an Almighty Power or Creator, the One Universal God of Creation, or Father of the Universe. The Rastaman simply refers to this God as "Jah-Jah," just as he would say "Papa" (or Father).

Like all folk creations, the term "Jah" is, however, quite obscure in its origin. Frank Cassidy, in his book *Jamaican Talk*, tell us that "Jah" was the term used by the Jamaican Maroons for God. Jah was also the shortened form for "Jehovah" as used in the English Bible between 1539 and

1758. The Jehovah Witness Bible also translated "Hallelujah" in Revelations 19 to mean "Praise Jah." It has also been suggested that the word "Jah" could have been a phonetic derivation of the Hindu word "Jai," which was commonly used by Hindus in praising their gods—Jai Rama, Jai Krishna, Jai Bhagwan. The term was used in Hindu communities to greet each other, as a term of respect.

In light of the close interaction between the Hindu indentured workers and African peasants, it seems reasonable to agree with Dr. Ajai Mansingh that "Jai" is a possible phonetic variation of "Jah," as he stated in the *Sunday Gleaner* of August 8, 1982. The emigration of 36,412 indentured Indians to Jamaica between 1845 and 1917 was indeed an important influence on Afro-Jamaican folks, who found that many Indian cultural aspects were congenial with theirs. In fact, their understanding of nature and its forces were basically similar. Thus some cross-fertilization of cultural ideas did occur.

Whatever the origins of the concept, Jah is now a powerful word-symbol for God, and it is used always by Rastafarians to denote the divine God-head, as in Jah-God, Jah-Selassie-I, Jah-man, Jahmaica. By use of this concept, the Rastaman shows that he is not ashamed or unconscious of the Almighty; by its use he shows instead that he is aware of the ways in which organized religions have departed from the original teachings of the Father. Rastas choose, therefore, to adopt the "new" name Jah as a symbol of Master, the Creator. By this name they express their own rediscovery of God. For them, Jah is not dead, but governs the Universe now just as in the days of old. All of what happens around us are manifestations of the workings of Jah-nature-God-the-Father.

I AND I

Outsiders are either fascinated or outright turned off by what has been termed the "I-Man" talk of Rastafarians which has given rise to a large number of "I-words." The personal pronoun "I" becomes a prefix for as many words as it is possible to alter by this insertion, as a way of emphasizing the importance of the first-person reality of conscious self.

In particular, Rastafarians always talk of "I and I." This refers to the unity of the speaker with the Most High (Jah) and with his fellow men. "I and I" simply refers to me and my God—one "I" is the *little I* and the other the *Big I*. The little I, or me, refers to the lower self of man, to his body and its ego, that part of him which is born and will die. It is this little I which experiences desires, ambitions, misery, happiness, performs actions and fears death. It is the outer garment of the Big I, an instrument by which the Big I manifests itself on the material plane.

The Big I is the ever-living, immortal or "true" self that was never born and can never die. It is the spirit of divinity and holiness residing in the depth of each. It is the soul or pure spirit or vital energy; it is the critical, all-seeing "third eye" or third dimension of the universal mind.

Thus the Hindu text, the *Upanishad*, describes this as the "Inner Controller:" "He who inhabits the earth is within the earth, whom the earth does not know, whose body the earth is and who controls the earth from within—he is your Self, the Inner Controller, the Immortal."

Jah is the Big I, or the great Spirit of Creation that must be worshipped in spirit and in truth. This Jah is "kind to every mankind," as one song intones. Thus the command from this higher plane to the Rastaman is unequivocal: "The entire Law (of Jah) is summed up in this one statement: Love your neighbor as yourself." (Galatians 5:14)

Knowing the Self for a Rastaman means moving towards merging the little I with the Big I, so that the little I of reality is lifted up in words and thought, and the person becomes a little I (like a child) in relation to the Greater I, the Father and Giver. A person must become a little I, in relation to this one great universal spirit on the highest level of thought. Speaking of this merger, Christ himself remarked: "...And I, when I am lifted up from the earth, will draw everyone to myself." (John 12:32)

As a doctor, Luke saw Christ as the great physician who united the upper half of the Self (the Big I) with the lower half (the little I). Simple as this sounds, it constitutes a powerful formula, understood by the Mystics.

Self-realization ("Inity") comes thus from the merger of the Big I and the little I, like Father and Son. Greatest freedom and power comes from one's ability to distinguish the true self from our ego, or our physical-mental personality. Self-awareness and self-development presses us always towards identifying our consciousness with the Big I. This results in spiritual strength, as the self is thereby opened up to the inexhaustible energy of the cosmos:

> Oh let the power fall on I, Fari
> Let the power from Zion fall on I
> O give I justice, peace and love, Fari

Reverend Henry Ward, O.D. and centenarian, was a pioneer theologian in Jamaica. As a child, this great local head of the Presbyterian Church taught us the meaning of I and I, in terms of a way of life and a meaning which is hard to forget. He recapped just before his death in May of 1979:

> Humbly, the story of my life is in very few words. Long ago came a vision of what man might attain, but that vision is only realized if one dies to self, dies to whatever may happen to self.

> So long ago I decided by the grace of God to live for the people, the children, the nation and to use Henry Ward as an instrument for that undertaking.
>
> Henry Ward died many years ago, and as a result of that was offered wealth and social promotion. But all these things passed me by. I was not interested.
>
> I was interested in our people, that we might build a nation for the glory of God."

In Rasta rebirth "I and I" becomes unified and is merged with truth. "I and I" refers to "me" in unison with my Creator/Nature/Jah. This unified personality was referred to by Khrumah and Edward Blyden as the original African personality, or what I have simply referred to as the "African I," implying unity and integration of self.

Christ's teachings called for this unity: the lower I must be integrated and proportioned according to Jah Nature's ordering:

> When you make the two one, and when you make the inside as the outside and the outside as the inside and above as below, and when you make the male and the female into a single one... When you make an eye in the place of an eye...then shall you enter the kingdom."
>
> *(The Gospel According to Thomas)*

To Salome, Christ said:
> If a man is identical (i.e., unified) he will be filled with light, but if he is divided he will be filled with darkness...

When you make the two into one, you shall become the sons of mankind. And when you say "mountain be moved," it shall be moved.

(The Gospel According to Thomas)

In the words of one Rastafarian:
> There is a book that was born in me, that has never been revealed. When such a book is open, a spirit which is divine inspiration, teach me things which I did not really know was within me.

While this is true in theory, the neglected secret knowledge which seems to have been left out of the Gospels relates to knowledge about the diverse blockages and stoppages within a person's mind-body structure. This definitely mitigates against a merger, the spirit of the little I sailing off into the Kingdom. These blockages often become so structured into the person ("takes on flesh") that he comes to defend these as his very own true nature, not being able after a time to separate this debased nature from this divine nature modeled on that of Father Nature. These blockages hold him back from seeing truth and reality as they really are.

REINCARNATION

The notion of reincarnation is one of those fundamental laws of nature that Rastafarians identify with. At the root of this belief is the ancient African belief in immortality and in the cyclical nature of the universe: "Whatever goes around, comes around." Each person eventually gets his just reward, somewhere along the road of life, which is very, very long for each spirit. Some doctrines of reincarnation stress the "transmigration of soul"—the belief that a person's soul or spirit must progress by taking in turn every earthly form, from gas to mineral an on through plant and animal to man, until all the "lessons" of mortal life have been learned.

Herodotous, the noted Greek historian, credited the ancient Egyptians with originating this doctrine, and its associated belief that it takes a soul some 3,000 years to reach the end of its cycle. African paintings often showed souls returning to each in animal form after having been judged by the God Osiris as wanting. Pythagoras learned this doctrine from the Egyptians and began teaching that souls never die but rather inhabit the body, passing on as need be.

The transmigration of souls was among the accepted doctrines of the early Christian Church, but it was eventually dropped by the Roman Catholic Church.

The African has never, however, dropped a notion which he knows intuitively to be true. Many will tell you that they have some vague recollections of life in other than human form, or of having a feeling of knowing a place without ever having been there is this life.

Rastafarians have revived this theory and have broken it down into providing a tangible framework within which the mystic unity and connectedness of Jah God creations manifest themselves. They see themselves as reincarnations of earlier personages, even of Christ. In fact, Christ and the ancient prophets can never die ("Jah live"); they live on by becoming reincarnated into other bodies. Many Rastafarians say that there have been some 71 appearances of God in man bodies, with His Imperial Majesty Selassie I as the 72nd and last reincarnation. This means for them that Haile Selassie, Christ, Solomon, David, Moses, Joseph, Aaron, and all the other God-men were one and the same Spirit. "The God-man is incarnated in many times and many places for those who have eyes to see him, and death has no place in the process.

This belief is often taken to its logical extreme by other Rasta-men who see themselves as a manifestation of this same Universal

God Spirit. The tendency of the society is, however, to dismiss such mystic identification with sarcastic humor, as this story shows:

> Somewhere in Jamaica, a few years ago, four members of the Rastafari sect, having just received a small quantity of the "wisdom weed," desired to find out which was the greatest among them.
>
> To achieve their ends, they sought the "mystic revelation from Jah Rastafari" (with a little help from the newly-lit chillum pipe). The first Rastafarian took a deep draw of the pipe and almost immediately discovered the truth: "I am Solomon, who built the temple of Jah."
>
> Now it was the turn of the second "dread." His probe into the far reaches of chillum brought forth the following revelation: "I am David, father of Selassie, elect of God."
>
> The third then said, "I am the greatest among you for I am Moses whom Jah sent unto his people with the Ten Commandments."
>
> However the fourth immediately disputed this, shouting: "Yu lie, ah no you mi did sen!"
>
> Needless to say this one was acclaimed the greatest.

The doctrine gives Rastaman faith in his own spiritual evolution and prompts him to emphasize his own regeneration and rebirth in this life. "Within life there is reincarnation, reconstruction. Life finds itself wearing down, doing wrong, and it regenerates itself, by living, regenerating exhausted forces, changing from wrong, and complying with truth."

LIVITY

This is a major Rastafarian concept, denoting his emphasis on everliving life. It is very much an African idea, expressed by the African word "Magara." According to this philosophy, man has an inalienable claim to a complete and happy life. A life without happiness is "death in life," worse than real death—which in fact only leads to another existence in this world. Magara was thus the "life force" expressed in the living person by prosperity and happiness. Since everything around us is linked, each person can only be happy when others are also happy, otherwise the Magara force is constantly flowing away from him and to the others: "When all have, it is sweet" (Yoruba proverb). Magara can be so reduced that life is no longer life but "death." For the slaves, magara was greatly reduced.

Rastas are quick to tell you that they "do not deal with death, only life." It is not simply living for the here-and-now, though emphasis is put on the concrete reality of now. It goes beyond this to a claim and a striving towards a certain quality of life which is essentially spiritual.

BABYLON

This is perhaps the most widespread concept evoked by the Rastaman to symbolize the negative or fallen condition from which the I-lect have fled. This theme is echoed by all Rastafarians and is most frequently expressed in their chants and songs: Rastas all want to leave "Babylon."

The Rastafarian imagery of Babylon is the first-person gut-level experiences of alienation and frustration under slavery, colonization and their legacies. It is not an imposed concept, but one that has grown out of the gut feelings and experiences of "souls on ice," and of dismembered beings. Babylon is the psychic image sustained by real life experiences, busted hopes, broken dreams, the blues of broken homes and of disjointed tribes of people trapped by history. It is an image of fire and of blood, of being on the edge, in limbo, in the wilderness, in concrete jungles surrounded by jungle animals of all shapes and sizes, particularly by "wolves in sheep's" clothing." It is a desolation in which man feels disjointed and out of line with the plans of creation. The body in this reversed order rules the head, and the horizontal now becomes the vertical, and the line put by Jah between man and woman is blurred.

This Rastafarian imagery of Babylon is also reinforced by both testaments of the Bible, and from the Jehovah's Witness's book, *Babylon the Great has Fallen*. Here Babylon symbolizes the powerful forces arrayed against the laws of Jah.

The name Babylon is derived from Babel, the name of the first Biblical city which flourished some 5,000 years ago, but which became so wicked in reversing Jah's natural order of things that it was eventually destroyed. In terms of Biblical symbolism, it is pictured as the Great Beast, with many heads and eyes, the Great Whale that swallowed Jonah. It was the city from which the prodigal son returned; it was the lion's den in which Daniel was thrown; the city where Delilah robbed Samson of his strength; the wicked city of Sodom and Gomorrah from which Lot and his family escaped before the city was destroyed; the same city destroyed by the great flood in Noah's time; it is the valley of Jehosephat, the land of dry bones and dismembered limbs.

The hallmark of ancient Babylon was its violence, its sexual and moral degeneracy, linguistic confusions, and the inability of its people to conceive of one God and one Heart, their widespread worshipping of graven images and "false gods," and the worshipping of the dead.

The shedding of blood and eating of meat was most common, though Jah ordered that "the soul of every sort of flesh is its blood" (Lev. 17:13). The Bible mentions Egypt at the time of its fall from grace as an example of Babylon:

> Their dead bodies will lie in the streets of the great city that is spiritually called Sodom and Egypt, where also our Lord was crucified. (Rev. 11:8)

The New Testament cites the Roman Empire of the day as a manifestation of ancient Babylon. Jesus incarnated himself in the very midst of this said confusion, for this very reason, so as to illumine the way out for mankind—to the lost sheep that went astray and was too blind to see their way home by themselves. Said Christ:

> I took my stand in the midst of the world. [But] I found them all drunk, I found none among them athirst. And my soul was afflicted for the sons of men, because they are blind in their heart-mind and do not see that empty they have come into the world and that empty they are destined to come forth again from the world.
> *(Gospel of Thomas)*

Likewise we find Paul castigating the Roman Empire of his time in words that are sociologically most relevant for today's Western post-industrial societies, and increasingly so to our own Third World societies:

> They altered God's truth into falsehood, and revered the creature rather than the creator... Their women perverted natural functions for unnatural, and similarly

> the men forsook their natural relationships with women and burned up with their lust for one another, men committing shamelessness with men…filled with immorality, depravity and greed, crammed with envy, murder, quarreling, deceit, malignity, slanderers, God-haters, insolent, proud and boastful, inventors of evil, disobedient to parents, without conscience, fidelity, natural affect and pity. *(Romans 1:23,31)*

The Gospel of Truth, a Gnostic text, described Babylon in terms of a nightmare. Not knowing God, people experienced "terror, confusion, instability, doubt and divisions," and disturbing dreams:

> Either there is a place to which they are fleeing—without strength—or from which they come; having chased after others, or they are involved in striking blows, or they are receiving blows themselves, or they have fallen from high places…Sometimes it is as if people were murdering them…or they themselves are killing their neighbors, for they have been stained with blood. When those who are going through all these things wake up, they see nothing, for they are nothing.

Rastas maintain that today ancient Babylon has resurfaced—reincarnated—cutting across both East and West, communist and capitalist, and finding its ideal expression in Jamaica. And they challenge our learned sociologists and politicians to refute this thesis. It is a chilling critique of Jamaican and world society, from bottom up, by poor Africans who see their life in the West as identical with ancient Israel's deportation and exile in ancient Babylon. Their criticisms of

Babylon go beyond the Marxian assault on capitalism, and extends as much to the communist regimes. Both are Anancy regimes. The Rastafarian sense of captivity and of alienation is expressed in the popularity of the Jewish song of exile, which has become a standard Rastafarian chant:

> By the rivers of Babylon, there we sat down,
> Yeah, we wept, when we remembered Zion,
> We hanged our harps upon the willows in the
> midst thereof, For there that they carried us away captive,
> required of us a song
> And they that wasted us required of us mirth,
> saying, Sing us one of the songs of Zion
> But how shall we sing the Lord's song in a strange land?
> If I forget thee, O Jerusalem, let my right hand
> forget her cunning
> If I do not remember thee, let my tongue cleave
> to the roof of my mouth. (Psalm 137)

Bob Marley, in song, described Babylon as the "bottomless pit" and as a "vampire system sucking the children day by day...Building church and university...deceiving the people continually...graduating thieves and murderers...and sucking the blood of the sufferer." Babylon is the "wicked sheriff" (policeman) whom Bob Marley shot down symbolically in song, and which even in the United States became a super hit song.

No wonder, then, that many Rastafarians call for actual repatriation out of Babylon. They are bent on "leaving Rome and the things Rome-men do." One familiar Rasta chant goes: "We know where we're going. We know where we're from; we're leaving Babylon, we're going to our Father's land." Peter Tosh, Rastafarian psalmist, cried out: "Stop that train, I'm leaving:"

> For so long I've been a lonely man
> Teaching those people who don't understand
> Even though I tried my best
> I just can't find no happiness
> Stop that train, I'm leaving.

Gregory Isaacs repeats the same theme in "I've got to reach the border," pledging to leave Babylon for "home." Marcia Griffiths is also remembered for her song, "Stepping Out a Babylon." Another Rastafarian singer resolved: "I and I gwaine beat down Babylon; I and I gwaine whip dem wicked men." The prayer on every Rastaman's lips finds expression in this chant:

> Oh Father, free us from the chains of Babylon!
> And make us free to walk in Zion!
> For we are pressurized, just like the Israelites.

CHILDREN OF BABYLON OR BALDHEADS

In Rastafarian folk terms, Babylon turns men into "baldheads," which is the same character type depicted in African folk culture as Brer Anancy. Conceived earlier as a folk hero by the populace, he is now pointed to by Rastas as a villain, particularly as he does not "know himself" and is thus spiritually dispossessed. His main motive is ego or self-gratification, and his magnificent obsession is to gain praise and material advantages.

In Jamaican folklore, Brer Anancy is described as "a little bald-headed man with a falsetto voice (bungo talk) and a cringing manner in the presence of his superiors," an "imitation man" without the constitution to be himself.

Originally "bald-head" was the nickname for the baboon monkey (Chinese equivalent of the spider), and sometimes for the peel-headed

John Crow, a scavenger bird common to Jamaica.

Baldheadedness has now come to imply both physical and mental stagnation experienced by the many, in contrast to the flowing vibrations and locks of the Rastaman and his spiritual uprising.

Rastafarians lead the way in criticizing Anancy ("Rasta nuh jester"); even non-Rastafarians say "Trouble deh a bush, but Anancy bring it a yard." Rastas themselves say that they are tired of playing this role, and as Bob Marley found out: "Jah would never give the power [spiritual power] to a baldhead." Again, much of this criticism, though personally attested to by each Rastafarian, is derived from Bible criticisms. There, Anancy is clearly depicted as the "wolf-in-sheep's-clothing," or as the "fiery serpent" or as the animal-man with many faces and many masks, the proverbial actor. The Bible tends to identify this Anancy character type with the Babylonian woman, as the snake-Eve who tempted Adam:

> For the lips of a loose woman drop honeyed words, and her palate is smoother than oil; but in the end she is bitter as worm-wood, sharp as a devouring sword...The path of life she does not consider...She sets her ambush and has a crafty mind."
>
> (Proverbs 5:6)

But the Babylonian man is also castigated for this role:

> Worthless man, winking his eyes, shuffling his foot, signaling with his two fingers."
>
> (Proverbs 6:12-13)

More explicitly, seven things were described as an abomination to Jah:

> "...haughty eyes, a lying tongue, hands shedding

innocent blood, a heart devising wicked schemes, feet quick to run to evil, a false witness breathing out lies…and sowing discord among brothers."

(Proverbs 6:17,19)

In our general folklore, Anancy is subject to a little criticism, but he remains basically the hero. Survival for him took precedence over loyalty, piety and truth. Anancy is a petty hustler and a schemer. He became an artist at psychological warfare, a tireless weaver, a trickster, a master of disguise and intrigue, a con-artist with his words, his tongue and his body movements. He constantly "works his brains" to further his schemes and is thus dubbed a "jinnal," a "scamp," a "rascal" or a "samfie-man." As a tactician he is indirect and circular. Even when he looks you in the eye it is merely an outward sham. He is a natural actor and dramatist who loves to be noticed. He believes in style and class and on the whole possesses a charmed life. You can never know his mind, for he is always up to some trick and always twisting his mouth and lying in the name of truth. He is an extrovert, more concerned with impressing others. You can never take what he says seriously; even when he laughs or agrees with you, you know it can be a trick or game calculated to achieve his particular goal, as he conceives it and which usually amounts to his getting a little bit more for himself and for his family or his tribe, from the system which overpowered him. So untruthful was he that in each Anancy story, the narrator excuses himself for Anancy's untruths by stating that the story has been told in the name of this insect-deity. Often Anancy stories would end with a comment: "Woe to one who would put his trust in Anancy—a sly, selfish and greedy person." Anancy compensates for his powerlessness by boasting, exaggerating and "mouthing." When he succeeded in maneuvering his way to becoming king, he turned out to be the wickedest king.

Bob Marley, in "Man to Man," tells us about the spill-off effect of Anancism—the severe paranoia:

> Man to man is so unjust
> Children you don't know who to trust
> Your worst enemy could be your best friend
> And your best friend your worst enemy.
>
> Some will sit and drink with you
> Then behind you dem soo-soo pon you
> Only your best friend knows your secret
> And only he can reveal it
> And who the cap fits, let them wear it.

There comes a time for the cultural awakening of a people, when they must cease taking themselves and their culture for granted, and must proceed to re-evaluate everything around them. The former Anancy hero has presently become our worst enemy, says Jah Rastaman.

He is the Trojan Horse within our gates. Baldheads eventually lose sight of the distinction between the true original selves and the veil of personality that constitutes its present costume, its current shroud. Anancies give themselves over to their present lines, unable eventually to remember previous roles, or to anticipate future ones. They become fixated, mentally enslaved from within, even when the chains from without are loosened. Yet only we ourselves can free our minds, from within our own dungeons.

ZION

Can the Ethiopian change his skin, or the leopard his spots? Then may ye also do good, that are accustomed to do evil.   (Jer. 13:23)

A central theme for all Rastafarians is the movement out of Babylon and into Zion. The Babylonian exile precedes the return to Zion. The fires of hell must precede the soothing waters of Zion. Zion is the Sun Vision, the Great Magnet.

Zion is Biblical in origin, and Rastafarians continue to use it in this tradition. Zion was established as "the city of David" around 1070 B.C. and became known as the "eternal city" or the "city of God" by the Israelites because the holy ark of the covenant was kept there, and those that were born there—like Solomon—were said to be blessed by this fact:

> The Lord loves the gates of Zion more than all the dwelling places of Jacob. Gracious things are told of you, O city of God…Yes, of Zion, it will be said, "This one and that one were born in her," and the most High himself establishes her. (Psalm 87:4-5)

Zion symbolizes peace:
> His tabernacle is in Salem. His dwelling place in Zion.
> There he broke the fiery arrows of the bow, the shield
> and the sword, and the battle." (Psalm 76:2-3)

One Rasta chant says of Zion: "No sin can enter in Mount Zion so bright and fair; No sin can enter there forever." Marley sees Zion as "the kingdom of Jah."

Ras Michael and the Sons of Negus remind us in song that "the kingdom of Rome is built on silver and gold" and that we should "make sure our gold-mine is found in Zion." The leading Rastafarian group called "Culture" says: "I and I want to go home, to look upon King Rastafari's pretty, pretty face" and that "the Black Starliner [Garvey's ship] will come to take us to Zion." Bob Marley hammers out this theme continuously:

> Zion train is coming our way...Oh people get on board...Soul train is coming our way...Oh man it is just self-control...Don't gain the whole world and lose your soul...
>
> I say fly away home to Zion...One bright morning when my work is over...I will fly away home."
>
> And so he did!

Rastafarians often explain that originally the Ark of the Covenant was kept in Jerusalem but that Jah, through Solomon's first-born Ethiopian son, ran off with the Ark to Ethiopia, back to its original place. Rasta lore has it that King Solomon had long had a vision, which he told to his priest Zobok, of how God would depart from Jerusalem to Ethiopia, the new Zion:

> That same night when Queen Sheba was there, Solomon saw a dream in which the sun came down from heaven and shone brilliantly over Israel, and then departed to Ethiopia to shine there forever. Then a sun far more brilliant came down and shone over Israel and the Israelites rejected that sun, and buried it, but that sun rose again and ascended into heaven, and paid no further heed to Israel. When Solomon understood the meaning of that vision, he was greatly disturbed and troubled in his mind, for he knew that the departure of the sun from Israel meant the departure of wisdom and God.

Many Rastas associate this new Jerusalem (Zion) with Africa, particularly with Ethiopia, and these Brethren think of repatriation as actually going back to Africa; others, however, locate Zion in Jamaica;

others do not associate Zion with any particular place but to the psychological and spiritual condition of being redeemed, to a condition of restored peace and wholesomeness, to finding the self as a result of following the will and the laws of Jah, the father of creation. The reward for this righteous and natural ("ital") way of living, says the Rastaman, is "ever-living life." Thus Zion represents the spiritual questing of Africans for spiritual fulfillment in their lives.

LION-MAN

The straight and narrow path out of Anancism (for Anancy) is the path of the Lion, say the majority of Rastafarians. They strive, therefore, to become lion-men.

Lionism is undoubtedly a major Rastafarian concept, very much tied in with Zion. Haile Selassie came in the name of the lion—as "The Conquering Lion of Judah" and as the "Man-Lion from Mount Zion." In Zion, Lion-man shall reign forever, sings Bob Marley, and "Culture" entreats us "to get ready to go to Zion to ride them lions," regarding themselves as examples: "Said I a lion, the righteous to Zion."

In the Old Testament, Jah was likened always to the lion. *Jeremiah* (50:44) depicts God as a lion:

> Behold [God] shall come up like a lion from the swelling of Jordan into the habitation of the strong: But I will make them suddenly run away from her: Who is a chosen man, that I might appoint over her? For who is like me? And who will appoint me the time? And who is that shepherd that will stand before me?

The prophet Hosiah also noted: "Therefore I will be unto them as a lion" (Hos. 13:7). In *Ezra* the Messiah is shown as the Lion of Judah at whose roar the last and worst beast—the Roman Eagle—

bursts into flames and is consumed. To the prophet *Baruch*, Jah revealed himself also as a mighty warrior—like a lion—who will bring the leaders of the Roman Empire in chains to Mount Zion and afterwards establish a Kingdom of Peace.

The lion as the official emblem of Ethiopia and the House of David has come to symbolize African manhood for Rastafarians. In Bible lore the lion is mentioned more often than any other non-domesticated animal. King Solomon entreated one of his women thus: "Come with me from Lebanon, my spouse...Look from the top of Amana...from the lion's dens."

(Song of Solomon, 4:8)

> And David said unto Saul, thy servant kept his father's sheep, and there came a lion and a bear, and took a lamb out of the flock; and I went out after him and smote him, and delivered it out of his mouth...And when he arose against me I caught him by his beard and smote him and slew him. Thy servant slew both lion and the bear.

The lion has also featured mightily in African folk culture as a symbol of manhood. Among the Hausas, the chief was often addressed as Lion (Ziaka), which for them represented power and dignity, and was a complimentary title for a chief, just as being called "bull" or "elephant" or "son of a wild beast" were compliments. Even in the Bible, God is sometimes addressed as "Abbir Y a'a Kob," literally meaning "Bull of Jacob," though this is often translated as "Mighty One of Jacob." Such early Egyptian rulers like Thotmes I and III, and Amenhotep I were also designated "Bull Kings" because of their greatness and power. The lion was the second member of the Triad of Gods at Memphis, and the loved and constant companion of the

God Ra himself. It was believed that around 2500 B.C. the Sun God Ra took the form of a lion, the Great Mau (Dr. Budge).

The lion is indeed an international symbol. The qualities of the lion and the tiger have gripped the imagination of men since the time of our oldest records. He is the acknowledged "king of beasts." In all of its aspects and in its total combination, the lion is the supreme international power totem—in its roar, hair, body strength and cleverness. Lions stress a kind of "moving territoriality," they stress "family pride," strong male/female roles and the training of the young, and family responsibility.

From anciency, every limb of the cat-lion was recognized as containing the potentialities of a god. The sacred cat-lion was described as possessing the "head of Ra, the eyes of Uraeus, the nose of Thoth, the ears of Neb-er-tcher, the mouth of Tem, the neck of Neheb-ka, the breast of Thoth, the heart of Ra, the hands of the gods, the belly of Osiris, the thighs of Menthu, the legs of Khensu, the feet of Amen-Horus, the haunches of Horus, the soles of the feet of Ra, and the bowels of Meh-Urit." (Budge)

The Sphinx at the Temple of Gizah is the largest monument in the world. It reveals two important traits: it is Negroid and it has lionized features. It is believed to have been built by the Black Pharaoh Khafre, and is said to be "an emblem of the strength united to understanding, of enlightened wisdom and true courage; in short, of the virtues which render man worthy of approaching the Deity and of entering his temples." The name itself—"Sphinx"—is said to be a Coptic (Egyptian) word meaning "a man who has his heart in his eyes, or is without disguise"—the opposite of Anancy.

Rastas start off as Anancies, but for Jah-related reasons they reincarnate themselves in and through the image of the dreaded African lion which they see as a more fitting Rasta ideal of Black manhood, expressing more of the natural and ideal spirit of Africans and offering a more wholesome definition of how they should live socially and feel inwardly. The lion thus represents the Brethren's symbolic yearning for power and wholesomeness to compensate for their powerlessness and their alienated existence. It symbolizes the resurgence of ancient African vibrations, ideals and definition of self. The lion symbolizes his own first person image of himself, as he transforms himself by discovering the secrets of getting more power.

So engrossed are Rastafarians with this lion symbolism that they actually see themselves as bearing the face, countenance, power, dignity, beauty, fearlessness and wholesome integrity which comes from the self-realization that he has it in him to become like the lion, if awakened enough. His "locks" are deliberately intended to symbolize the mane of the lion, and his dance form is referred to as the "lion skank." In spite of all their variations, Rastas seek to embody the face, strength and fearlessness which comes with the powerful self-realization formula: "I am Lion-Man." This is not talked about as if it involves only a mental resolution, but rather implies a real revolutionary change of the individual at the organic level. I can tell a Rastaman by looking at his overall vibrations, and after a few exchanges his level will manifest itself to me clearly.

Pictures of lions adorn Rasta music halls, their dwellings, their record shops, and they sing about the lion as a psychic exercise. It either accompanies the picture of the Emperor, or takes his place in Rastafarian representations. In fact, the facial features and presence of the lion has become more firmly implanted in the consciousness of Rastas than the face of Selassie, particularly since the Emperor was removed from his throne by the communists in 1974. The lion totem (by itself) is more and more being used to symbolize the ideals of the movement.

Both in Jamaica and in Guyana, in recent years, we have had reports of Dreadlocks trying to re-enact the experience of Daniel in the lion's den by attempting to cohabit the local zoo with the lions—sometimes getting killed in the attempt. The *Gleaner* of November 3, 1979 instanced this.

Lion symbolism also gives us a clue to the origin of the Rastafarian expression—"irie"—which is used to signal positive vibrations. But irie seems to derive from the Jewish Bible terms "Arieh" (lion) and "Ariel" (lion of God). So when the Rastaman feels irie, that means that he is feeling like a lion.

LAMB-MAN
"Many are called, but few are chosen."

While the majority of Rastafarians identify themselves with the dreaded lion, it does come through their overall movements and symbolisms that there is yet a higher level that is possible: that of the lamb.

In Eastern philosophy, this lamb-level is defined in numerical symbolism as the seventh level of consciousness, an internal clairvoyance stage in which one clearly sees and comprehends everything through infinite time and space, and manifesting itself as universal love and the capacity to embrace all opposites and turn them into complements.

In ancient Japan, this journey to discover the Kingdom of Heaven within ourselves is called *Do*, in India *Yoga*, and in China *Tao*. *Taoism* originated at the time of Confucius. By cultivating stillness through yogi practices, a few key individuals in each community could become perfect receptacles for Tao, the basic power of the Universe. Thereafter such persons could radiate a kind of healing, harmonious psychic influence over the communities in which they lived. The Taoist believed that successive deposits of toil and worry have so silted up our souls that it was necessary to work back through these layers until "man as he was meant to be" was reached.

Through this path or through others, man becomes divine when he trains his mind to a state of continued unbroken consciousness throughout waking, sleeping, death and onwards to the next incarnation upon this earth. With such wisdom, the individual can withstand every and any temptation to misuse power. For this reason, traditional African priests also trained over a period of 25 years. Power without wisdom is death. Babylon politics.

Vera Stanley Alder described this seventh level elite thus:

> Very advanced students become unaffected by heat or cold, wounds and poisons. They are able to perform feats usually considered as miracles, and they appear to have access to regions of wisdom and felicity undreamt of by us. People of this type move about us unsuspected. They do not advertise themselves; they are under a law which forbids them to help unless help is asked, or to give out knowledge unless it is sought and will be properly understood. They are ready and waiting for the time when a growing number of people sense their secrets and beg their help. When the general public have sufficiently advanced they will insist on being governed by persons of such attainments, and this will indeed begin the Coming of the Golden Age."
>
> (Alder, *Finding the Third Eye,* p. 25)

Anancy and Lion are both more extrovert and more like actors than the innocent and meek lamb. Both Anancy and Lion call each other Brother ("Brer") while simultaneously trying to outdo each other. But not the lamb, which is symbolic of a higher plane. The lamb is the gentlest of creatures, symbolic of innocence and truth, unchanging in its nature, a friend of children, and a world of contrast to Anancy's tricksterisms and dualisms, or the warring aura of the lion.

Moreover, lions are leaders and do not lend themselves to being easily led. Lions were often used in Roman times against gladiators and Christians in Roman arenas.

In Bible lore the lamb does symbolize Christ's level of spiritual power, though in the Old Testament the roaring lion takes on greater divine significance. Bible scholar H.S. Lewis, in *The Secret Doctrines of Jesus*, had this to say of lamb symbolism:

> Throughout the ages the Lamb had been the symbol of a great mystery, and its blood had been spared for special sacrifice at times and in places in cycles of unfolding civilization when the populace had never realized the spiritual or mystical significance of the ceremony, and it had remained the mystery of all mysteries, unrevealed to the greatest lights that had hinted at its significance. Jesus's mission was actually to demonstrate the mystery, rend the veil asunder, and expose to the soul of all mankind the process of purification and the way of salvation. (p. 70)

Thus, like a child the lamb became the symbol of innocence and the salt of the earth. When its innocent blood is shed, it becomes the nourishing salt of the earth. The lamb is the proverbial sufferer, the "child of sorrow acquainted with grief."

Coequal to the lamb in its symbolic meanings is the "dove" and the "child:" "Like as the arrows in the hands of the giants; even so are the young children."

(Psalm 127:4)

Christ prayed: "Father, Lord of Heaven and Earth, thank you for hiding all this from the learned and intelligent and revealing it to babes."

(Matt. 11:25)

> The wolf also shall dwell with the lamb, and the leopard shall lie down with the kid; and the calf, and the young lion, and the fatling together; and a little child shall lead them.
>
> (Isa. 11:6)

The New Testament indeed depicts Christ as the "Lamb of Calvary," the "Lamb of God," the "Good Shepherd," and his followers are regarded as his sheep.

In Revelations, John tells of the "Lamb's Book of Life" which records the names of the righteous. Christ said: "My sheep listen to my call. I know them and they know me" (John 10:25). "...I am the door for the sheep..." "I am the Good Shepherd who lays down his life for his sheep" (John 10:11).

To his immediate followers Christ said: "I am sending you out as sheep among wolves" (Matthew 3:16).

According to our rendering of John's Revelations it was the "Lion-transformed-to-the-Lamb" who opened the "seven seals" and was accordingly praised by the elders. The lamb has a kind of spiritual power lacking in the lion; for Christ's (the lamb) fists and hands were indeed more powerful than those of Mohammed Ali. The sheep is more like the lion asleep.

The lamb mentioned in Christ's teaching is thus the same "Lion of Judah" transformed into the lamb. That a lion can become a lamb is evidenced by the lion's returned kindness to the slave Androcles in the famous story of his lamb-like kindness at the very time when he was supposed to tear Androcles to pieces in the Roman arena; and it is also evidenced by the famous story of the young lioness, Elsa, told by Joy Adamson in *Born Free*, who had become so lamb-like that she had to be taught to kill before she could be returned to her native bush. It is also symbolized by the "tamed" lions who (like lambs) sported in the court of Haile Selassie.

The Book of Revelations makes it clear that it is the lamb who will be the eventual victor, the one who will inherit the earth:

> The lamb who is in the center of the throne will shepherd them and lead them to springs of living water...And God will wipe away all the tears from their eyes. (Rev. 7:17)

> They will war against the lamb, and the lamb will conquer them, for he is the Lord of Lords and King of Kings; while those with him are called chosen.
> (Rev. 17:14)

In ancient Egypt the sheep was a sacred animal, and Egyptian priests were not allowed to handle wool. Christ was pictured as a Good Shepherd holding a sheep in his left arm. In fact, there in ancient Egypt, from where this symbolic interpretation first arose, the term Shepherd designated the rule of a peaceful king, whereas Bull designated a warrior king.

Thus the proverbial "black sheep" is the original black Christ. Garvey took his image of the Black Christ Shepherd from the Ethiopian Coptic Church, which is the oldest Christian church in existence. Garvey himself was quick to recognize the guiding spirit of Christ: In his famous speech at Liberty Hall, New York on December 24, 1922, Garvey stated:

> For man to see his God, for man to face his judgment and become one of the elect of the High Divine, of the Holy One, is for man to live the life of Christ—the spotless life, the holy life, the life without sin, and that is a journey everyone in the Christian world is called upon to make...Man has fallen so low, so far, from his high estate, as created and given him by God, that even now man does not know himself except in the physical, but the physical does not make the man complete...There can be no peace until that peace reflects the spirit of the angels of nineteen centuries ago—the real peace actuated by love, love as that which Christ came into the world to give us.

Many Rastafarians today recognize the heights of lamb level. They nickname one species of herb "lambsbread." A number of such Rastafarians will be instanced to make the point. While the militant Peter Tosh was very much lion, Bob Marley in recent years went on up ahead, to the spiritual heights of the lamb, at the highest regions of Mount Zion High. The Ethiopian Coptic Church also recognizes the lamb, which it uses as its emblem.

Coptic Rastas or *members of the Ethiopian Coptic Church* take the position that Coptic civilization (ancient Egyptian) is primordial with creation and Christ, and which they say is symbolized by the Lamb rather than by the Lion:

> The Coptic way of life is thousands of years old and has not changed from the perfect principle of creation. We are herbalists who live a Bible life, a natural civilization of Godly self-government whose foundation is the moral laws of God.
>
> (*Coptic Times,* Vol. 2 No. 3)

They regard their Coptic priests as Shepherds and brethren who came down into hell (Jamaica) to civilize and Christianize the African descendants of slaves. They have declared: "The promise of redemption is now fulfilled in living glory embodied within the mystical brotherhood of the Coptic Church." Many Rastafarians dispute the sincerity of the Coptics, however, who many feel to be only an organization making money off herbs. It is not for me to judge.

Rastafarians are very conscious of differing levels of movements, of "ranking" and of "heights." The Lamb rank or "heights" is a measure of how far the lion-man has traveled out of the bottomless pit (of Babylon). At this level, he is qualitatively changed in the direction of greater spiritual awareness and power. There is a de-emphasis on outward symbols and rituals, including locks and herbal smoking, which were so important in his initial movements. The more certain he becomes of his own mental liberation, the more certain he rises to the spiritual heights of the lamb. At this level he might even forego his locks without feeling devitalized. For Coptic Rastas this is even viewed as necessary on the grounds that:

> A courageous man is a spiritual lion and does not require one to have matted and tangled hair. Locks is a symbol of war.

While this is true, at a certain stage locksing dramatizes one's break with conventional society, signifying greater independence.

Prince Edward Emmanuel heads the Rastafarian Melchizedek Orthodox Church, and his lamb-like character is revered by his followers as the reincarnated black Christ. Said he: "We only seek our daily food until the hour that the seven miles of Black Star Line come to take us home."

Stanley Beckford, founder of the politically insignificant "We

Party" of Jamaica, declares himself a prophet who has seen God face-to-face and to whom the secrets of the scroll were revealed, one of which being that Jamaica, if it is to attain peace, must be governed by a black lamb-king, for "he that killeth with the sword must be killed with the sword." For him:

> The strength of Africa is in the patience, faith and love for the lamb...Jamaica's throne will be great and her land with joyfulness will sing praises to God and the lamb.

The Rev. Claudius Henry is very much the example of a well-known Rastafarian who has gone through the recognizable stages—from Anancy to Lion to Lamb. A man given to receiving visions and scriptured inspirations from an early age, he was instrumental in deifying Haile Selassie. He was born in Jamaica, but while living in the U.S.A. he reported that in 1957 "an angel of God" appeared to him in a vision, instructing him to return to Jamaica, giving him the power to deal with these hard-hearted people; he also received a new name, Cyrus, "the son of righteousness." Wherever the name Jesus appears in a song or a verse his followers substitute Cyrus. His other titles include "Repairer of the Breach," "God's Approved Prophet and Israel's Leader," "Implement of the Holy Trinity," "God's Watchman Over the Nations," or simply "Another Moses leading Israel's scattered slaves back Home to Motherland of Africa." He holds that neither justice nor peace is to be had in heaven after death but is right here on earth, and preached the need for a "Leper's Government," which sounded like madness to many—and in fact Henry was examined for lunacy but was released.

Henry once called for the death penalty for violations of the Sabbath, which he said must be kept holy, and so he preached against the established churches for breaking this law of Jah.

In 1959, calling themselves the "Seventh Emmanuel Brethren," Henry promised immediate repatriation to Africa, printing cards as "substitute passports" which he sold for a shilling and which read: "Pioneering Israel's scattered children of African origin back home to Africa. This year 1959, deadline date, October 5th. This new government is God's righteous kingdom of everlasting peace on earth, creation's second birth." Many people sold their houses in preparation for repatriation. For this phase of his work he was sentenced to six years imprisonment, while in 1960 his sons took to the hills like lions or Anancies to train in guerrilla tactics. One witness for the Crown in this petite guerrilla uprising stated that Henry told him at the early stage of the plot:

> This is blackman's time. If we don't get what we want we will not stop until every black man is dead. Blood is going to flow and the white man or black man who tries to stop us will be killed. I am going to train an army stronger than lion and I am going to free Africa and go home. (Quoted by Barry Chevannes in *Repairer of the Breach*, an excellent discussion of this prophet and his role.)

Today Claudius Henry declares himself to be a lamb, the prophet standing in the gap, and anointed by Jah to "take over where His Imperial Majesty Haile Selassie left off." Like Noah, he said he was instructed to bring back the Ark of the Covenant to Israel. Jah instructed him to build a majestic house in Jamaica which he has named "Bethel." Out of this house, in which the spirit of the great and ever-living Jah is now resting, will spring forth miracles which the world has never seen before. The peace from this house, Bethel, located in Jamaica, will invade the whole world and free mankind. Bethel is for him the birthplace and headquarters of God's righteous government, a new world of love and everlasting peace.

HERBAL MEDITATIONS ("INITATIONS")

Rastafarian rituals include singing, chanting, dancing, drumming, reasonings, and the smoking of ganja. Often their ceremonies are referred to as Nyabinghi.

Rastas strongly believe that they follow Christ's example and have discovered the mystery of everliving life promised by Christ—that spiritual birth not born of woman. Rastas see the usage of herbs, particularly its smoking, as the catalyst for this spiritual rebirth. They are quick to point out that John's prophecy makes mention of this: "And I John saw the new Jerusalem... And he showed me a pure river...on either side of the river was the tree of life...And the leaves of the tree were for the healing of the nations." (Rev. 22:2)

Rastas have tested and experimented with ganja and reason that this must be the tree of life on the basis of its experienced effects.

Rastas thus come together around the usage of ganja, which they use for smoking, eating, drinking and sniffing as an holy herb. So omnipotent is this ingredient of their culture, and so positive is their estimation of its value to man, that they call it the wisdom weed and the spiritual food of the movement. Symbolically for Rastas, herb grew out of the grave of Solomon and, because of its wholesome effects, has the power to heal the nation by bringing every man to self-knowledge appropriate and fitting for everliving life.

The Ethiopian Zion Coptic Church (with chapters in Jamaica and Miami) reveres ganja as their holy eucharist and spiritual intensifier with Biblical, historical, and divine associations. Biblical justification for its use is found on the first page of the Bible (Genesis 1, verse 29). For the Brethren, ganja is the mystical body and blood of Jesus—the burnt offering unto God made by fire—which allows a member to see and know the "living God," or the "God-in-Man." They derive their moral authority to use the herbs from their personal experiences with the plant and also from the Book of Genesis, which approved the usage of "every herb bearing seed."

Rastas, through the use of ganja, feel themselves to be divinely inspired, experiencing the same magnificence of spirit and oneness with nature which Moses must have experienced high on the mountain top in the form of the burning bush (herbs), as did Jesus high on top of Mount Sinai.

Every Rastaman has experienced, to varying degrees, the wholesome effects of herbs. They talk of this all the time. That is the only reason for using it.

My initial report on the meaning and observed effects of herbs within the Rastafarian movement was first published in the Jamaican *Daily Gleaner*, and was later described by the Ethiopian Zion Coptic Church as "one of the more truthful articles about ganja," and was reprinted (without my knowledge) in their newspaper, *Coptic Times*.

Here is a section of that report, called "Ganja and African Consciousness:"

> ...The individual's usage of "herbs" have the wholesome effect of stimulating and facilitating one's return to "roots" vibrations, to energy source. In fact, this is the main significance of herbs at the individual level: it resurrects and stimulates dormant African vibrations. It helps some Rastas to find their way back to the "lost" Africa of the "I." It can stimulate the development of a vibrant body-power akin to those felt by the African ancients starting off with the lung expansion movements which the inhaling of the herbs stimulates.

In their desperation and despair blacks "rebel" by calling upon the powers of herbs which give them a glimpse and taste of original African vibrations and power. Herbs thus constitute a healing force according to Rastafarian Theory and experience. Used in its many forms and with proper understanding it can become a vehicle through which an ancient original power and spirit infuses the body with a primeval source of energy such that the "I" becomes more at one with his ancestral spirit. Two years of intensive observations of many different Rasta groups and individuals form the objective basis for these generalizations.

Original African youth vibrations can be stimulated back to life under the conscious usage of herbs. It unleashes a flow of energy in the body by showing the "I" a glimpse of the true heights of many splendid possibilities: most Rastas recall the workings of a powerful energy source on their minds and bodies, restoring them back to their more wholesome originality and potentiality, through many complex processes, interconnections and movements.

From my observations and studies I have seen enough to be convinced that in such a journey back to one's I-roots, one can retrieve such lost aspects of one's natural system like voice, rhythm, and creativity. Herbs, as used by Rastas help to rekindle African original vibrations by helping to break down the mental and physical stumbling-blocks in our physical unconsciousness. The brown or white skin Rastas are only responding to the African vibrations within their systems and must be judged no differently than other Rastas.

As the Rastaman experiments with herbs, using the prism of his own being and his own senses as the major judge in his experimental movements forward and inward, he learns to define what is good for the "I" and he thereby comes to know the "I" and he can work this new consciousness into his physical structure through a system of physical exercises. New dimensions and original vibrations of his being become stimulated back into action.

As one succeeds in traveling further back into one's essence, to the "I" one arrives at a subconscious layer of primeval energy and creativity which links the "I" to Africa and to the Universal. No wonder the untutored Rasta artists (poets, dramatists, painters, musicians etc.) come up with unmistakable African patterns, portraits and images, though like Marcus Garvey, they have never set foot in Africa.

Rastafarians thus use the holy herb to take them inwards, to their inner temple. This inner (spiritual) development is tantamount to finding Jah-God, when successful.

From experience, it has also been found that herbal usage is more essential and necessary in this inward journey at its initial stages. But as the Rastaman succeeds (many do fail) in integrating the positive effects of herbs into his body, his personality changes—deepens—and he reaches a higher level in which he no longer relies upon the sacrament (of "lambsbread" and "kings-bread") to reach this level. Eventually he is restored to a natural high resulting from his restored breath and the unity of I and I. This is the settled experience of Rastafarian folk prophets who flourish in the hillsides of Jamaica.

But supportive evidence comes to us also from others. The Don Juan described by Carlos Castaneda is really the Mexican-Indian equivalent of the Rastaman. This mystic used the "little smoke" (as he termed it) as a vehicle for taking him to "Mescalito," his ally or God. Said Don Juan:

> The smoke takes you to where the ally is, and when you become one with the ally you don't ever have to smoke again. From then on you can summon your ally at will and make him do anything you want.
> *A Separate Reality*, p. 45)

This secret knowledge is what constitutes sorcery in Don Juan's scheme. Most interestingly, Don Juan discusses two different levels of sorcery which are in fact equivalent to the Rastafarian movement from Anancy-to-Lion-to-Lamb. In Don Juan's scheme the stages are hunter, warrior and then "man of knowledge;" however, emphasis is placed on the second and third stages.

What the Rastaman designates as *lionism*, Don Juan calls the *warrior* stage, which causes a man to live strategically, to overcome fear of his own death, to take responsibility for his acts, and to develop his willpower and the endless capacity for struggling. The height of sorcery is, however, to be found at the stage beyond that of the warrior, according to Don Juan, though this warrior stage is a necessary prerequisite, just as the Rastaman finds that lionism is necessary before moving on to the higher regions of Mount Zion High. Don Juan tells Castaneda:

> My teacher was a sorcerer of great powers…His will was magnificent. But a man can still go further than that; a man can learn to *see*. Upon learning to *see* he no longer needs to live like a warrior…Upon learning to see a man becomes everything by becoming nothing…This is when a man can be or can get anything he desires…But he desires nothing, and instead of playing with his fellow-men like they were toys, he meets them in the midst of their folly.
>
> (*A Separate Reality*, p. 160)

The *man of knowledge* (equivalent to the lamb) is thus the *sorcerer* who perceives the world with his senses, with his will and with his "seeing." Once such a sorcerer is able to "see" he does not have to live like a warrior, for he can see things as they really are and direct life accordingly. He does not have to change (i.e., force) things but uses such forces by redirecting himself and adapting to their direction. However, the warrior stage must precede the ultimate stage: the lion must lay the foundations for the lamb. He warned: "To see without first being a warrior would make a person weak; it would give one a false meekness, a desire to retreat; and one's body would decay."

Chapter 5
THE GREAT GANJA CONTROVERSY

And God said, Behold, I have given you every herb bearing seed, which is upon the face of all the earth, and every tree, in which is the fruit of a tree yielding seed; to you it shall be for meat. (Genesis 1:29)

And I John, saw the New Jerusalem...and He showed me a pure river...on either side of the river was the tree of life...And the leaves of the tree were for the healing of the Nations. (Rev. 22:2)

You have five trees in Paradise...whoever knows them shall not taste death. (The Gospel According to Thomas)

If you know the story of all the leaves of the forest you would know all there is to know about the gods of Dahomey.
(Herskovits, *Dahomey*)

THE RASTAFARIAN THESIS:
"HERBS FOR THE HEALING OF THE NATION"

It is a well-known fact that trees have played an important role in mystical movements dating from remotest times, particularly the "Tree of Paradise" (or "tree of life") which is sought after in Jewish, Babylonian and African lore. Moses saw God through burning tree leaves: "And the Angel of the Lord appeared unto him in a flame of fire out of the midst of a bush...the bush burned with fire...God called unto him out of the midst of the bush, and said, 'Moses, Moses.'" (Exodus 3:2-4). Countless myths speak of the derivation of man from trees. Osiris was once "enclosed" in trees. Goddesses were often worshipped as trees.

From the Yorubas of Nigeria, the Kikuyu of Kenya, to the Pygmies of the Congo, Africans once held the notion that trees are sacred, that they are alive and full of ache (power), that each is endowed with a soul, and that each moves about, eats, and has a particular Orisha (spirit) as its guardian. Every Santerio priest among the Yorubas was a competent herbalist who could cure almost every disease with an herbal brew, or cast a tremendous spell with a few flowers.

In Jamaica the Rastaman has searched out among the available plants and roots to find that plant with the greatest ache, and he has discovered that it is ganja, which he ranks way ahead of its possible contenders: ahead of the sugar cane, banana, bread-fruit and coconut plants. There are Jamaican folk songs elevating each of these other contenders for the throne, but songs about ganja outnumber and outshine the others. Some songs about its contenders often make strong claims: "Coconut water makes you strong like lion." Most Rastafarians will tell you that while these other plants were used earlier to enslave blacks on plantation colonies, herbs have come to liberate them; "King Sugar's" rise to the throne meant black enslavement, as everyone knows.

Rastafarians come together around ganja and the usage of herbs in general. Ganja (also known locally as "cannabis," "weed," "hemp," "marijuana," "pot," "kali," "grass," "I-lley," and the "I-cient tree") is used as food, as drink, for sniffing, for massaging and for smoking. A very potent ganja oil is also extracted from the plant with the aid of a very strong alcohol in which it is boiled down and reduced to oil and is then used to coat regular cigarettes, smoked usually by wealthy foreigners. This is not a method among Rastafarians.

Herbal usage is all-pervasive among Rastafarians. They and herbs are like twin brothers, both outlawed or orphaned by official society. It forms the substance of their communion, their major source of income, the fountain of their inspiration, and the symbol of brotherhood, manhood and wisdom for them.

Over the past 50 years Rastafarians have "tasted" herbs and have proclaimed, on the basis of its effects, that herb is a force for the "healing of the nation"—physical, mental, spiritual and social.

For them, ganja is not a chemical drug but an herbal plant divined by Jah for the healing of the nation. It is a spiritual food or wisdom weed having the power to bring its users to the self-knowledge appropriate and fitting for an awakened and healthy life. For the Brethren, "God is a living man, and herbs is his gift of love for the healing of the nation."

Looked at from the political angle, this thesis declares herbs a non-violent means of achieving genuine liberation and de-colonization, and the sweet guarantee of increasing one's consciousness of life in general and not just class consciousness.

Rasta lore has it that ganja was removed from the Bible by mistranslations and by deceit, that there were references to King Solomon's priestly garments being made from ganja fiber, and that the original Hebrew religion involved use of herbs as an intoxicating incense.

Mr. Edward Seaga's work on the Congo heritage in Jamaica reveals that "Baba C," a 70-year-old "Kongo" man and a prominent transmitter of Kumina to Jamaica, knew of ganja—which in the Kongo culture of his memory was called "Mungwa." (*Sunday Gleaner Magazine,* 5/12/82)

This I-cient (ancient) tree is revered mainly for medicinal reasons, and Rastafarians over the past 35 years have bred progressively higher strains of herbs, as measured by its strength—its psychoactive ingredient, which varies from .2% in bush herbs to 6% in the seedless sensimilia herbs. The pricing of herbs varies with this sought-after THC content, ranging at source price from $20 per pound for bush herbs (low in THC content) to $400 per pound for sensimilia, which is the highest in THC content.

For Rastafarians, kali heals the trinity of body, mind and spirit, lifts them upwards toward the higher levels of spiritual consciousness, and makes them aware of the importance of their personal identity to their functional wholeness, health, and growth. It is used by them for lifting depression and easing hypertension, and is almost always prescribed for such common diseases as glaucoma, asthma, bladder irritation, ulcers, constipation, insomnia, malaria, and muscle cramps. Vera Rubin's study of the Rastafarians (*Cannabis and Culture*) reported some 30 ailments reported curable by marijuana, including asthma, colds, stomach disorders, fever, rheumatism, and muscle spasms. Rastas reported in this study that ganja made their blood strong, and that it gave them energy. Many had been smoking it regularly for 35 years, according to this study, without experiencing any signs of ill effects.

This practice is not an isolated element, but part of a way of life. Rastas have revived the African herbal tradition, giving rise to what they popularly refer to as the "Ital" tradition, which centers on the eating of herbs, grains, fruits and vegetables to the exclusion of meats, salts, artificial chemicals and sweeteners. It is also related to the keeping of the general commandments of Jah-Jah. So say the Nyabinghi Rastafarians, who represent the "purest" practitioners of this culture. All over the world, up until the 1850's, the medical treatment of illness and disease was based mainly upon the use of herbs and plants. Up to that period doctors as well as chemists produced their own medicines, but gradually medicine manufacturers took over the production. In fact, with the swift progress of the chemical industries, medicine based on plants were replaced by the "purer" synthetic preparations. In recent years, all over the world, there is a tendency once again to use herbs and plants in medicine, because many of the important ingredients of the natural plant cannot be produced synthetically and are destroyed by such treatment. Thus conceived the ital tradition of the Rastafarian is both preventive and curative medicine. The smoking of herbs for the Rastaman cannot be singled out from this herbal tradition as a whole, and is very much a part of the same world movement now afoot towards greater wholesomeness and spiritual power based on ancient precepts.

Rastas in fact emphasize that the international herb, along with reggae music, has played an important role in bringing together and grounding people of different social classes and varying racial origins and cultural traditions. Reggae is now on Broadway, they say. It draws as big a gathering at St. Peter's Square in Rome as an address by the Pope. Rastas sing, chant, and reason about the magnanimous power of herbs all the time. Over the past two decades in particular, reggae musicians have immortalized the herb in such popular hit songs as *Rita Marley's* "One Draw," *Peter Tosh's* "Legalize It," *Sugar Minott's* "Please, Mr. D.C.," *Bob Marley's* "Rebel Music" and "Easy Skanking," *Paul Hurlock's* "Someone Cut it Down," *Freddie McGregor's* "Natural Kali," *Jacob Miller's* "Tired fe lick weed inna Bush," *Black Uhuru's* "Stalk of Sensimilia," and *Culture's* "The International Herb." Those who can't sing quietly hum and chant its praises.

One of the foremost Rastafarian defenders of the herb was Peter Tosh, who dubbed himself the "Bush Doctor." In our epoch of mounting crisis and tensions, the Bush Doctor administers to himself as his own-self medicine man, democratically applying herbal potions (not only ganja) to attain bio-energetic equilibrium and balance, a state of private internal harmony. Peter Tosh was recognized and honored by a well-known health institute for his contribution to holistic health.

The usage of herbs by the Rasta Bush Doctor (on himself) gives him a personal power and personal dimension unknown to the non-experimenter. As Peter Tosh testified in song: "Anything you can do, I can do it better, I'm the toughest." The creative and artistic vitality of the Rastaman offers ample proof of this.

Through the growing physical-mind-self-awareness which the herbal potion induces and stimulates, the Bush Doctor moves to the center of his being, to his essence, to his Big I, and thereby discovers more of himself in its anciency and primeval wholesomeness and power. To reach this state, vast layers of European and African indoctrinations (which cloud over the Big "I") have to be transcended. Peter Tosh, Bush Doctor superstar, understood all of this, and made himself a major exponent in the movement to legalize the plant. Through his songs he educated the populace into the consciousness that cigarettes are bad for their health while ganja is good. After all, even in the U.S. the Surgeon General warns on each packet of cigarettes sold in that country that the stuff is dangerous to one's health. With patience and time, a handful of herb seeds can multiply almost as if by magic, whereas alcohol is produced only after several long and expensive processes.

Like Dr. Freddie Hickling, the Senior Medical Officer at Bellevue Mental Hospital, Peter knows that "it is the only cure for glaucoma," and that it is good for asthma and many other mental and physical ailments. To deny this would mean to deny himself and his discovered truths, just as Judas did toward Christ.

The Rastafarian thesis concerning the herbal effect was summarized by the author an earlier appeared in Jamaica's *Daily Gleaner* under the heading "Ganja and African Consciousness," and was later reprinted in *Coptic Times* under the caption "One Step Closer." It has appeared here in Chapter 4.

THE INTERNATIONAL HERB

Similar claims about the curative and holistic powers of ganja have been made by many others in many other countries and traditions. Precisely because these claims stretch from the most ancient times to the present, they cannot be dismissed without imposing a great injustice on ourselves. It was a staple medication in many remote Asian, Arabian and African communities. Ancient Chinese, Persian and Indian texts indicate that since pre-history cannabis has had diverse medical usages: relief of pain, countering appetite loss, acting as a mood elevator and tranquilizer. Indian texts refer to it as "vigahia"—"the source of happiness"—and as "anada"—"laughter-provoker." Historical records show its earliest use in ancient China. The legendary Chinese emperor Shen-Nung encouraged his people to cultivate the plant and taxes were paid in hemp stalks in 500 B.C. China.

Not even the Japanese can be left out, as one Japanese ode goes: "I would have O Aze' decorated like a young pine tree with pieces of hemp hanging on the branches." Herodotus was the first Greek scholar who made mention of hemp (c. 460 B.C.), noting that the inhabitants of the Siberian mountain regions made clothing from it and also breathed the vapors of its burning seed. In his travels to the East, Marco Polo was also introduced to the herbal experience and was informed that it would take him to paradise.

It was even known in the New World among the Aztecs—long before the coming of the Europeans. At the beginning of the

Christian era, hemp was the main source of clothing for the known world, and the ships that sailed the seas had ropes and sails made from it. Among the items which King James I instructed his New World subjects to grow were hemp, flax and silkgrass. And in 1630 half of the winter garments in America, and nearly all its summer clothing, were made from hemp. But with the advent of steam power for ships and the invention of the cotton gin in 1793 (which made cotton growing efficient), the usefulness of hemp began to decline.

Throughout this earlier period, the medicinal and psychological aspects of hemp were known by a few. The plant was used commercially for uses other than for smoking. New Orleans was the first American city where hemp for smoking became a great fad in the 1920's, based on easily obtainable Mexican herbs. But by 1936 Americans became frightened when herbs began to be stereotyped as "causing" crimes. In 1937 the Federal Marijuana Tax Act came into being.

The main commercial growing areas today are Columbia, Mexico, Jamaica, India, Pakistan, Afghanistan, Morocco, Lebanon and Thailand.

The *first major historic report stressing the medicinal side of ganja* was by a physician named O'Shaughnessy, who in Calcutta in 1843 tested hemp on all his patients and reported that it was effective as a pain reliever, a muscle relaxer and an anticonvulsant. In no uncertain terms, it was reported that: "The leaves make a good snuff for deterging the brain; the juice of the leaves applied to the head as a wash, removes dandrin and vermin; drops of the juice thrown into the ear allay pain, and destroy worms or insects. It checks diarrhea; is useful in gonorrhea, restrains seminal secretions; and is diuretic. The bark has a similar effect; it destroys phlegm, expels flatulence, induces costiveness, sharpens the memory, increases eloquence, excites the appetite, and acts as a general tonic; the powder is recommended as an external application to fresh wounds and sores, and for causing granulations; a poultice of the boiled root and leaves for discussing inflammations, and cure of erysipelas, and for allaying neuralgic pains."

He tells us, moreover, that the powdered leaves check diarrhea, are stomachic, cure the malady named Pitao, and moderate excessive secretion of bile. He mentions the use of hemp smoke as an enema in strangulated hernia, and of the leaves as an antidote to poisoning by orpiment.

In India there were licensed agents responsible for its growing and distribution. Along the River Ganges, kali was smoked when invoking the favors of the great, terrifying black earth goddess—Kali Mam—for the attainment of the impossible and for inner strength.

For similar reasons, ganja was smoked by the Shiva worshippers in India, but it is most visibly used today by the *peyote cults* amongst North American Indians. These Indians have organized themselves into the Native American Church and practice a kind of love-feast where slices of peyote take the place of the sacramental bread and wine. They regard this cactus plant as God's special gift to the Indians, and equate its effects with the workings of the divine spirit. For these Indians, religious experience had to be direct and illuminating. In short, they sought mystical experiences. Under its influence they see visions or hear the voice of the Great Spirit; sometimes they become aware of the presence of God and of those personal shortcomings which must be corrected if they are to do His will.

The Central American Indians are also notable for the importance placed on hallucinogenic plants. This comes to us most systematically through the writings of Carlos Castaneda, a UCLA student who became a scribe to Don Juan, an Indian mystic and man of knowledge. These writings include *The Teachings of Don Juan* (1968), *A Separate Reality* (1971), and *Journey to Ixlan* (1972). Don Juan taught Castaneda about two such plants which furnish people with insights on how to live. There is "datura," which gives the ability to divine, through visual and auditory hallucinations, and which gives a sense of extreme power but creates a dependency in those who use it. Then there is the "little smoke" (Don Juan's), which creates a state of bodilessness from which one can transmute oneself into a crow, fly through space and perceive from above, just as a crow does.

It is surprising for many to hear that the growing of hemp was very important in the earlier days of America's Protestant heyday, at the earlier days of her colonization. There were 28 medically approved marijuana preparations on the U.S. market from the mid-nineteenth–century until 1937, when the marijuana tax effectively ended the medical use of hemp.

OPPOSITION TO HERBS
Commenting on the Federal Marijuana Tax Act of 1937, Robert S. de Ropp, a noted doctor who has studied the herbal effect, stated:

> Scientists who have studied marijuana agree it is a very innocuous drug, non-poisonous, non-addicting; and does not even produce a hangover. As an example of a prohibitive legislation at its worst, the Marijuana Tax Act can hardly be improved upon. It is founded in ignorance, nourished by superstition, and pervaded by a spirit of vindictive self righteousness that places it on a level with the old laws relating to witchcraft. A myth, the Marijuana Menace, has been created that has about as much substance as a medieval succubus. In the name of this myth otherwise respectable citizens are thrown into jail like common criminals for having it in their possession..."

(Don Wakefield, "The Prodigal Powers of Pot," *Playboy Magazine,* August 1963)

In Jamaica, as in most countries around the world today, the cultivation, sale, distribution, possession and use of ganja is a "criminal" offense. This has meant that people who have discovered the medicinal powers of herbs are defied, harassed, "busted," and put behind bars with other types of criminals without any distinction made between them. For instance, in September 1978, the well-known reggae superstar and Bush Doctor Peter Tosh was severely beaten and eventually fined $250 (or three months' imprisonment)—on top of his broken arm and an injury to his head. There are continually many cases where even old people, and particularly the ordinary "little man," are fined and humiliated in the courts and on the streets of Jamaica today for the possession of an ounce of herbs expressly used for private administration. And why? What do some people have against herbs?

Herb has been accused and charged for bringing about negative effects—effects which are contrary to the Rastafarian thesis and against the mainstream experiences of the Rastafarians themselves. Among its alleged "dangerous" effects are charges of chromosome damage, testosterone deficiency, and other harmful effects on the sexual and reproductive functions; it is ominously indicted as increasing one's susceptibility to disease: "Precarious effects on lungs...produces sinusitis, pharyngites, bronchitis, emphysema...a cause of psychosis in Jamaica ...Increase in impotence (20%)...negative personality changes..." rants a recent medical practitioner.

It has also been linked to "crimes," "guns," "violence," etc., and is seen as contributing to the upsurge in crime over the years. No one can deny its linkage with the criminal underworld, but the reason for this accusation has more to do with the persons who enter this field to exploit the high cash value of herbs, and has nothing at all to do with the inner content of the herb itself. Because of its illegal status and high cash value, the herb industry is a factory and school for

Anancism. Racketeers and outright criminals, most of whom do not even smoke the herb, but traffic in it purely for commercial gain. They use violence to protect their interest when necessary, and involve themselves in the high level of corruption of political, security and business officials, as well as dealing in "hard" drugs. An equally large network of police and military personnel exists, supposedly to close down this international herb business. However, it would seem that the herb trade is partly sustained by the cooperation of significant numbers of security officials who wax privately in conspicuous affluence. A Penguin paperback by Barry Cox called *The Fall of Scotland Yard* (1977) exposed the extent of this involvement in British society, and is a Revelations text in itself. In 1978, according to the U.S. Drug Enforcement Administration, cannabis ranked third as a big business—behind General Motors and Exxon—and was far ahead of Ford and Mobil Oil or the liquor, wine and beer industries.

No one can deny these kinds of negative intrusions and the takeover of the herbal field by profiteers, but this kind of problem is not the same as the problems and dangers attributed to the smoke itself. The so-called "scientific studies" which indict herbs for all kinds of maladies are themselves most deficient and distorting of the reality, much more than the herb itself.

But who indicts these scientists and calls this bluff? Most of these accounts are usually very bitty ("middle-range," in sociological language) and are conducted in artificial (laboratory) situations; they are not done over time to see the long-term effects and many are conducted on rats and like creatures that do not reason or meditate, which is the decisive mediating aspect in the case of human beings. One's mind and its power can and does *guide and affect the herbal effect*, medical and otherwise. It constructs a kind of safety-valve margin to protect itself. A sick mind in a sick body can indeed be overpowered by the "forces" or spirits in herbs, in which case it is the weakness of the man's mind that is at fault rather than herbs per se.

Addressing herself to some of the charges against herbs, a very perceptive white anthropologist, Dr. Carol Yawney, who wrote her Ph.D. thesis on the Rastafarians in Jamaica, remarked:

> The Cannabis high is not to be identified with its symptoms. It is not synaesthesia, dichotomous thinking, euphoria, love, dissociation, sensuality or time and space distortions, though all these features may be involved separately or in combination. All these are epiphenomena; *the essence of the experience is to realize the arbitrariness of one's customary codes by exaggerating their contents out of proportion…Providing the individual does not fixate at some point his consciousness gradually comes to detach itself from the grids and codes imposed upon it…*This detachment leads to greater volitional control…
>
> It tends to dissolve the boundaries imposed upon consciousness by Culture, forcing an awareness of the redundant and arbitrary content of social interaction.

Dr. Vera Rubin conducted a large-scale field study in Jamaica in 1974 and found that there was no evidence of these deficiencies among the users of herbs, and that herbs constituted a benevolent alternative to alcohol. Several groups of Coptic smokers were examined in Jamaica by teams of U.S. doctors with the aid of a Jamaican neurologist, Dr. Lampart; none of the Coptics examined exhibited any harmful effects from ganja smoking; the group had no trouble concentrating, there were no significant memory disturbances, no evidence of psychopathology or cognitive disorders. Most of these people had never seen a doctor, according to this report, as they enjoyed remarkable health and excellent physical condition.

CURRENT USAGE OF HERBS

In spite of its illegal status, the people's choice towards herbs is indicated by the lengths to which they will go to procure this substance and to break the "law." This trend, however, is allowed for by the spirit of the Jamaican Constitution and that of the U.N. Declaration of Human Rights, not to mention its consistency with the spirit of Africans. The *Jamaican Constitution* states:

> Except with his own consent, no person shall be hindered in the enjoyment of his freedom of conscience, and for the purposes of this section the said freedom to change his religion or belief, and freedom, either alone or in community with others, and both in public and in private to manifest and propagate his religion or belief in worship, teaching and observance.

Article 18 of the United Nations Declaration of Human Rights similarly states:

> Everyone has the right to freedom of thought, conscience and religion: this right includes freedom to change his religion or belief, and freedom, either alone or in community with others and in public or private, to manifest his religion or belief in teaching, practice, worship and observance.

Ganja pervades Jamaican society from the squalid shanty towns of Kingston to the exquisite beaches of Montego Bay and Negril. At least half of Jamaica's 2.1 million citizens think that life goes on better with ganja, according to Dr. Carl Stone's survey, known as always for its stunning accuracy and reliability. For those Jamaicans, smoking a joint carries about the same moral weight as a coke for an American, according to Dr. Stone's survey. I would add that every joint smoked is a people's vote for the Rastaman's thesis. Herb is regularly used at many public events in the presence of prime ministers, the highest ministers of government, and top-notch police officers and ministers of security.

Ganja plants can now be found growing not only in the hills and in ghetto gardens, but also in well-to-do suburban and residential flower beds. Ganja soaked in rum is a basic folk medicine in Jamaica, recommended and used widely for colds, fevers, throat and stomach infections. Jamaica has been described as a "virtual laboratory-museum of a cannabis-based cultural lifestyle." Every reggae lover is either a smoker or a potential smoker of the herb, and by supporting reggae music ("music to the King"), they are supporting the herb.

The widespread use of herbs is now diffused to the non-Rastafarian population as well, both in Jamaica and in metropolitan societies. Its widespread usage internationally is attested to by the various post-war international commissions specifically set up to study what was usually perceived as "the growing epidemic of drug abuse:" There has been the National Commission on Marijuana in the United States (1972), the Wooten Commission in Britain (1968), the Canadian Commission (1970, 1973), and several others in Western countries, including Jamaica.

The trend has been towards an upswing in its usage, and there doesn't seem to be any turning back. Herb smoking is more than a passing fad. "Between 1965 and 1970 the number of Marijuana offenses in the U.S. increased 1,000 fold. In Canada convictions for the possession of Cannabis rose from 25 in 1964 to 10,695 in 1972." (John W. Commissiong, *Ganja*)

The World Health Organization estimates that there are over

200 million people around the world who use ganja, with some 30 million smokers in the U.S. alone. Its usage has now become a cross-class and cross-race cultural habit, even to the point where foreign princes and princesses, sons and daughters of presidents, and wives of prime ministers have been noted in the press as having "tried" herbs. The Canadian Commission, as early as 1970, suggested that "the middle class Canadian housewife is now the typical abuser."

The widespread selling of rolling papers, pipes and other smoking aids in confectionery stores in Europe and America, as well as the continuing and surging popularity of reggae music and the movement of Jah Rastafari, are certain proof of this twilight region of the mystical herb.

"A sort of bootleg pot procurement operation seems underway," reported one writer, "with nice old ladies with glaucoma 'scoring' from their grandchildren and learning how to roll and smoke joints. Cancer patients unable to gain relief from standard drugs are using herbs, not for fun, but to help relieve the nausea caused by chemotherapy."

There is growing evidence that even the medical profession is now catching on. Pure derivative and synthetic variations of cannabis are being tested for their ability to relieve pain, asthma, epilepsy, multiple sclerosis, glaucoma and the side effects of chemotherapy treatment for cancer.

Following the report of Jamaican fishermen that their exceptional night vision was due to the drinking of white rum soaked in ganja, Dr. Manley West, in association with orphalmologist Dr. Albert Lockhart, both from the U.W.I., set about developing a medication—Canosol—which has been reported as a "breakthrough" in the treatment of glaucoma. Glaucoma is a leading source of blindness, caused by excessive pressure within the eyeballs due to an imbalance of ocular fluid. Dr. West is also experimenting with herbs as a treatment for asthmatic patients and has already reported that canosol has been found to work "like magic" as it relieves breathing almost immediately and increases one's air intake, with general improvements in lung functioning. Ganja smoking causes a dilation of the bronchial tract. Asthmatics suffer from bronchial spasms that constrict the bronchioles. The THC (psychoactive) element in ganja actually helps in bronchodilation.

Now medical doctors in over 20 North American states are legally able to prescribe cannabis where necessary, while health-conscious naturalists increasingly use it as a safe home remedy. A growing number of the world's youth are also using the herb as a functional equivalent of the more dangerous cigarettes and alcohol.

Other possible therapeutic applications for the herb which have already been acknowledged by some doctors and pharmacists include its use as an antiepileptic, an antibiotic, an appetite stimulant which also lowers stomach acidity, and as a sedative and pain reliever. In addition, work is proceeding on the use of cannabis to treat menstrual abnormalities, migraine and headaches.

Czechoslovakian scientists have surveyed thousands of plants for antibiotic activity and found preparations of cannabis among the most promising. Preparations of this sort are applied to the skin and mucous membranes as a salve or as a spray. The University of Missouri has a five acre ganja farm used for experimental purposes, under the direction of the National Institute of Drug Abuse.

The personal use of cannabis has already been decriminalized in Colombia, Holland, Italy, Alaska and at least eleven other North American states, with decriminalization bills pending in over twenty other states. In Holland, a shop operates legally where monitored quantities are legally sold over the counter. Such is the trend. But in Jamaica? The truth will set it free.

What is a dream when you can't
remember your dream.
What is a song when you can't
sing your voice sounds like
broken glass.
What is love when you can't
understand love is like
the bitter night.
What is a smile when your
face is always in a frown.
What is a cry when there are
no tears.
What is pain when there is
no hurt.
What is feeling when you
can't feel your feeling.
What is emptiness when
your body is unwhole
 What it is
 what it is
Is the dream which you remember
and afraid of its beauty
afraid of your dreams
 What it is
 what it is
Is the song which you like
to sing and dance and afraid
of its rhythms, afraid of the beat
 What it is
 what it is
Is the love you have in your soul

and you are afraid to share it
afraid to express it
    What it is
    what it is
Is a smile which lives in you
in your heartbeat
which you are afraid to open
    What it is
    what it is
Is the cry with the joy
which has to be seen
    What it is
    what it is
Is the pain which has to liberate
you towards your freedom
is a pain which has to be expressed
    What it is
    what it is
Is the emptiness of the day
Fulfillment of its God creation
giving thanks to every living thing
    What it is
    what it is
Is a fear that everyone
hides themselves in their own mask
    What it is
    what it is
Is a selfishness that breeds
within your body stopping
yourself from growing
    What it is

what it is
It is a human trap in slavery
trapping every living life creation
    What it is
    what it is
It is a madness—madness
Man-made madness—madness
    What it is
    what it is
You got to set yourself free
free yourself from your own slavery
    What it is
    what it is
You got to unmask yourself
to be free unmask yourself
    This is it
    that is it
    what it is
    this is it
    THIS IS IT
    Unmask yourself
    Free yourself.

        Frank John

Chapter 6

ON THE GANJA TRAIL: ENTER MY STORY

"Do not criticize your brother until you have walked for a mile in his moccasins. Or, at least, hear what he has to say." (Indian saying)

PERSONAL TESTIMONY AND SOCIOLOGICAL METHODOLOGY

What is the real truth about herbs and its effect? How do we go about discovering the truth about herbs and how can we ensure that this is indeed the truth? It seems that the matter needs serious investigation and that all ingenuity should be applied to discovering this truth very quickly.

Why are so many people of different races, ages, classes and stages using it, while so many are so against it? Herbs today is like the "lover who stands accused of love and is found guilty." People are very confused in their minds about it; it has been accused of leading to peace (or apathy) as well as to aggression, sexual impotence as well as sexual lionism, activism as well as docility, the road to heaven as well as to hell.

Faulty methodology and differing values are no doubt the main causes for this confusion. In sociological language, research into herbs needs to be "grounded," as the only way of arriving at sure truth about the matter. A great deal of information about the personal effects of herbs and about its economic aspects are available from the subjective and business experiences of its users and growers. It seems tragic, however, that up to now so little scientific and economic use has been made of this experience and knowledge.

This view is shared by an increasing number of people today. While all kinds of artificial (laboratory) experiments are conducted to test the Rastaman's thesis (with distorting results) we continue to ignore the simple testimony of its users who have interacted with herbs naturally and have either been successful or unsuccessful in taming and integrating its spiritual powers. In either case, their stories and experiences, and the analysis of this data, is the surest scientific route to knowing this plant.

My experimentation with herbs draws its strength from this position expressed so aptly by Makeda Lee: "The ganja experience must be respected foremost by the testimony of those of its users who have been fortunate to receive the blessing of its wisdom and through it, come to a closer understanding of the full power of God-liness that resides in each human waiting to be put to maximum use."

Unlike the majority of our present-day black intellectuals, I do not find it impossible to combine the role of responsible and sensitive human beings with that of scientist. Thus my personal experiences and research with herbs form the primary data on which my conclusions are based. I have no other basis for drawing my conclusions, other than those furnished by biographical experiences.

My work with herbs has taken place over the ten year period 1972-1982. I will therefore, in this chapter, recall and analyze the effects of herbs as part of my total life-process over this period of time, and these will be checked against the experiences of others. In this way I hope to show both the negative and positive spirits that can be aroused by herbs. My experiences will then be placed in the next chapter within the theoretical framework of what is known in the Orient as the chakras, as a means of systematizing and illuminating the general effects of my study on the total human being.

As I am committed to the scientific quest in the study of man, I was very conscious throughout my study with ensuring the maximum accuracy and reliability of my participatory observations. Of necessity, my methodology had to adapt to the nature of the subject matter being studied. In this case the technique had to be creatively indulgent, often to the point of placing me on a limb or placing me in circular movements (which others could not understand) just in order to see and feel certain things for myself even if they were dangerous or were defined as "criminal." Because the cultural context in which I operated was based so much on Anancism, it would have been most unscientific to rely on the simple, straightforward and conventional methods of interviewing and questionnairing people. I had to design and apply a creative methodology in order to extract the healing spirit from herbs and to see the reactions of others as well as myself—a process that was more like wrestling with a power until it yields its power; or why it would not.

A combination of techniques and approaches were used in order to ensure as much objectivity or truthfulness to my conclusions as is possible. Much patience, curiosity, doubting, questioning, circular movements, meditations, checking and cross-checking were involved.

This by itself demanded much deintellectualizing on my part, and a return to groundings.

My general method might be called bio-social feedback or bio-social cybernetics. It consisted of using primarily the reactions of my own biological system, cross-checked against the external reactions of others, in pursuit of some predetermined goal—in this case health and peace of mind. This is the methodology of what might be called "I and I;" it involves being one's own supervisor, doctor and psychoanalyst. *But for this process to be effective, the experimenter's mind must always remain in control—directly, watching, noting, double-checking, and measuring these changes upon the body and upon the mind itself. Only a mind governed by Truth (the higher self) can measure and steer these changes successfully, a mind that strives to distinguish between truth and falsehood, between the little I of our lower self and the big I of the divine God-head, and sees the supremacy in the big I.*

I relied heavily upon my own bodily feelings and upon my senses in monitoring the daily effects of herbs: my ears, eyes, nose, touch, and feelings were all brought into the operation and became sensitive monitors, watchful and vigilant in registering the herbal effect on my mind. These sense monitors and their findings were constantly checked one against the other. In this way I developed concrete organic sign-posts as organic indicators and proof (both internal and external) that I was following an effective path, thereby placing my faith (in herbs) on solid foundations. Faith returned with clearer understanding of this journey into self-exploration, attested to by my own self-growth which I myself could see, touch, smell and feel—even if others did not want to note these or were too blind to see them.

Effects that I observed on myself were constantly compared and checked against the effects on others, and as these were perceived by others. I watched myself through other people's eyes, through their general reactions in words, body-language, gestures, and thought. I began penetrating the herbal impact from all sides and angles—as I felt it, and as others saw it and conveyed it to me, either consciously or unconsciously.

My brother and an attorney-at-law, I-Roy Forsythe, figured importantly as my control element, one of those significant others whose reactions provided me with a significant and unique *mirror*. He accompanied me on many of my field trips into the most offbeat places, and as a non-smoker his presence was *built into* the cycle of my Rastafarian movements most naturally, as a control unit and as an alert stand-by force outside the dynamics of my own herbal trip. I know that he could be relied upon for sound advice; and that if I faltered or showed any tendency to fall off the deep end of my research, he would be the first to show intelligent concern which I would take seriously. I would then withdraw, as I have never regarded myself as hard of hearing to intelligent counseling and wise guidance. He, along with my other brothers, also provided a very important and unique opportunity for constant comparisons as the various indicators of the herbal effect registered their effects on my body and mind structures. Most times they were not aware of what was going on and what was underneath my movements. This bio-social feedback technique meant that everything that happened to me during this period became data. I looked forward to each new day and every encounter as data. It was partly for this reason of collecting feedback data for my thesis that I wrote a weekly column in the Jamaican *Daily Gleaner* for a year, and took it in to them *personally* as a way of drawing forth responses to the Rastafarian thesis, which I began to identify with and systematize in this weekly column. Whichever way people reacted to it and me (even by ignoring it) was data. The sought-after reactions to this thesis was frequently voiced in the Jamaican *Daily Gleaner*, as I expected, and there were often some lively polemical exchanges centering around this Great Ganja Controversy.

My personal interaction to herbs has been such a highly dynamic process that the effects of herbs were ever-changing, constantly posing new challenges, generating new vibrations and effecting new life situations, some of which themselves come about when people come to know that you use herbs and they then start acting differently towards you. *To tap the effects of herbs on my own person and the task of finding a suitable language for organizing and communicating these effects to others—as well as the lionism to tell a part of this story, was itself the greatest intellectual challenge to date in my life.* How should I tell my story (both outer and inner), a story involving so much guerrilla experimentation in this underground terrain? How much of it should I tell? What concepts must I use in translating this inner mystical experience induced by herbs? Such was the challenge. My method boils down to that of simply telling my story as it happened, as the process was revealed to me.

THE PRE-EXPERIMENTAL STAGE

I grew up in a cultural environment in which herbs was used all round—in the making of beverages (as tea), for massaging and bathing, for smoking, eating, divining the spirits of the dead, or simply as medicine. Ganja was, however, put in a category all by itself and was taboo.

I was too disciplined as a child ever to have dared touching the taboo "devil's weed." Moreover, as I saw it then, and felt (even to this day), my major problem then was how to move up in this world, away from the squalor and misery of my youth to a better mode of existence. "Better" meant moving far away.

Precisely because I come from a poor, non-literary folk background, I was overschooled to the notion that a proper education was my only crutch—my Jacob's ladder, stretching from the mire—from the bottomless pit, to heaven of being a somebody with a comfortable and secure life. The school and the church were thus inseparable, both in their effect and in their administration. Both were central forces—outside my extended family and community—which shaped my youthful life. In those years teachers were giants. They were folks that forward-looking children could look up to with respect, in appreciation for guidance to their helpless souls that were in need of firm guidance. "Silver and gold may vanish away, but a good education will never decay" ... "Early to bed, early to rise, makes a man healthy, wealthy and wise" ... "A child should be seen and not heard" ... "Spare not the rod and spoil the child" ... I grew up under these maxims and their tried—and often tired—applications.

In spite of the nagging and awesome discipline, which I experienced as hurt and downpression in my youth at the hands of hard-pressed adults and an overly disciplinarian community, I accepted the high value placed on proper education. It was my only hope in getting away and rising upwards. Getting away to *where* was not then my main concern. I could see in those early years that my brightness stood me in good stead with adults, I could make points with girls and use it to win favors from bullies. School days—such were they! Mirrors to all our futures. My primary objective at this stage of relative innocence, my primary and rightful objective, was the acquisition of a suitable education that would provide me and my family with a secure avenue of social upliftment from the mire of the squalid and humiliating poverty which I knew intimately in those most delicate and formative years of childhood. There was no one else to blame for the condition of my birth, nor did I know this modern antic of always blaming everyone but ourselves.

Second to education in my life was religion and the church. For me, this meant unceasing Sunday School attendance, Sunday services, prayer meetings ("meet-hims" for the girls!) and gospel meetings. If my 70 year old great-aunt could not attend church on a particular occasion, she would make sure that I reported on the specific sermon that she had missed, just to ensure that I attended church and paid attention. Religion for me in those days meant being lured away to street corners and off-track places to listen to the religious sects that populated rural communities in those days, pulling us to them by the pulsating ridims of drums, clapping, singing and the mystery of spirit possessions. At the age of fourteen I was ordained as a member of the local Presbyterian church, but I remember distinctly that we had to be circumspect in our movements: no clapping, not the slightest tendency of getting carried away, and definitely no drumming. Yet I was an African in essence, needing the same expressions then as my ancient forefathers of old—of ancient Egypt—who worked out the original contract between God and man, and who decreed music to be good.

These were my dry, non-smoking, opposition-to-herbs years. They were necessary. I believed them, and I do believe still, that the individual should exercise complete responsibility for what he does all the time and what happens to him, and that one should not impair one's self-control and one's center of judgment.

THE NOVICE STAGE: THE NORTH AMERICAN HIGH

I was 26, I had finished my training as a sociologist at McGill University, Montreal, and was already an established lecturer, when I began experimenting with herbs. I felt the need for it then, and felt also that the same spirits and the same intelligence, reason and mind that had guided me thus far in the choices I had to make from boyhood up could also be relied upon to guide my usage of herbs and had earned me this right. I was thus not afraid of it and never felt that it could harm me in any way, but I approached it, nevertheless, with the caution of a cat.

Intellectually I was astute enough in reasoning that in this world of confusion one must sometimes work things out for one's self, as the truth has to be hunted down and searched out at times. As a sociologist this was my role. I reasoned that anti-ganja laws could very well be like the other Establishment laws (from the top) which have been used in the past to suppress aspects of African religion and culture, for fear that their cultivation and articulation will unleash some feared African spirit or power which would make Africans henceforward more uncontrollable or more threatening to white power. Like the laws instituted in the Caribbean against black involvement with limbo dancing, Obeah and shell-blowing in the 18th Century.

I had become intellectually broadminded enough and secure enough economically to break the taboo on smoking herbs, as the next stage in my intellectual pursuit for truth and personal quest for happiness.

This was the stage of the "North American high," with emphasis on pulling the smoke up into one's head rather than down into one's lungs. It was the stage of the occasional spliff, the stage of contact highs. We usually smoked only on weekends, and if we smoked in the week it amounted to a total of around two to four joints for the whole week. It was too expensive to exceed this dosage (given the structured and disciplined priorities I had), plus I did not have, nor did I feel the need for, a larger amount. I smoked usually in the company of two or three colleagues, each of whom would take turns in sorting out and procuring supplies of ganja even when the season went dry. Mexican and Colombian grass fetched the highest price in those days, and created the greatest excitement among us, as we waited to see if each procurement would bring about some good internal experience.

The effects which these occasional smoking sessions had on us was noticeably nice, otherwise we would not have continued using it.

It did something for us. We noted that smoking had the effect of making colors and lights more luminous—it raised colors to a higher power and made us aware of the innumerable fine shades of differences to which at ordinary times we were blind; our appetites were noticeably affected by what we referred to amusingly as the "munch," or craving to eat. Our minds became more introspective and inward-looking as a result of smoking, and we acted more spontaneously, laughing one moment, retreating inwards into silent introspection the next, followed by outbursts of more laughter, and then the sharing of our thoughts and reasonings with others.

Even at this stage of the American head high, the psychic spiritual effect of herbs was evident to members of our smoking confraternity as this aspect of our experience became a frequent topic in our reasonings. We interchanged our experiences so that we could learn from each other and thereby re-enforce each other. It was quite noticeable even at this stage that the people who experimented with herbs were very similar in important aspects and were tied together by some invisible bond, partly induced by herbs. Our rates of vibration were more akin. On countless occasions our group manifested unmistakable demonstrations of a group mind or spirit: when all five individuals in the room burst out from their separate silences simultaneously with the same idea or thought that was not even related to what was being discussed in the room! This was the group mind at work.

We looked forward to these sessions as periods of great illumination, as indeed they were to us at the time. Ideas did flow in a fantastic fashion, in almost uncontrollable sequence at times, as if Some One were directing these at a rate which was too fast for the brain to coordinate or for it to be recorded externally. Effects and memories obscurely hidden were often brought to our minds, although we found that events and things only a few minutes old were often forgotten as trivia. Sometimes a lightness and freedom pervaded our whole body so that the physical body lost all of its weight and was dissolved into pure mind-energy, from which we derived greater sensation and intellectual powers. Herbs smoking, for these brief moments, "made everything more."

The following description by a white liberal contemporary summarizes the herbal experience in images that we then shared as smokers and intellectuals. This author reports:

> Being high is one of the most pleasant sensations available to mankind. Every day is suddenly Saturday. It is to be like a child; to perceive events with clarity; to look into the gates of paradise; to completely enjoy whatever you might be doing; to smile so hard and long that you jaw muscles get tired. Being high is to laugh at the silliest things; to understand things that have seemed absurd before; to have the aloofness of a cat; to afford a kingship with God. Being high makes life seem terribly good. Being high is simply grand.
>
> (John Rosevear, *Pot,* 1967)

In no way did we see ourselves as indulging in "abuse" or in a criminal activity. For us this was very much in keeping with the intellectual training of our minds, which was our raison d'etre. For me it was a rational individual choice, based upon my felt needs at the time. I kept my herbs exactly where I kept my aspirins. Smoking herbs for me became more and more my conscious alternative to swallowing such chemicals as aspirins or taking any number of alternative paths such as alcoholism, or the path of sowing wild oats as a means of reaching the much-needed relaxation and escape, if only for a short spell, or continue as I was—on ice—until I broke from a heart attack.

Aldous Huxley, the author of *Brave New World,* experimented with herbs and reported in his book *Heaven and Hell* on the deeper reasons which prompt people to smoke, including such intellectual stalwarts as John Stuart Mill, Alexander Dumas, and William James. Said Huxley, speaking for this group:

> Most men and women lead lives at the worst so painful, at the best so monotonous, poor, and limited that the urge to escape, the longing to transcend themselves if only for a few moments is and has always been one of the principal appetites of the Soul. Art and religion, carnivals, dancing have all served as Doors in the Wall.

That herbs smoking brought on an improved state of feeling and vitality was not a theory for me but an undeniable fact. It was an experienced reality which I could not deny, any more than I could deny the frustrating and boxed-in condition of my life at the time—a time when my personal and family life was in crisis and yet the demands of my roles and office, as well as my own disciplined and structured nature, meant that I had to keep on going, keep on moving, and using my mind to forget my aches and pains. Herbs helped me in resting, in taking a break from my personal problems so that I could keep on going. But my soul was on ice, and my body was as if it was wrecked and was not really mine.

Climbing the academic ladder as quickly as I did left my body and mind tired and drained to the point of feeling wrecked and severely depressed. Sitting in libraries all my life—being in the same posture and subjected to academic uncertainties and competition—does have a distorting effect, particularly if it goes on for all of one's life. A special kind of intellectual alienation results, which is schizophrenia in its own right. The frequent changes in climate and food also had an effect on my overall structure. But who studies these effects, and who cares? All of these factors contributed to painful marriage experiences and to the feeling that marriage was a prison. I felt unfulfilled and trapped in spite of all the worldly signs of middle class success. After a long series of ups and downs in my marital life, and soon after our temporary separation, my wife at the age of 25 developed the terminal disease known as Lupus. This has since become a major trauma in my life, for this was like a death-blow delivered against me from the inside which penetrated to my core, to my every fiber, and I felt agony and despair. It became a major psychological blow, a trap which I had to overcome if I was ever to move on and discover life.

It was *only then* that I began to really understand the psalmist crying out in despair thousands of years ago:

> My Soul is filled with troubles and my life is nearing death's portals. I am reckoned among those who go down to the pit. I am a man without manly strength.
>
> (Psalm 88:3-4)

Where was my Isis or my third eye? Who would search for my dismembered pieces and put them back together so as to save me from certain death?

I had reached this stage of crisis apparently because I had not been "conscious" enough in knowing that when strains and frustrations persist for prolonged periods of time, various disturbances in the functioning of our glands and organs are bound to develop. Ignored or suppressed, these symptoms will ultimately result in chronic pathological and degenerative changes in a person's body. But I was too busy with my abstract intellectualism in those earlier years, too other-directed, too narrow and naive to understand that "what goes around comes around," that "what was hidden in darkness will come to light." My blame is not individual, it is cultural. Even my tendency to search for my Isis externally in the form of a woman was a cultural legacy which so many men share.

I was seriously and frequently plagued during this period with nasty colds and coughs, headaches, stomach aches, neck aches, lower back pains, inward growing facial hair, tonsillitis, hair loss a serious scalp problem, increased blood pressure, recurrent nightmares, allergies to plants, dust, cats, dogs, milk and cold beverages. All of these and more were cues that something was fundamentally wrong with me, particularly as I could remember a time when I was free of these ailments and was lion in body, mind and spirit.

Ironically, none of the many doctors who treated me in those years really offered me any long-term relief, nor even came close to giving me any hope of ultimate relief. As narrow specialists, they could not see the whole me (the holistic I) nor gain the necessary total perspective on me that was necessary if I were to live well and happily. They were more concerned with profiting from my sickness, and each concerned himself with some very limited manifestations of my general ill state. They were not interested in the trinity of body, mind and soul. This was not their fault; it was the prevailing bias in Western medicine. Thus, in spite of my costly allergy treatment, the removal of my tonsils, chemical treatments for gastric indigestion, and many other expensive remedial medical treatments which I underwent during this period, my overall health deteriorated.

I decided to take my health into my own hands. Exercising, herbs smoking, massaging, and a great openmindedness were the major tools in the self-help natural medicine which I found myself getting into naturally. It began dawning in my consciousness, as I smoked and reflected, that man is an organic part of the biological and cosmic universe and subject to all the unchangeable and irrevocable laws of nature. Man's disregard of these laws in respect to his environment, nutrition, physical and emotional needs leads to disharmony with the lifegiving biological and spiritual universe, resulting in disease, decay and death.

At this stage, herbs smoking for me did not mean any expressly Rastafarian identification. I was living in Montreal and Washington, D.C. at this stage, far removed from any contact with Rastas. I smoked because I tasted it and found that it brought personal relief and personal insights which I knew I needed badly. Moreover, it is written: "I, wisdom dwell with insight, I find out knowledge through deliberating" (Proverbs 8:12). "People of insight have knowledge from a Crown" (Proverbs 14:18).

It was pointed out to me (later on) by several individuals close to me at the time that whenever there was a fuss in my life (and there were many) and I smoked herbs, I automatically moved away to a quiet corner and started a series of gentle movement-exercises and "got into myself"—presumably, meditating for truth in my own way.

THE STAGE OF IN-DEPTH PENETRATION: THE JAMAICAN HIGH

> The man who comes back through the Door in the Wall will never be quite the same as the man who went out. He will be wiser but less cocksure, happier but less self-satisfied, humbler in acknowledging his ignorance yet better equipped to understand the relationship of words to things, of systematically reasoning to the unfathomable mystery which it tries forever vainly to comprehend. (Aldous Huxley)

Upon returning to Jamaica in 1977, I was led into a more systematic and in-depth self-application and exploration of herbal usage as a result of a great number of forces and pressures. It was as if this was to be my destiny: testing the Rastafarian thesis by using my own experiences.

By 1977 I felt that the time had come for the "prodigal intellectual" to return to Jamaica after being away half of my life. I returned intending to make my contribution to the national effort under Democratic Socialism. The definitions of myself then as a "Black Marxist intellectual" and as a revolutionary were uppermost in my consciousness, compounded by the beating of nationalism (my need to identify) in my soul. I had great expectations that somehow everything would work itself out miraculously upon my returning to Jamaica. I was then unaware of what the environment would subject me to before this coming together could take place.

Within a fairly short period of time upon returning to Jamaica, the blues began. I started experiencing frustrations, oppositions, and stumbling blocks in all forms and from all spheres and at every turn. It was as if a whole society began conspiring to drive me out of the country and to test my manhood, my strength and my ingenuity in the survival game or racket that was Jamaica. In spite of all the lip-service and entreaties to West Indian migrants to return home, such migrants soon found this return filled with tragic traumas, so that a good many found it necessary to re-emigrate or simply ended up broken or even mad. The period that I chose to come back was such that the odds were against me from the start. Jamaican politics during those last days of Michael Manley's second 5-year term of Democratic Socialism had reached an all-time low in morals and finance. The general effect was all-around alienation, political violence, economic and social stalemate, and bankruptcy.

The Rastafarian communities (separate and apart from the two-party system) were strikingly different in their pulsation and strivings. Though the name of Rasta was so badly defamed at the time, I began to sense and feel a unifying power emanating from that source, a healing power which ran underneath all the negative stereotypes, and beneath all its outer masks and symbols. This difference had to do, it appeared, with how they, as Rastafarians, answered the *identity question*, as attested to by their non-partisan level of consciousness. Philosophy, not ideology, was the major preoccupation of these conscious brethren. "Rasta nuh deal in politricks, him deal wid truth"—this was their motto. While dealing with "truth," they were also forced to hustle and scuffle in order to survive.

In the ghetto community of *Majesty Pen ("Back-to")*, where I spent a good deal of my waking hours, I began to see the differing images and definitions of Rasta. It was there that I began discovering the pulsating message and truths of Bob Marley, Ras Michael, Peter Tosh, Jimmy Cliff, and the scores of others who were generating a similar message and vibrations. It began dawning on me that I was witnessing and participating in something wonderful: the miracle of triumph through unavoidable sufferation, for out of the ghettoes of Jamaica was emerging a redemptive philosophy and a powerful peace movement in the form of Rastafari. I was bent on penetrating this movement and its definitions to see where it would lead me.

I was fortunate to have met a number of elder dreads who offered wise counsel. I felt very comfortable and very at home in the ghetto yards. I tracted in their midst, much more so than in the intellectual world of the university to which I was officially attached during the first four years of my return.

Herbs smoking was central in the daily lives of the Brethren, and its varying effects were a major subject in our reasonings. Among the Brethren there was notably less of the usual egotistical chit-chat centering on wine, women and motor cars. There were constant reasonings on life and on their personal problems and of their beliefs and knowledge about the world, of ghetto realities and of what they planned to do in order to survive and cope in Babylon.

I was particularly intrigued about the way in which the Rastas contrasted my intellectual knowledge, derived from the university, with their intuitive understanding derived from adversity, herbs and Jah Rastafari. They set about instructing me on how to bridge the gap and combine both types of knowledge in order to increase my power. They were able to see me from a perspective from which I could not see myself, and I learned from this.

After a while I could easily distinguish the levels and types of herbs and Rastamen. Hierarchy and class was acknowledged, but this was not expressed as a person being "higher" or "lower" or "better" than another, but of being "forward" or "backward" of another. They were most creative in the terms and concepts and images they used to relate and interact with each other. Many such Rastas bore the unmistakable imprint of Anancy in the way they spoke, dressed, looked, acted and related to each other and towards me. Others were like the playful and gentle lambsmen, while others were lion-men varying from the regal type to the wild dreadlocked lions. All the different types or vibrations of Rastafarians could be found in this community.

The daily intake of ganja varied according to how much each could afford, how much his personal system could absorb, and on the strength (power) of the particular "cup" of herbal brew. On average, each of the Rastamen who caught my attention as being a seasoned smoker inhaled about half a pound of ganja weekly. A good many had been doing this from 15 to 35 years.

In learning how to spot these differing types of characters and of how to survive and handle myself in this harsh and mystical world of ghettoism and Jahdom, and of how to read their symbols and meanings, I was aided by a group of elder Rastamen—Sata, Tonton, Brother Mac, Uncle Harry, Ras Michael, Jah Mike, and others too numerous to mention.

I began retreating and withdrawing with the Rastaman into his world, into his definitions and into his movements.

If I could use herbs to heal myself like the model Rastaman, then this would kill many birds with one stone. It would validate the Rastaman's thesis, fulfill Christ's directive to man to heal himself, and also serve as a therapeutic model of importance. I would also be validated in terms of my private traumatic life story. I felt that this quest was justified and necessary all round, particularly as Jamaica was also caught up in the grip of a terrible, nightmarish crisis which could not be dealt with by blaming the imperialists or the Russians. Our general crisis reflected something beyond mere economic forces: it reflected a malaise at the level of self in relation to Jah and in relationship to everything else around us. And this called for drastic revival at the individual level, particularly of the leadership class.

I was bent on riding the herbal train to Zion and returning with embodied proof (an idea clothed in flesh) of what was involved, as well as knowledge of the processes and of the wisdom derived therefrom, knowledge of the "I am." It would not be enough, I reasoned, to get high in the North American "head" fashion, for in this way a person only smokes over the symptoms while remaining the same in physical constitution. My aim was deliberately to use herbs in such a way as to gradually extract and work its positive vibrations into my mind-body system. By this very process, I would transcend any "addiction" to it by making sure I used it to progressively become a person that did not need to use it.

If ganja was to be my therapy (and not an excuse), this had to be its ultimate aim: *the eventual restoration of my mind, body and spirit to their original and natural state, and an eventual graduation of one's personality from the Ganja University.* Since this world of ours and its problems (hell) is all around us, the personal challenge was conceived as one in which I had to become lion in my body and mind so that I could cope and withstand whatever the external pressures bearing down on me.

As I began to move among Rastafarians, I began to feel the pulse of the Rastafarian movement, and I became more and more in agreement with them as I penetrated their meanings. The missing ingredient for the healing of the Jamaican personality and of the nation as a whole could largely be sought and found by distilling and sorting through Rastafarian images and creative outpourings and insights. *I began to see the movement as the nucleus of an emerging Third World force beaming across a formula and a definition of evolutionary revolution from which the whole world, starting with Jamaica, could draw from. It offered itself as a model movement for fundamental changes,* and importing a fresh and lively perspective more consistent with the experiences of the African in the society and also with the spirit of Truth. More and more I began to see myself as a microcosm of the Rasta movement, and this movement as a microcosm of Jamaica, and Jamaica in turn as a microcosm of the Caribbean and of the Third World. How I personally resolved the dilemmas of my own personal life—how Rastafarians learn to transcend these dilemmas without compromising their manhood and integrity—became for me a real model for positive change in the Third World, and the pathway for breaking out of deadlocked systems and situations.

THE SPIRITUAL POWERS OF THE RASTAMAN
 "Jah would never give the Power to a Baldhead."
(Marley)
 "The body without the Spirit is dead."
(James 2:26)

My Rastafarian friends were quick to instruct me that: "If you have not taken the chalice, you are keeping malice, with King Rastafari and will not see HIM in His palace." They also instructed me in rhyme, that "the spliff makes you drift, but the chalice makes you fit." Perhaps the greatest of the esoteric truths which I learned from my Rastafarian brethren was the overall importance (for attaining Rasta heights) in moving on from smoking the spliff (the North American head high) to the stage of smoking and mastering the chillum water pipe (chalice). Not only was this practice healthier (as the smoke is filtered through pure cool water), but more fundamentally, *this transition (which Rastafarians talk about) from the spliff to the water pipe or "kutchi" contains the secret root source of much of the Rastaman's mystic powers,* resulting in the resurgence of an organic power shooting out from the navel and crown, all of which is evidence of an awakening body vibrancy that can be known only by the actual experience of making this transition successfully. In one sense, at the physical level or in physical terms, this transition or acculturation is equivalent to the metamorphosis from Anancy to lion. In order to pull herbal smoke into one's lungs to full capacity, one must invariably slow down, move inwards, and discover how to work inside of one's mind and physical structure in ways suggested and guided by the smoke itself, by the Big I (Eye) of Jah Rastafari—so that the person can see, bypass and eventually remove the thousands of internal physical and mental blockages that impede the smooth intake of the herbal energy into the fathom depth of one's lungs. The intake of the smoke becomes a most accurate measure of the depth and vitality of one's respiratory process and the vitality of one's organic life process as a whole. This does not mean, however, that people with big lung capacities are invariably more vital, healthy and good.

Rastafarians invariably become most conscious of their breathing and of their lungs as they attempt to inhale as much of the smoke into their lungs as they can, and holding it in as long as they can in order to achieve the high. This "high" is different from the North American head high. In fact, it is truthful to say that Rastafarians do not smoke to get high, as they have already passed such limits. They feel vibrant but not "high." By watching, seeing and feeling the differing amounts of smoke inhaled and exhaled from the lungs, the

Rastaman measures and compares his lung capacity and breath with those of others, and, more importantly, with himself over time, as a measure of his own expansion. This is the ancient bio-social-feedback process at work. This smoke provides him with an objective test, a smoke signal visible to himself and to others. Rastafarians are very proud when they can pull the chalice so deeply and so rhythmically that the herbs in the kutchie light up in a fiery glow, like a ball of fire, bathing the surroundings with a gentle moon glow.

While the immediate and most conscious or *intended aim* for smoking is the upliftment of the Rastaman's consciousness and feeling, the inevitable and unconscious effect of this exercise is its deepening impact on the user's lungs and minds. Through this a general dispersion and mobilization of vitality to the body, generated from the enlarging of one's lungs and minds which develops from the constant deep inhaling and exhaling of the smoke. The *mechanical rhythm* or movements of the lungs by themselves is sufficient to produce some expansive effects on the body, starting in the engine room of our lung sacs. This physiological effect of the Rastaman's heavy usage of herbs has been completely neglected by all our scientists, who are supposedly concerned with the science of herbs. They are in fact concerned only with its chemistry. They have neglected its effects in stimulating one's breathing back to its rhythmic state, and in expanding one's lung capacity—consequences which by themselves are usually enough to negate/balance/ outweigh/control its negative organic defects.

A number of Rastafarian brethren patiently demonstrated the rhythmic technique of drawing the pipe ("sipping the cup"). To reach the level where my body and lungs opened up to the deep, smooth rhythmic intake and expiry of the smoke involved me in a long, painful, arduous, mystical journey into my "self," into my body and its parts, and into a meditative search into the past history of these body parts.

Although I had spent an earlier three years studying the art of karate, in which the importance of breathing was greatly stressed, I did not discover or master its secret, and at the end I was worse off than when I started, with my breath having become more depressed and shallow.

In Jamaica I discovered that by way of smoking, Rastafarians also emphasized the power of the breath, the power of the parts as well as the greater power of the whole breath. Herbs became for me the Sesame, the lamp that lighted the way inward towards the unfolding development of my breath. In this way I came in from the cold, thus substantiating the Rastafarian thesis, for the discovery of one's breath is the greatest discovery of all.

For my lungs and breath to be deepened to its abdominal depth, a great number of blockages within my overall system had to be located and gradually removed so as to make possible the greater flow of energy in my body, and my rib cage had to be loosened up terribly to become what they were meant to be—"floating ribs." Herbs became a powerful ally which set me free to see, experience, and traverse the boundaries of this inner reality. Herbal meditations allowed me (my consciousness) to follow the smoke into my lungs, and into my heart, legs, toes or any other part of my body, and allowed me to "know" these parts by feeling them out and by generating vibrations in these parts. By means of such internal concentration, focus, and movements which the smoke sustained and generated, I was able to see, feel, and actually identify and touch the internal blockages within my personal system as the first step to removing these blockages. These blockages became identified and were felt as a certain kind of pain and as a certain kind of muscular tension or sensation which I could also externally identify through touch. Painful and stressful vibrations, tremors or fears are indicators of such internal blockages. In my meditative state I gained insights into the origin of these blockages and of the impulses which they block, as my mind developed the keen ability to travel back in time. Some refer to this as "astral traveling." For me, this was a most painful trip into my past. This ability, and the insights that I gained on the specific formation and origins of these blockages and how to overcome them, became the basis of a new faith in myself, as it allowed for the reordering of my lower self, sickly and frail, and its control by the higher self or Big I; and with this integration, greater energy and livity emerged.

All this inward meditation meant for me an increasing awareness of the spiritual life, for *spiritual life is really the inner life of the body as opposed to the outer material world of the body*. Those people focusing all their energies and feelings on the outer world, through their outer eyes, lose much of their potential spirituality. What we see with eyes closed possesses a spiritually higher significance that what we see with eyes open. Hence the phenomenal wisdom and genius of the physically blind I-dren *Stevie Wonder*, whose spiritual visions are those of the universal third eye. From the overflow of his heart, our soul brother Stevie Wonder sings and feels, "sees" and shines.

By this inward focus, then, the Rastaman becomes more aware of himself in his various dimensions—physical, spiritual, intellectual and emotional, and he becomes more sensitive to their disharmonies. They say that one's body is the holy temple in which the Great Spirit of Jah dwells. The biggest surprise of all is that the smoking actually brings out the God in man, by making the smoker more and more conscious of his own powers and with this, the source of power itself.

BLOCKAGES
These deserve special notation, for in my journey inward they constitute the major stumbling blocks leading to a compounding of my worries and troubles. They can become inbuilt, ingrown, and

structured—that is when they are easily overlooked, until they disrupt in disease, death and decay.

Blockages constitute an ingrown system of automatic defensive armoring in one's body—ingrown shields against painful and threatening experiences within one's personality or those threatening from outside. They have been caused by sitting in the same position for very long periods, or from too much direct physical pressure on parts of one's body, or even from long and harsh routines and/or from threatening situations. A "sin," or the breaking of Jah's laws, results in a blockage of one kind or another. The very existence of these structured anxieties prevents us from relaxing voluntarily when we are told to relax, and when we genuinely desire to relax but find that we cannot. We tense the very muscles we need to relax. For this reason, transcendental meditation cannot offer much help to those people who are blocked up internally.

Even without being aware of it, we often respond to felt pressures by increasing our muscle tension—a process called "bracing." This is the muscle act which the body goes through when preparing to defend itself by alerting all its appropriate action stations. Considerable degrees of tensions—even "knots"—can develop in the muscles. They are one stage in the beginning process of most organic diseases that affect the human body.

Facing anxieties, a person will brace himself by increasing his heart rate, sending up his blood pressure, and flooding his body system with adrenaline and other potent hormones. This bracing reaction not only affects performance and creates discomfort, but over a long period, it will most certainly lead to pathological tissue deformity. The person who has inappropriately braced his nervous system and body may well have succeeded well is his social role as teacher, father or minister, so he may continue to repeat this error at every performance, sometimes leading to the point of paralysis. Bracing often results when we continue to expend energy in a way that was once appropriate but no longer serves any purpose. Chemical drugs do not alter the underlying response tendencies of the organism, and often lose even their trick-ameliorative effect in time.

During the tension-producing situation, such muscle tensing is scarcely recognized. It is only when the conscious attention is not concerned with the emotional situation (i.e., during meditation) that the muscle tension becomes significantly appreciated and understood.

Muscle tensions can become so structured (as flesh) that they become a part of one's body system, and we become so unaware of them that they become a part of our lower self and we then begin to defend this as part of the "I am."

The psychologist Gardner Murphy has pointed out that "self deception is usually accomplished by body movements that prevent unwanted information from reaching the mind." Wilhelm Reich called this "character armoring." Says Murphy:

> The striped musculature of the arms, hands, trunk, neck, and by implication, other parts of the body may be conceived to be used all the time in the battle of thought, especially the battle against recognition of information, and most of all against information unfavorable to the self."
>
> (Gardner Murphy in T. Barber, *Bio-feed Back and Self-Control*)

If our muscles are not given relief from tension by relaxation or change of activity, the muscle fibers physically adapt to the state of increased tension. Continued stress and reflection on stress does not allow our muscles to recover completely from their increased tension, and the tension becomes sustained at higher levels. As blockages are chiefly internal, one must of necessity develop the internal eye of feelings by means of which we become conscious of these internal blockages as the first step in the long process of removing them.

Blockages are often experienced as chronic muscular tensions in the body and are expressed ordinarily in such folk terms as feeling choked up, having a broken heart or having one's heart in the wrong place, having a chip on one's shoulders, being tight-fist, closed mouthed, stiff necked, etc. Blockages induced by sustained tensions of all sorts could manifest themselves in a rigid thoracic cage which restricts one's breathing, or they could lodge themselves above and around the waist, neck and shoulders, all of which fundamentally restrict and distort one's breathing and the free flow of one's blood (and spirit).

The muscular spasticities and tensions experienced, which are stimulated into our consciousness by smoking, are signs that energy is dammed up unevenly inside, and that pulsations and *feelings from the heart to the surface of the body are blocked off. A person's heart can become so armored in by these muscular tensions that love impulses are blocked off from the surface of the body (from outward expression) so that although the person talks of love—and imagines that he loves—he is not biologically and spiritually loosened up enough to reach out in the full expression of love.* Your body has to be conducive to love. Bob Marley asked the profound question: "Could you be loved and be love?" Being closed off in himself from within, by muscular armoring brought on by years of pressures and tensions, a person so affected will invariably locate his problems in the external world, outside himself, on to others, and he will be incapable of truly loving on secure foundations.

A person can become so armored, for instance in the midsection region (around the waist), that there is a disassociation of the upper half of the body from the lower half, thus providing the biological foundation for schizophrenia. Blockages are in fact the basis of illnesses of all sorts. Clearing these blockages is referred to by the folk as "straightening one's self out," "opening up," "hanging loose," and "getting one's feet on the ground." An analysis of Bible texts will confirm the importance of this kind of cluesome body language talk which gives good pointers to the vital points of man.

Every therapeutic method must bring the person in touch with these tension areas, as a prelude to removing them. Herb smoking was the instrument which I used in this monumental task. I became a mystic man and learned that one cannot find Jah, nor keep His sacred commandments, without overcoming these blockages. The heart might be willing but the flesh weak, like Peter's. The merger of the Big I and the little I into the integrated Self can only occur when we remove these structured blockages, which is a prelude to fusing body and soul, mind and spirit. Only then can the little I can meet the Big I face to face and become unified as One.

THE PROCESS: HERBAL MEDITATION AT WORK

I do not wish to reveal the exact quantity of herbs digested, nor the amount of time I spent in experimentations, nor any of the other actual techniques or internal maneuvers which I used in this process of wrestling with the spirit of ganja. These are Nyabinghi secrets. My aim here is not to offer a manual or guide to herbal meditations, although I do believe that such a guide should be written, as it would serve a useful purpose. The Ganja University was not founded by me, nor am I recruiting students for it. Suffice it to say that I used enough herbs and spent so much time to myself, locked away, that to many (including the "me" of yesterday) I became an oddity, an eccentric recluse, an enigmatic man.

Quietly I was involved in an intense process of herbal meditation in which I was bent on using herbs to explore the interaction between my mind and my body, and I began to discover the remarkable extent to which my mind could exert a powerful healing effect by altering my body structure and functioning and in controlling the so-called *involuntary functions* of my body: my heart rate, breathing, blood pressure, muscle tone, endocrine glands, skin temperature, orgasm flow, etc., which were all believed to be generally beyond a person's control. In this process of herbal meditations, I created tensions to deliberately disturb my organic system in order to accelerate processes of organic alteration within particular regions of my mind-body structure. With gentle lung movements, stimulated and sustained by the smoke, which functioned as the *anesthesia* keeping me fixed, I focused and concentrated on this path of internal herbal meditations for a whole decade.

The process of herbal meditations engendered in me an exceptional degree of physical consciousness which constantly impelled me on towards the search for physical wholesomeness and breath. This was the feedback signal which the extrovert physically oriented culture in Jamaica directed me to do: to become more physically conscious in order to balance my intellectual consciousness. Each level of my physical consciousness, breath, and health in turn stimulated a more balanced and fitting intellectual and spiritual awakening so that after a time the spiritual quest and awareness itself became more intense and more assertive. The resulting long journeying into myself which the weed stimulated and sustained resulted in the unfolding of Rasta within. Before this process I knew myself only *abstractly*; I could not yet define the content and substance of being an African and a man. But the successful application of herbal meditations gave me the opportunity to know myself in the real sense of the term and to ground my feet on reality, both present and ancient.

Herbal meditations enabled me to feel the vibratory tensions (felt as stress, pain or tingles) generated in those areas and regions constituting blockage points to the free intake and flow of the energized smoke in and out of my body. This meant that my mind had to become very conscious of my body and learn to become sensitive to its feelings and vibrations. Thus throughout the process my mind kept a record of the different rates of vibrations—negative and positive feelings—generated at specific points and in the whole body over time, or those associated with specific physical-meditation maneuvers. Through my mind function I was able to direct my energies to the different tension points in my body in order to heal them, sometimes by tediously shifting around my internal organs and restoring them to their original meant-to-be positions; at other times by stretching them and massaging them through gentle internal movements. The result was the straightening out of my posture, and a discovery of the tremendous elasticity of the human body, and the increased power which derives along with increased elasticity.

The discovery of these crucial blockage points is really three-quarters of one's problem. But knowledge of these points or regions is discovered in an evolutionary and dialectical manner: The discovery of blockage point A will lead to the discovery of B, and B's discovery clears the way for us to discover blockage C, and C leads to D, etc. The point being made is that from the position of blockage A, a person most often cannot see any other blockage but B; when he sees this and clears this, he discovers others more deeply structured in him. Sometimes the smoke will point to the source of a blockage at a point far removed from the region where the spasm or stress manifests itself. The pain in one's head is sometimes rooted in one's body or feet, or vice-versa.

As one journeys deeper into the self, touching deeper sources of energy and removing blockages, things start happening to the person to indicate that something fundamental is happening. These changes occur in bits and pieces, sometimes in cataclysmic shifts, sometimes as a silent unfolding felt deep within.

Don Juan, the Mexican Indian mystic, gives a graphic description of what happens as one's blockages are removed and one's centers of power are touched and are rekindled by the little smoke:

> One day he succeeds in performing something ordinarily quite impossible to accomplish. He may not even notice his extraordinary deed. But as he keeps on performing impossible acts or impossible things keep happening to him, he becomes aware that a sort of power is emerging. A power that comes out of his body as he progresses on the path of knowledge. At first it is like an itching on the belly, or a warm spot that cannot be soothed; then it becomes a pain, a great discomfort ...Sometimes there are convulsions for months, the more severe the convulsions the better for him...When the convulsions cease the warrior notices he has strange feelings about things. He notices that he can actually touch anything he wants with a feeling that comes out of his body from a spot right below and right above his navel.
> (Carlos Castaneda, *A Separate Reality*, p. 159)

These itchings and convulsions noted by Don Juan are growth pains. They are not confined only to the navel region of the belly, but are often experienced around the neck and throat, on the crown of the head, in the chest and at the coccyx region of the lower spine, and even in the palm of one's hands. Sometimes the whole surface of the body becomes temporarily ablaze with a sweet irritable itching sensation, deep underneath one's skin and within one's muscles where it cannot be soothed with one's fingers, but waited out with patience until the healing cycle completes itself.

With the aid of herbs I developed the technique of *using stress to defeat stress, of deliberately inducing additional stress and pain in the body, so as to accelerate certain processes of growth and decay.* Carol Yawney, the Canadian anthropologist, remarked on this theme of growth pain:

> In every breakthrough and understanding there is correlative pain in the form of boundary disturbances. This is what the researchers tend to seize upon—the decay product of the transition and not the fact of the transition itself. There has been little recognition given the fact that for consciousness as well as for society there are liminal states: flights of passage.

Outsiders to my experiences, understandings, meanings, and intentions—even some people very close to me—took all the external embodiments of these changes as signs that I was going mad. They could not understand the nature of mysticism despite efforts on my part to explain to them what was happening to me deep down, and as they happened.

Mr. Morris Cargill, Jamaica's most noted white author, apparently picked up my own growth pains in a vision, which he reported as a bad dream to the *Daily Gleaner* of November 22, 1979.

This *nightmare*, as reported by this author of the book *Jamaica Farewell*, involved a mystical press conference called by Michael Manley, then Prime Minister. Mr. Cargill sarcastically reported: "Everyone was there, even my colleague Dennis Forsythe, structured historically, looking fit, full with vigor, energy and patriotism. Lucky man. He had his 'I' with him on one side, and a dozen or two great philosophers whose views he anticipated. Even Plato and William Shakespeare were kneeling at the feet or our great thinker; and Descartes was heard to mention to George Bernard Shaw that here was a Sociologist to end all Sociology. 'He is no abstract category or statistical unit,' said Karl Marx, 'but is full of insights, outsights, foresights and backsights. Trouble is, he is downpressed and totally deadened in body and spirit.' 'Why?' asked Lord Russell, 'Has he been drinking anesthetic?' 'I'll tell you later,' said Marx, spitting into a flower pot."

Eventually, by the end of this bad dream, Mr. Cargill "accidentally" put his finger in my "I"—presumably to destroy the vision and consciousness which the "I" had come to symbolize for the Rastaman. This "I" constituted the basis of an alternative perspective or "third eye," without which I would have remained a mimic man, fixated in the traditional Left-Right compartmentalization of the world. But Mr. Cargill would not have been able to understand what was going on in my world and in my space. But he saw the *vision*.

Only a poet or artist can capture the sense of exhilaration that I felt as I learned to master my body waves through mind control. All our lives we are led to believe that we cannot do anything about our *involuntary nervous system*, until the lucky few of us start discovering otherwise for ourselves.

This mystic trip, encompassing all these discoveries, is long, arduous, and lonely. The eleventh hour, just before the dawn of the expected big breakthrough, is when the clouds get darkest. At the summit points, however, the sense and feeling of vitality returns, sometimes in such an intoxicating outrush that I raised my arms and voice in thankfulness to Jah for having allowed the little I to sight and work towards this ecstasy and power of feeling and thought which so many will never come to know and feel in this life. From the blues I could now sing the redemption songs of Jah Rastafari.

Yes, I felt pain. I knew this, and I deliberately accelerated the pains and stresses in particular regions as part of my therapeutic model, using herbs as my *anesthesia*. Processes were set to work underneath my skin which were altering and readjusting my internal structure. People who were physically very close to me knew of things which clothes hide. When they could not deal with these changes they often ran away to spread propaganda against Rasta and the weed, taking with them my "good name." The smoke gave my mind an internal eye and angle on these inner processes. During peak points in this process my voice returned, like the opening up of my soul. Even more remarkable was the fact that after eight years of herbal meditations I repeatedly *saw* a huge glowing cross during the heights of my meditations. Nowadays this can be easily seen at my internal center, without the great mystery which accompanied its earlier discovery in my depth. It appears as a luminous cross occupying the center of my inner core of blackness. With my eyes closed I repeatedly began to see two thick luminous beams of fluorescent light-glows, one running vertically downwards along the center of my spine and the other running horizontally across my shoulders and neck. Together these beams constitute a beautiful and hypnotic image that lured the outer I inward like a magnet.

In the last four years of my research work I have also experienced a tremendous range of body changes, witnessed by those closest to me; but many of which I kept away from the eyes and the understanding of others, because this knowledge could be used by sex hustlers to sharpen their rapacious claws in the fleshmarkets of Babylon.

As this process of herbal meditation deepened, I learned to feel my heart for the second time around in my life and to control my heart beat, speeding it up and down at will. And even if I am only 50% along the way, I am now certain about how to finish the rest of the journey—just keep on going forward. The dangerous irregularities of my heartbeat (called "PVCs"—premature ventricular contractions), which were severe in my case, had programmed me as a candidate for a sudden heart attack or stroke paralysis in the years to come. But the smoke contributed to my mind development, which provided the important mediator force just at the right time.

Layers and layers of my skin constantly peeled off over the years, preceded always by intense itchings. My hands and fingers also underwent many rounds of internal changes until they became like hands unknown to me. My ears, also, and my feet. So much had they changed in size, texture and capacity to feel and transmit vibrations. There were periodic breakdowns and collapses in my body which I regularly looked forward to as I saw these as enforced relaxation phases demanded by my body as a result of placing additional stress on my body through too much physical and mental movement which I was engaged in constantly, day in, day out, according to plan. I could confidently look forward to these collapsed phases as they would be invariably followed by a stage of greater vitality and structure aroused to a higher pitch and greater lionism. I understood all of this and was thus not alarmed when these came on, leaving me looking very broken at times.

My lung capacity in particular registered the most lasting impact of herbal smoking as it expanded many times during this period, and with this rediscovery of my breath I was able to conquer the many silent fears that haunted me since childhood and which had remained knotted up as blockages and a distorted and limited breath power. With the return of my breath came greater internal harmony, psychological security and peace, and with this the abolition of my dependency on M.D.s and their chemical prescriptions. I am not as easily affected by any of my many former troubles, aches, pains and nightmares that had rubbed shoulders with me all my life; but as I discovered them and became more conscious of them I became very disturbed, sometimes over things which happened to me decades ago and which were now being revisited in search of Truth and knowledge of Who I Am.

I discovered that my nightmares were the result of blocked impulses inside, for each night I used the smoke as an alarm clock to wake myself at those very moments of nightmares when my spirit became trapped inside of my body and could not travel freely. These blockages then had to be removed at these points and moments through herbal meditations before I could rest and sleep again. My spirit could then move again—always traveling, over rocky mountains, valleys, and deserts, as if in perpetual search of a cool running stream which it knew is to be found somewhere, as it had passed at some time long, long ago.

My eating habits changed with this process as my taste buds themselves became more discriminatory. My body became overall more discriminatory with foods, colors, words used, and friends chosen. All round I became a more conscious man, and these changes were no longer more intellectual resolutions; they are now real, and embodied in the return of my breath.

My sexual energy rose with the breath, and this energy moved upwards, like the tree of life, towards the Seventh Level, beyond flesh-based love to the heights of spiritual love—loving with all of one's heart, soul and mind, and loving one's neighbor as one's self. At this level Eros could be controlled by will power, rather than by the blockages which caused a downward rush to the Earth.

The remarkable transformations which I underwent during these mind-body interacting alterations had the most remarkable effect of transforming my outer appearance so that physically I became almost like a twin with my younger brother in appearance and physical stance. After the process of herbal meditations had worked itself successfully through my system, ironing out my blockages (like the exorcist), I returned to a more fitting outer form, as exemplified by the physical image of my brother who had not suffered the particular distortions, strains and blockages which I had suffered. He suffered his own and to his own unique extent, which he has dealt with in his own way, which, although different, does not run counter to mine.

By the middle of my transformation period, many people began indicating that in real life I did not look anything like my picture in the *Daily Gleaner*. "You should sue the *Gleaner* Company for that picture of you. It doesn't look anything like you!" was the expression of many. Jah Rastafari had in fact transformed the visible I, just as I knew He would, from the start of the process. This picture was long in my mind.

The return of my breath and the physical image of self was accompanied also by my ability to understand many other things, including the mystery and the power of the Dance which had mesmerized me from the age of seven to twenty-seven. Now I have discovered the power of the Dance. I became most aware of my blockages during dancing when my mind and spirit gave command and my body responded haphazardly and out of tune. After the process, I became a dancer, naturally. One Gnostic text (the Acts of John) in fact hints at the importance of dancing to the spiritual life, as it tells that Christ intoned this mystical chant in the garden of Gethsemane on the night of his arrest:

> To the Universe belongs the dancer…He who does not dance does not know what happens…
> Now if you follow my dance, see yourself in me who am speaking…
>
> You who dance, consider what I do for yours is this passion of man which I am to suffer.

Prof. Rex Nettleford in the *Caribbean Quarterly* (March—June 1968) said almost the same thing:

> Of all the arts, Dance is probably the most neglected. The Art form continues to elude many of the most

> intuitive in an audience, including the critics. It has taken us a couple of generations to begin to perceive, in this phenomenon of the Dance, an activation of subconscious and sleeping resources in the phantom limb of dismembered slave and God. An activation which possesses a nucleus of great promise—of far-reaching poetic synthesis.

Wilson Harris made a similar point regarding the importance of the dance. In *Caribbean Quarterly*, June 1970, Harris wrote that the dancer is "a dramatic agent of the subconscious. The life from within and the life from without now truly overlap. That is the intention of the dance, the riddle of the dancer." Herbal meditations gave me the physical-mental capacity to see and understand this truth. Man's inner power is displayed in his ability to coordinate his mind, body and breath so as to reach perfect unison with God through gracious rhythmic movements.

Why does a person have to use herbs in order to explore one's self and to find God? Couldn't a person explore himself without running the risk of its dangers? These are indeed legitimate questions asked all the time.

I doubt that I would have become as conscious as I now am without the usage of herbs. Even though my mind would have willed certain things, my body weakness would have said no, largely because of accumulated depression.

A depressed body is one that suffers from a diminution of natural energy because of blockages in body or mind. The de-energized body generates the need and feelings for the smoke as the smoker knows of the relationship between energy and ganja smoking; so he endeavors to take in more and more of this enriched breath as this generates nice heightened feelings and sensations, as the smoke moves around like a spirit within him, adding some fire to his sleeping impulses, like a warm fire within our gates on a dark windy night.

Moreover, there is evidence that many yogis have used it to hasten and intensify the meditative process. These advantages can only be known by its users.

Herbal meditation is one approach complete in itself and sufficient in bringing about its intended effect. It seems particularly fitting in a colonial cultural context like Jamaica where the exploration of self is generally lacking. Using herbs sooner or later brings one closer towards self exploration. I have used herbs as my ally because I found it to contain a powerful spirit which provided added energy to the already depressed air which my depressed and overly stressed body breathed. Scientists refer to this psychoactive element in ganja as THC. Through herbal smoke, this THC element is added to the air inhaled to enrich it, no different from the joining of any other two natural elements by human creativity for added strength and vitality—like the adding of spice to one's food, of heat to carbohydrates, or of kerosene oil to damp coal. That is how the folk-mind sees his own smoking of herbs. Aldous Huxley's conclusion is a fitting note on which to end this chapter.

> To be shaken out of the ruts of ordinary perception, to be shown for a few timeless hours of the outer and the inner world, not as they appear to an animal obsessed with survival, or to a human being obsessed with words and notions, but as they are apprehended directly and unconditionally, by Mind at large—this is an experience of inestimable value to everyone and especially to the intellectual.
>
> (Aldous Huxley, *Heaven and Hell*)

At the stage that I have now reached, I believe in angels, miracles, and prophecies, as I have seen these things with my own eyes and have been a part of these wonderful processes all the time. At my present stage I can see a Creator, a Universe, a Father—not in the image of man, but in the image of a ball of energy-fire-intelligence which issues forth from itself...Sons, in its image like Christ, to light the path for humanity. A Creator that issues forth judgements continually, in all forms.

Chapter 7
RASTAS AND THE CHAKRAS

*"The veil of Isis sevenfold to him as gauze
shall be; Wherethrough, clear-eyed, he shall
behold the Ancient Mystery."*

(Ancient Egyptian riddle, quoted in Peter Rendel,
The Chakras)

INTRODUCING THE CHAKRAS

My experiences with herbs, particularly its effects in taking my consciousness (my mind) inwards towards spiritual power and spiritual understanding (i.e., of making my mind aware of itself in relationship to Jah above and the earth below) will now be discussed with the aid of what Hindu and Oriental mystics and philosophers refer to as the "Chakras," or the chain of seven sleeping forces within us. Though not a Rastafarian concept in origin, the idea of the Chakras is very African; in fact it is a universal idea system pertaining to the makeup of the self. One which provides a most relevant conceptual framework by means of which I can intelligently tell the inner story of herbs, both its positive and its negative potentials, as I have discovered these to be.

Back in childhood, long before I became an intellectual capable of understanding the Chakras as a mystic-scientific concept (which is only recently), I was intuitively aware of the beautiful inner reality which this term represented. And I had grown to silently wonder about its disappearance and the meaning of this. Herbs smoking and herbal meditations took me to this realm and reintroduced this long-forgotten reality of the Chakras to me, this time with greater clarity and understanding and power. Quite literally, the smoke touched or baptized my Chakras and stimulated their growth by forcing them up into my consciousness. What are these mysterious Chakras?

The Chakras are the sleeping centers of power within us. This is not the physical power contained in our muscles. They are our subtler psychic sense organs which may appear to us during meditations, when we turn our eyes (mind) inwards. They form our internal zodiac system. When they are undeveloped, they appear as small luminous circles, or as stars, crosses, or as flashing light beams, or as other flashing objects glowing dully in the fathom depth of the ordinary man. When awakened and vivified they become large blazing whirlpools of light, like miniature suns, within our deep dark inner space frontier.

The famous 17th Century German mystic, Gichtel, discovered his Chakras through what he termed "inner illumination." He described his book, *Theosophia Practica*, as "a short exposition of the three principles of the three worlds in man, represented in clear pictures, showing how and where they have their respective centres in the inner man; according to what the author has found in himself in divine contemplation, and what he felt, tasted and perceived."

These Chakras are certain inner body centers or regions that have enormous concentrations of power and energy—more like the electrical transformers or storage batteries in our body system, functioning as the connecting links between our mind and body, between the material and nonmaterial realms.

A chain of seven Chakras make up the energy system and fields in one's body at the different levels of experience or consciousness. They include such vital energies in the body like physical energy, mental energy, sexual energy and energy of the soul or spirit. In its ideal condition, man's body energy system and its network of Chakras is in exact correspondence with the universal energy system: "As Above, so Below," so says the folk mystic, who pictures the universe as an infinite energy system.

As a person gets to know himself from the experience of inward journeying, he comes to realize that all life, starting with himself, is energy in its different states or different rates of vibration or movements. The body from this view should ideally function as a finely tuned instrument for receiving and dispatching infinite vibrations. The energies seated at these levels manifest themselves through these vital force centers (the Chakras) in one's body, and together they constitute the essence of one's inner being.

This concept of the Chakras and the reality it expresses bring out man's intimate and delicate connectedness to the universe around him, pictured as a vast energy system or magnetic field. The mystics and alchemists conceive of the world as a great magnetic field in which the sun was the major pivot, with the earth revolving around this great magnetic center, Ra. The Chakras are the body's own duplicate internal energy system which link the human organism to the universal energy field or outer space. Our entire body was conceived as being charged constantly with "CHI" or environmental energy originating from our surroundings.

All the meditative sages (Buddha, Don Juan, Christ, etc.) had knowledge of the Chakras and all left words pertaining to them, as knowledge of them constituted for them the most certain basis of self-knowledge and of finding God. The Bible most certainly makes reference to them, but often in very veiled and symbolic terms. They are the mysterious Seven Seals mentioned in the *Book of Revelations* which, to be opened, is the formula for reviving the living dead: "Be awake and invigorate the things that remain, that are at the point of dying." Revelations 3:1). Zechariah translates the seven Chakras as the "seven eyes of the Lord which runs to and through the whole earth." The symbolism of the seven-branched candlestick refers to the same thing.

The historical monuments in ancient Egypt show that they knew of these secrets, and indicated the "Third Eye" on the statues of their gods by a knob on the forehead; their priests were trained in the use of this psychic center in their temples.

In Egyptian mythology, Chakras were the "Seven Wise Ones" who came forth in the form of seven hawks from the pupil of the eye of Ra.

Likewise, the Babylonians spoke of the seven planets as *seven stages in the purification of the soul*: To attain superiority, the soul must first give up all its pride to Marduk (Jupiter), all its anger to Nergal (Mars), all its lust to Ishtar (Venus)—through all seven deadly sins.

The seven Chakras come down to the Yorubas of West Africa to mean "the Seven Orishas" or the "seven African Powers," the "Magnificent Seven" deities who are believed to be the most powerful, and who together control all of human life: *Obatala,* as king of purity, represents Heaven and brings peace and harmony; *Oduddua* represents earth and the female principle; *Chango* is symbol of sensual pleasure; *Eleggua* opens all the doors of opportunity and removes all obstacles; *Oggun* is god of war; *Yemaya* is the goddess of fertility and maternity. The union of the seven orishas is believed to bring invincible power. Each of these Yoruba deities was represented as ruling a particular spiritual (inner) force center. For instance, *Oshun*, as goddess of love, marriage, gold, and of the river, is seductive, unlimited in her powers, and rules the abdominal area; she is often invoked during pregnancies.

All seven schools of Yoga recognized in India accept the existence and importance of the Chakras, and each school has its own methods of concentrating upon and developing them.

Western science has been quite unwilling, up until recent times, to delve into this inner mystic realm, but they recognize the seven physical equivalents of the seven Chakras in the form of their seven corresponding endocrine glands: pineal, pituitary, thyroid, thymus, pancreas, adrenals, and gonads. All of which they recognize as being vital to the functioning of the body and to the maintenance of one's health.

All of which goes to suggest that this concept of the Chakra and the reality it represents is most important, as it bridges the gap between mysticism and science and shows the essential unity between them, and may indeed provide us with the intellectual bridge between heaven and hell.

THE SEVEN CHAKRAS OR ENERGY CENTERS

In traditional African thought, the abstract structure of the universe was conceived in energy terms (in terms of "spirits"), and the universe as consisting of conscious and unconscious energies, with conscious energy (or thought) being of higher frequency, intensity and power, with Divine Intelligence seated at the summit of Power. Jahn, in his book, *Neo-African Literature*, summarized this African conception of the universe. The universe for Africans, he stated, consists of a structure of living forces which are hierarchically arranged with each having its own spirit or power. The "thinking forces" are the most powerful forces by virtue of their control over the magic of the word, the *nommo*, and they are superior to all other forces, to the "thing-forces," to the forces of time and space and of the "how." The thinking forces include living people, dead people, deified people, the ghosts and the gods. In the hierarchy of thinking forces, living people are on the lowest rung, yet the whole universe of forces depends on them. For it is only through them that all other thinking forces can go on affecting the world.

The ancient Chinese, at the height of their glory and splendor, also explained the universe most systematically, simply and scientifically in terms of *vital energy* or *CHI*, which it saw polarized into two basic types: positive and negative energies, Yang and Yin.

This classification was their all-pervasive classification and the basis of their religion as well as of their science. I will state this energy theory of life as fully as I can comprehend it, including the theory of the Chakras, and then I will proceed with the story of herbs and of Rastas within the framework of the Chakras. As a clear and easily obtainable summary of this most important concept is not easily available to John Public, I have endeavored to elaborate on this concept more than is really necessary for completing the story of herbal meditations, which is really the process I am primarily concerned with highlighting—in abstract. Since more and more people are nowadays talking of vibrations and are smoking herbs, a discussion of this area is most useful and timely.

The whole universe, according to this Eastern-African theory of life, is built upon the fusion of positive (yang) and negative (yin) energies. Western science recognizes these with the name electromagnetic currents.

Yin is the negative or magnetic, expansive, receptive quality in things which attracts and holds power. This includes woman, the moon, night, cold, dark, the interior of the body, our blood, alkalis, the horizontal, the left side of our bodies and brain. *Yang* is the positive or electrical, contracting and acting side of nature—like the sun, male, day, light, muscles, the exterior of the body, and the right side of our bodies and brain.

Throughout the whole of creation, according to this ancient conception, from the greatest to the tiniest, the same universal process of creation is going on all the time: The female magnetic power attracts the male electric force (or vice versa), fusion occurs, and creation takes place. The two sides or poles have to be brought together for action and creation. Yang actuates Yin, and Yin produces Yang, with health depending on their harmonious balancing. Thus all human life is maintained and is activated by these two primary forces: a centripetal force coming into the magnetic core of the earth from the stars, constellations, the sun, the moon, other celestial bodies, the atmosphere and infinite space itself (heaven force); and a centrifugal force generated upwards by the earth's rotation.

The universe was thus conceived as composing of billions of units, all sizes, each having its own center or pole, having an electrical side (running to its right) and a magnetic side (running to its left). When the magnetic side of the pole contacts the electrical current combustion takes place, power is generated, power is given off, a spark is lit, and creation in the form of fire takes place.

The human body is analyzable—and was done so by the ancients—also in terms of this energy conception. In terms of this theory (with such offshoots as acupuncture), the universe (or heaven) generates centripetal force which enters our body through the hair spiral, charges our midbrain with images and thoughts (the way TV receives images), and proceeds downwards in our bodies, vitalizing all the organs on its way, then exiting to the earth through the genitals. Earth's upward-moving centrifugal energy enters our bodies through the sex organs, rises upwards, creating spiraling tissues like the ovaries and breasts wherever it meets with the descending sun rays of positive energy, then finally exiting through the hair spirals on the top of one's head.

There are 12 pairs of meridian lines (which Western science now recognizes with the aid of its machines) which are the channels created as a result of the electromagnetic charge existing between both forces in the human body (as well as in all things). Both forces run deep within the body along the one central channel of the spine, and they collide at certain areas, producing intense outward radiation of energy at these points. The areas where this charge is most intense are one's midbrain, throat, heart, stomach, and small intestines. These five colliding areas, plus the entrance and exit regions of our bodies, form the holy Seven Chakras, the sleeping forces within and around us, that link or ground us in the wondrous universe around us, if only we could see.

In his *Introduction to the Chakras*, Peter Rendell explains them to us thus:

> We are children of the earth as well as of the sun. And these two forces—heavenly and earthly—must meet in us and work together for our evolution. In man there is a voltage and current between his basic polarity of Crown and Root. The potential difference between these two poles gives rise to the flow between them. This flow gives rise to the magnetic *aura* which surrounds a person. In man's occult anatomy there are two currents of energy which flow on the right and left sides of the spinal cord, which are positive and negative.

Each Chakra is a vortex of energy which revolves under the influence of a positive and negative current acting upon it.

The stem of the Chakras starts from the Spinal Cord. Into the open mouth of each Chakra an energy force from the higher Solar World is injecting its life force, a divine energy pouring from above, from the first Sun God Ra. The positive energy current is life-giving, while the negative energy current is life-receiving and conducting. As long as the two energy flows are in equilibrium, the individual will be mentally and physically well; but as soon as his consciousness becomes too one-sided—either too much towards the physical or too much towards the spiritual plane—he becomes susceptible to illness.

The Hindu mystics used the lotus flower as symbol of the Chakras. The rate of energy vibration is symbolized by the number of petals or spokes in the *lotus flower*. The number of petals is determined by the amount of power attributed to each center by men of knowledge, and these rates of vibration rise as we ascend the Chakras' ladder from bottom up-wards: the root or base Chakra has four petals, while the highest crown Chakra is attributed with 1,000 spokes or petals. So variable are these centers in their relative power! The petals in any particular center are either active or not, depending on whether or not these force-centers have been aroused. What is most important to note is that *they can be consciously aroused*, but with dangers to the unguided.

THE SEVEN CHAKRAS

Each of the seven chakras is said to be connected with one of the four basic elements of the universe: earth, water, fire, air (and ether). The chain of seven has been subdivided into three broad types, and these chakras will now be discussed in the order of these three broad divisions. There are (i) 2 lower physiological chakras, (ii) 3 middle-personality chakras, and (iii) 2 higher spiritual chakras, forming altogether seven rungs on this Jacob's ladder linking heaven and earth.

Sigmund Freud translated and applied this Eastern system somewhat in his psychoanalytic theories and practices. These three broad chakra types were renamed by him the *Id/Libido/Eros* (corresponding to the 2 lower chakras), the *Ego* (the 3 personality chakras), and the *Superego* (equaling the 2 higher spiritual forces). Freud reacted to the sexual repression of his own childhood, foisted on him by his culture. The mystics on the whole, and Christianity in particular, placed greatest emphasis on the higher powers, as did Plato in his ideal Republic.

From bottom up, we have *first the lowest root chakra*, which is located at the base of the spine, just below the region of the genitals. This center is symbolic of earthiness, solidity and grounding, of youth and libido energy. It is the seat of sexual or animal energy (Eros), the home of the coiled serpent fire energy—Kundali—which comes from the earth, and by whose activity it is believed the other centers are aroused to their maximum growth. A person feels at all levels but the lower chakras, particularly the root chakra, gives rise to the most intense physical feelings, expressing lower and slower rates of vibration and feelings.

The *second center is in the sacral region*, centering on the spleen, and is responsible for receiving the intake of vitality from the sun. The watery feeling of ripeness in our bodies is governed by this center.

The third center is the *solar region, located at the navel*. This is said to be the seat of physical energy (the element of fire) in our nature, and this region governs our sight and the brightness of what we see and the lustiness of our eating (which can be viewed as combustion).

When awakened, this particular center brings the power of feeling and a sensitivity to all sorts of influences. It is at this level that we experience the duality of expansiveness, warmth and joviality in ourselves. Laughing from our belly or gut is taken as a very healthy and positive sign by psychologists.

Don Juan alluded to this particular center in his teachings to Carlos Castaneda:

> Every man is in touch with everything else, not through his hands though, but through a bunch of long fibers that shoot out from the center of his abdomen. These fibers join a man to his surroundings; they keep his balance; they give him stability.
>
> (*A Separate Reality*)

To the Eastern mystics, this is the Hara region and is of great importance for the maintenance of health and strength.

The *fourth center is the heart chakra*, located over our own heart. At the heart level we ideally experience the qualities of airiness, gentleness and lightness, as well as the sense of touch. When awakened it gives a person the power to comprehend other vibrations of other astral entities. Through the direct access of the heart to the divine spirit of love and truth flowing from above comes those intuitions which are always more reliable than the thought processes of the brain. Christ as model mystic said: "As a man thinketh in his heart so is he…Where a man's heart is there will his treasure be." But he also said to Thomas: "Blessed are those who have been persecuted in their heart—these are they who have known the Father in Truth."   (*The Gospel According to Thomas*)

Not only Christ but all other yogis stress the importance of this center. Don Juan, for instance, told Carlos Castaneda: "For me there is only the traveling on paths that have Heart, on any path that may have Heart. There I travel, and the only worthwhile challenge is to traverse its full length. And there I travel, looking, looking, breathlessly."

(The Teachings of Don Juan)

The rhythmic beat of the heart is a model of universal rhythm and is replicated in the drumming beat of Africans and the importance they attached to this.

The *fifth center is the throat chakra,* located at the front of the throat. It is at this center or level that we ideally experience the quality of space—the feeling of freedom, the feeling of flying like a bird. This is the "ether," space itself, within which air, water, fire and earth (all the four basic elements) exist and come together. This center is the crossroads of the body, where both the higher and the lower selves meet. Through this throat-ether the lower elements are controlled. The throat and thyroid gland located in this region is the seat of much creative power. The sense of sound is derived from this center and constitutes the highest expression of this center. Voice is thus a clear measure of a person's development, and it is indeed through sound—word, speech, voice, and language—that man differentiates himself from the lower animals. Through language communication that his social nature develops: "In the beginning was the Word and the Word was Jah."

When awakened, this throat center gives a person the spiritual power of hearing on the astral plane. When you can hear a certain sound beyond complete silence—"the sound of silence"—you are at the level of the ether chakra. When highly developed, it endows one with the power of hearing voices and sounds from the other realm and from Jah.

The sixth center is the brow chakra, or the mind, known also as the organ of our second sight, our mysterious "third eye," which was regarded as the window to the human soul. By looking into a person's mind (not the physical eyes as is popularly believed now), you could tell what manner of being a person was. For it was believed in those days that man was constituted by the Father in such a way that "as man thinketh so is he." The emphasis here being on the mind— on consciousness and the search for truth, reality and "holism," the All and Now in all of us. What is the mind?

The mind is much more than the *physical brain* and its physical accumulations. The brain is only its vehicle or shell. The mind is a super intelligence system (or a real ideal existence) in its own right, but whose actual development in a particular individual case is dependent on many factors and "movements," including the values and vibrations it receives from the society. In this process, social and self-discipline in the right degrees are most important. Also the stimulation and development of the pituitary and pineal glands in our foreheads contribute to the development of the mind, a mind whose upper limits is that of a linkage with the Godhead itself and knowledge of how this conversion or renaissance takes place. It provides a kind of radar-like vision into things, from the simplest to the greatest.

Many mystics actually bored holes in their foreheads in search of a physical third eye, as they were often greedy or led astray. But for Rasta it is a state of radar-like consciousness, their far eye which they are bent on cultivating and which is responsible for their deep intuitive penetrations and creative outpourings. This third eye or far eye (or foresight) gives them tremendous range, distance and depth— in short, wisdom.

The sense of seeing and power of vision to human beings is indeed of unsurpassable value. Experiments in psychology of sense perception have shown that without the use of both eyes, without binocular vision, there can be no awareness of space's third dimension, and we could not well adjust to the world around us.

The Father thus provides mankind with a third eye (far eye) to supplement and make up for the short-sightedness of our physical pair of eyes, so that we can avoid harming ourselves and others by coming up with a better and a more realistic understanding and picture of ourselves in relationship to things around us and with Jah. But we have to be able to see and know that this does not mean looking. It has been appropriately said that the only thing that is good without qualification is this extended vision of mind development, the enlarging of one's understanding and awareness of what reality is ultimately all about—as energy at different rates of vibration.

The *seventh and highest spiritual center is the crown chakra*, which is the seat of the highest frequency of energy vibrations in our bodies, and having the greatest creative force. "At seven one reaches heaven," the stage of unity and bliss when one's spirit becomes eternal light—or life. At this stage one's mind reaches its higher levels of development, so that it controls the vibrations of the five lower chakras, rather than allowing itself to be controlled by them. As a person progresses on the path of spiritual advancement, the crown chakra (wisdom) increases until it covers almost the whole top of the head, at the stage when he realizes himself to be the king of the divine light. On this plane the individual consciousness fuses and becomes one with the Overself, or God. "He anointed my head with oil, my cup runneth over with joy." (Psalm 23)

To attain this level of unity and bliss, the lower chakras have to become completely united with the higher centers and the energies of these lower chakras transmuted into energies for the higher centers and more universal goals.

The symbolism of the "seven-branched candlestick," referred to in the Bible, alludes to this phenomenon of the seven chakras which according to the theory and symbolism is directed by the Seventh One: "We six are lights which shineth forth from a seventh. The seventh light is the origin of us. For assuredly there is no stability in those six save what they derive from the seventh." For all things depend on the seventh, like the sun (central body of the solar system) which gives its light to the moon and to the other five visible planets which have no light of their own.

At this seventh (spiritual) level there is only the grand and wonderful experience of the "I AM." One has achieved oneness with the spiritual and universal principle (of Truth) within one's self. One can speak from the universal level because one has universalized one's consciousness. Consciousness at the crown chakra level brings the experience of complete union with one's source—with the divine reality within one's consciousness—and the resulting feeling of bliss and unity with all of life. One emerges into a higher realm where one is closer to all beings and is more solid in his unity with all. At this level time does not exist—all is new and yet ancient at the same time. At this stage he can indeed love his brother as himself.

When this level is reached, the man of knowledge is able to leave his body in full consciousness, and also return to it, so that his consciousness will be continuous through night and day. Eventually neither death nor sleep will break this continuity. His spirit lives eternally, and will reside with those of the Great Spirits.

At this stage the God-man can then use his body as a vehicle for manifesting the spirit of unselfish love, as he has filled his body with the highest energies.

This kind of charismatic spiritualism will give the individual the power to mold, as he can lead his fellow men with truth and with effect. In agreement with this theory, Aldous Huxley wrote, after studying the phenomenon:

> The contemplative whose perception has been cleansed, does not have to stay in his room. He can go about his business so completely satisfied to see and be a part of the divine Order of things that he will never even be tempted to indulge in the "dirty devices of the

world"...Contemplatives are not likely to become gamblers, or procurers, or drunkards; they do not as a rule preach intolerance or make war, they do not find it necessary to rob, swindle, or grind the faces of the poor.

KUNDALI AND ITS AWAKENING

A very important and special kind of energy is sexual energy. It is in this area that symbolism was most often used to convey that which was known (or not known) about this vital Force, to veil knowledge about it, and to mystify the ignorant.

Freud often referred to this energy force as Id or Eros or Libido. Oriental mystics referred to is as *Kundali*, concern with which found a special place within their overall theory of the chakras, just as concern with it stood at the center of Christianity, which tells us that man's first human relationship in the Garden of Eden was marred when this forbidden fruit of life was given by Eve to Adam on advice of the Serpent. In the *Osiris* legend, the libido problem was central to that story, taking the form of the constant breaking of the incest taboo by all members of the holy family, who were cursed and punished by Helios in consequence. Sexual anarchy became a central theme in the fall of ancient Babylon. This problem seems to have been with us from the very beginning, and is now back with us. Recently the psychologist Abraham Maslow found that self-actualized people (i.e., those who know themselves) seem less preoccupied with sex than the others. Though orgasm was important to them, they did not seek it out for its own sake. And because fully integrated people experience love on a higher level than most, they felt no dependence on sex but simply enjoyed it when it occurred. Among these Maslow found less possessiveness and jealousy of their partners. For these it is a choice, rather than a drive. For a few seconds sex makes some feel worthwhile and powerful, but after a time the feeling quickly subsides, so we seek it out repeatedly, like a junkie looking for a fix.

The control and regulation of sexual energy or Eros is central to most religious systems, and indeed many mystics believe that the loss of semen is destructive to mental powers and that sexual energy can and should be transformed into energy of the mind. Others, however, believe that some loss of semen is natural, normal and necessary, but that it should be completely regulated and controlled by mind and will—by the Big I, for Eros without Spirit leads to gross animalism and to all kinds of sexual excesses.

Along with their understanding of the chakras also went an understanding of this force and the challenge of awakening or arousing this force Kundali, the earth spirit, pictured symbolically as a serpent of fire, lying coiled at the base of the human spine. Kundali or the female or earth energy is said to be like liquid fire as it rushes upwards through the body when summoned by the mind or will (the male principle) in quest of the "mystical marriage" or universal conception.

In African lore this root energy (Kundali) is pictured more as the lion which moves upwards to marry the lamb. "The doctrine of the 'Encircled Serpent' or the 'Coiled Lion' was dear to the heart of the Egyptians," wrote W. Oldfield Howey in his book *The Cat*. It was also often pictured as the "Tree of Life," rising up from the earth in response to the heavenly sun.

Sexual desire (libido) is created in the brain by impressions received through the senses. Impulses are then sent out from the brain, through the spinal cord, to the sex center in the lower part of the spine (the "moon region" or root chakra) and thence to the nerves controlling the sex organs. In reverse, local stimulation of sex organs sends impulses to the brain which registers these sensations as pleasure. Sexual energy is a creative force, whether it be used for physical or mental ends, whether it be directed upwards or downwards. Its use depends on us.

To the material-minded it is used purely and quickly for procreation or sensual gratification. As man aspires to higher ideals, as he yearns to create mentally and live in the spirit, the force is gradually drawn upwards to the creative principles in the brain. He can magnetize this force upwards through the channel of his spine, until it reaches the masculine-feminine principles of the brain and fires them. Inspiration and wisdom then follow. As this energy filters upwards through the other centers (i.e., as it is retained and controlled rather than discharged) it vivifies the life (feeling) of these other centers, raises the person to a higher level of consciousness and enhances his life in general. If and when it reaches the brow chakra, it confers the power of hearing the voice of the higher master and obeying its command.

After its upward journey, this serpent fire is led back to the base of the spine energized by the higher spirit, much stronger in quality and type as a result of its upward journey and this mystical marriage. At this stage one's sexualism is at the seventh level (physical discharge is at the first level). It is then that one loves at the seventh level divinely, with all of one's heart, soul, and mind.

Mystics use techniques for arousing Kundali such as will power, fasting, modes of breathing, mantras, postures, and movements. They say that sexual desire in its lowest animal form keeps the mind to the earth, and prevents it soaring to the highest planes of consciousness. Sexual desire is a distracting power or spirit that must be controlled to increase the power and vision of mind concentration and our general magnetism. Sometimes it is aroused by accident prematurely, in which case there can be dangers and even pain resulting from underdeveloped passages and the unpreparedness of the body and mind.

Central to the teachings of Christ (no less than in that of Don Juan) is this theory of the arousing and awakening of Kundali; Christ's basic teaching being: Until all the passions of the body (of the brain and senses) are subdued, and until the inherited and acquired instincts of the flesh can be controlled and until all the unconscious reactions and stimuli of the physical system are curtailed and the physical system made immune to the stimuli (temptations) of nature's worldly (physical) powers, man cannot be a moral angel. In Galatians we find this stated most clearly: "Behave in a spiritual way; then you will not carry out your fleshly cravings. For the longings of the flesh are contrary to the spirit and those of the spirit are contrary to the flesh." (Galatians 5:16-17)

HERBS AND THE CHAKRAS

Rastafarians in the majority are roots folks, and as such few are consciously acquainted with the concept of the chakras. Yet, when one listens and penetrates the Rastaman's reasonings on herbs and when one keenly observes its effect (body and mind) it becomes clear that they are speaking of the same inner reality which the concept of the chakras denotes.

When one further experiences this reality for one's self, this thesis appears even more convincing: There is a whole universe of power inside of us, and the herbal trip, if and when successfully steered, is the Rastaman's way of achieving increased consciousness of these inner (spiritual) body centers. With this the increased spiritualism (energy) allows them to transcend Babylon and become one with Jah Selassie I, in Zion, in the spirit realm. In doing this they are neither cheating nor stunting themselves, as this spirit realm is of a higher value in the overall scheme of the universe (the Father). This is the Rasta ideal, amounting to a most realistic repatriation movement back to the lost Africa of integrated "I and I." While many Rastafarians continue to think of repatriation as physically going-back-home-to-Africa, the new trend (particularly since 1977) is the movement back to Africa *internally*, through the mystic passageway of our chakras. Of our minds through the concrete rhythm of our breath. It is there, at the summit of a rhythmic breath, that real and lasting love, health, wealth and happiness are to be found. The greatest truths are the simplest. This is one of them.

The Canadian anthropologist Carol Yawney also noted that among Rastafarians the distinction between mind, body and soul is most important. She noted:

> Being the descendants of transported slaves, the Rastas conceive of their physical selves as existing in a condition of exile...Rasta ideology conceives of consciousness as being potentially free regardless of physical circumstances; that one characteristic of a truly free consciousness is that it can journey unhindered about the earth. Thus while their physical structures remain separate from the heartland of Africa their consciousness can return at will given certain conditions. The purposes of these flights is to gather energies to fight the fight in Babylon until the time when mind and body are finally harmonized in Zion...The smoking of herbs lubricates the slippage between body and mind. (Carol Yawney, *Herbs and the Chalice: The Symbolic Life of the Children of Slaves*, 1972 paper)

While Western scientists are more concerned with the chemical components of herbs, Rastafarians view it in its wholeness as an ally or spirit used in the process of self-analysis, self-healing and as a stimulant for their subtler psychic sense organs—the chakras. This inner nonmeasurable world is one which Western scientists have ignored until recent years. Eyes are now looking more towards the East—to Africa, China and the Bible—for they are now realizing that this inner reality is dynamite and the source of our power.

That herbal smoking affects the chakras was alluded to by Don Juan, the Indian man of knowledge who taught Castaneda how to see, that is, of penetrating the aura, and of seeing more than what meets the naked physical eyes—physical eyes which look but do not see, as Don Juan himself explained:

> Men look different when you see. The little smoke will help you see men as fibers of light...Yes...fibers, like cobwebs. Very fine threads that circulate from the head to the navel. Thus a man looks like an egg of circulating fibers. And his arms and legs are like luminous bristles, bursting out in all directions.
>
> *(A Separate Reality)*

As a concentrated energy force, ganja smoking affects the user at all his force centers or levels of his consciousness—physical, mental and spiritual. It leads the smoker's consciousness towards these body centers, and through circular feed-back and interaction, it helps in stimulating our awareness of them and by this very awareness of them, stimulates their growth and development by way of improving the rhythm and depth of our breathing and the quality of our lives in general. The dynamics of breath and the integrated effects of herbs smoking in this process is referred to here as *herbal meditations*, consisting of gentle movements stimulated by the Great Breath.

THE GREAT BREATH

Breath is life. With it starts life; it is necessary for conception to take place. Legends have it so. Ra, "Father of the Gods," is said to have first created Shu, the *Wind-God*, as a personification of himself. In the *Osiris* mystery religion it was Set (known to the Greeks as

Typhon), meaning a windstorm, who destroyed Osiris. His wife, *Isis*, then hovered over the dead body of Osiris in the form of a sparrowhawk, and caused breath to enter into Osiris' lifeless form by the fanning of her wings, so that the dead god entered upon a new existence as king of the underworld.

Growing up as I did in a very African way in the rural heart of Jamaica, I remember well how I and my brother, being spirited enough, ventured out to hide among trees near a number of graves, watching to see if smoke, symbolic of the spirit or ghost, would rise out of the graves three days after burial. In the folk mind, smoke (the wind) and spirits have long been associated, and this association goes back to antiquity.

Christ himself promised everliving life or immortality *in this life* to some: "Verily I say unto you, there shall be some standing here, who shall not taste of death, till they see the Son of Man coming in His Kingdom." This power of eternal life granted to the elect has been linked to the great breath, for on conferring this power of the Holy Spirit on them, Christ "breathed on them." This breathing on them was a very sacred and divine procedure and was the only occasion during the whole life and history of Christ that he ever breathed upon other human beings. Perhaps he also did so in arousing Lazarus from the grave! It comes out also in the Nicodemus story. This wealthy official (Pharisee), who was in search of redemption, was given this formula by Christ: "Except a man be born of water and of the Spirit, he cannot enter the Kingdom of God…Ye must be born again from Above…But this Second Birth is not from a woman's womb…But from the fructifying breath of the wind (in Greek, Spirit and Wind are expressed by the same word)."

Even in Western biological sciences, breathing is recognized as the most important function of the organism, affecting all other body activities most directly. They too agree that knowledge of the rise and fall of breath comprehends all knowledge and is the highest of all the sciences. It is the essence of knowing one's self and the basis of self control, including control of libido. All living things breathe, but at different rates. Each has its own ideal rate in relationship to time.

It is a known fact that very few people make the fullest possible use of their potential capacity for breathing. Complete breathing involves a combination of abdominal (deep) breathing, middle breathing, and upper (or shallow) breathing. Shallow breathing is the most uneconomic form and corresponds to the lowest stage of life. It is linked to "first level" sexualism. Psychologists have shown also that shallow breathing is a response to stress and fear, for by slowing down one's breath a person blots out some of their awareness (life), including the awareness of the ensueing dangers and pain. Short breath is associated with weakness, tiredness, short life, disease and death; long breath has been associated with long life, stamina, and vitality. This is an important focus for the sociology of medicine. What are the social, historical and biological factors affecting breath?

In the correct or effective breathing, the whole chest should be uplifted at the intake of the breath, and this movement should then raise up all the internal organs from their stagnant and depressed positions. At the exhalation the diaphragm muscle contracts again upwards, dragging up still farther the organs below. Correct breathing in this manner assures a continuous gentle massage and a stimulation of the digestive organs.

It is also most important that one's speed and rhythm of breathing be slow, deep and gentle. It is quite impossible to become overexcited if one breathes slowly. If one's breathing is slowed down to ten or twelve breaths per minute it will become impossible to feel overexcited, irritable and nervous or even to feel pain. If breathing can be dropped to, say, three per minute, then all the bodily vibratory activities will become so subdued and harmonized that the more delicate perceptions will be discernible, giving us inspiration and premonition, and more spiritual power.

All yogis know from actual livity experiences that only by the conscious regulation of our breathing can we achieve the resistance which assures us a long life free of sickness. When we consciously develop our breathing, we set up an equilibrium between the positive and negative energies in our system. In holding in our breath for a time, we focus our consciousness in the center of our self, uniting both energies, and creating the basis for complete equilibrium. By holding in breath we clean all the little airsacs in the lungs and stimulate them towards increased activity. Well aired lungs transmit more oxygen to the body, circulation becomes more vigorous, our endocrine glands are regenerated, the whole body is vitalized and peace of mind flows naturally.

By gradually lengthening the period of retention of breath, we generate a spiritualizing effect on our consciousness. By emphasizing the in or upward breath, one is spiritualizing or regenerating oneself. The science of the chakras is the art of proper breathing. Patient observation of one's own breath stream eventually leads to the ability to control the vital forces and focus them at will at the different levels. Gradually one learns to recognize the changes in vibration which occur as breath or life force passes through the different levels. The ultimate step in control is when breath can be suspended altogether and one can leave the world of form and withdraws into the spiritual realm, the universal consciousness. The adept who has learned to control his breath completely is able to suspend it and withdraw from his body, without abandoning it. He is also able to return to it again as he likes.

All disease is merely a restriction of the flow of the life force (Chi or Prana) or ache (air and blood) in a particular region as result of structured blockages. Air is one major channel by means of which this life force enters our bodies. Lifelessness and disease in particular areas of the body result from insufficient breath (life force) to those regions. Tuberculosis, for instance, results from insufficient breath, as does asthma. The stomach, the brain and mind, the spine and our entire nervous system is affected by our breathing, adversely if our breath is defective in any number of ways. Our minds (responsible for integrating self to reality) are oftentimes the most clogged up chakra needing the expansive and grounding effect of the smoke, clogged up by false and decrepit images induced by decades of miseducation, false indoctrinations and sheer smoggy ignorance.

When our energy channels are purified and cleared of blockages (lodged in our musculature as knots, strings and hard ossification), and the forces in our systems are balanced, the energies can flow freely through them. We cannot get in touch with the highest and most powerful vibrations of the spirit within ourselves when our bodies and brains are a mass of struggling, fighting, inharmonious or ossified vibrations.

Unfortunately, most people are not conscious of breathing handicaps which have become second nature to them. And even doctors report on how difficult it is to develop deep breathing in most people who have lost touch with their bodies and with this original truth of the Great Breath.

Thanks to the power of herbs and Jah Rastafari, I have regained my breath…or on my way, merrily. Herbs was the mystical lamp that lit the way. The way was the way of the breath. Herbs was, in effect, an earthy University of the Air with the real educational effect of expanding my consciousness in the most certain and universal way—through the breath.

From curiosity and "kicks," herbs passed on to becoming an integral breath therapy, and eventually moved on still further to being my sacrament to the Most High, in thankfulness for discovering the inverse correlation between breath and death: more breath, less death.

DANGERS: GETTING LOST IN THE MAZE

Though I am so positive about herbs, and my story is one of triumph, this does not mean that there are not negatives along the way. I endeavored to see these also, so as to avoid them.

There are two categories of dangers associated with herbs. First, there are those dangers which outsiders of the herbal experience talk about, and secondly, there are some real dangers which objective Rastafarians themselves know about. Outsiders, including many scientists and medical "experts" in the West, have up until recent times condemned herbs, claiming harmful effects on organ tissues, body structure, brain cells, and at times they linked it to a host of modern diseases, in a scapegoat fashion. In this regard it is blamed for a range of socio-psychological attitudes, values, behavior forms and lifestyles which are then denounced as sick or pathological—all as a way of denouncing Rasta. The most persistent charge by outsiders is that "it drives people mad…It makes people go off." This is the most serious scare charge against herbs, and so strongly is the charge believed and acted upon by outsiders, that they cluster into a causative force with the effect of driving the "weaker" smokers of herbs toward real fear, paranoia, and even to madness itself. It is a charge which gets to the heart of the whole confrontation in our society.

In a post-colonial society like Jamaica, where day-to-day frustrations and pressures are the order of the day and equal to the sun's heat, herbs have become an easy scapegoat. I put it as part of my present thesis that, had it not been for herbs, there would have been far more madness in the island/world today, as there would be less coping energy available to deal with the particular achings and itchings that summon this particular agent of relief.

I have seen no evidence that herbs make people mad, but it can most certainly accelerate the tendency towards breakdown and madness under certain kinds of conditions. This fact cannot be denied. So we must examine the argument as carefully and as consciously as we can. There are dangers to herbs. Therefore, our discussion of herbs, if it is to be really scientific, should most certainly deal with this question of its possible dangers, as well as its possible strengths, for the sake of our children.

The lighting of a match or the crossing of the street are fraught with dangers; so too is herb smoking. By knowing the specific nature of the kinds of dangers, we are better able to deal with such dangers. However, these dangers can only be known by the insiders themselves, particularly if these dangers are related to personal health, feelings, and people's energy levels.

There is wide variation among human beings, no less than among Rastas, in their individual response to herbs as in anything else. Herbs is not a chemical -specific drug. Its effects depend not only on its inner content (THC), but also upon the context and manner in which it is smoked, as well as on the mediating condition of the user's mind chakra and other force centers.

The physical condition of a person is an important consideration for us to begin with. It is not advisable that people suffering from certain kinds of sickness should touch herbs without the support of a specialist. For example, it is not advisable that people with cardiovascular problems should smoke without proper guidance because of the accelerating effect of the smoke on the heart rate. Also, if one already has a mental disturbance, smoking without proper guidance can worsen the problem, because of the introspection which results. Individuals can fall off the deep end and never return from some of the twisted inner meanderings which inevitably accompany smoking, particularly at certain stages of effects. They can become trapped in the maze by the smoke. One has to know what the hunter is looking for in the maze, or the hunter can become trapped by the spirits in herbs. Only when a person is committed to the greater Spirit of Truth through inner resolution can one most certainly avoid the dangers and pitfalls inherent in the use of herbs. In smoking herbs, one has to be guided by this greater spirit, a guiding framework, an all-powerful model, a Don Juan, a Christ, a system of ideas—or else one can be trapped in the mist and become lost.

The guiding framework of I and I is that herbs is the tree of life, the mystical threads or ropes sent down to the earth, to Anancy (the black sheep who went astray), the fallen angel, by means of which he can climb (parachute) back up to heaven, through the maze of the smoke—like the caterpillar which discovered how to become a butterfly so as to fly. Truth and reality has to be the guiding framework throughout, for unless Anancy is committed to truth he will become trapped. In spiritual questing, "Many are called, but only few make it through."

Even the truth-seeker is not without dangers. He who seeks truth and is determined to uncover and master the secrets of the universe for himself is treading a path beset with many pitfalls, dangers and illusions. *The real dangers have to do less with the kinds of effects Westerners stress and the way in which they see these effects coming about. The dangers, as I see them, have more to do with its unguided arousal and disturbance of the various body powers or chakras, and of altering one's accustomed internal energy or Zodiac system. Of throwing them into disorder and confusion at a stage when the mind is not developed enough to integrate these changes.*

There is the danger of being overwhelmed, of disintegrating under the pressure of a new and more powerful reality, greater than a mind accustomed to living most of the time in a cozy world of symbols and make-believe could possibly bear and deal with.

Some smokers have become overwhelmed by fright and fear at certain points as they begin the journey inwards and begin sensing and feeling strange inner rumblings and energy re-adjustments. One's mind or will-power must be strong and self-conscious enough to will itself to return at any time or the smoke can take one away into the astral world; and even if this trip takes the smoker back to Eden or the Nile Valley, his spirit could never be intelligently steered back to tell us here in twentieth century Babylon of his trip to this twilight zone of yesterday and tomorrow. Herbs smoking can awaken a particular chakra, giving rise to fright and unsettling feelings, particularly if the smoker does not have an overall understanding of what is happening to him and to handle these changes if and when they arise, and how to remain grounded, or detached, as need be.

Herbs can in fact bring out schizophrenic tendencies in a person, although it can also help the schizophrenic. For by arousing and awakening particular chakra centers without at the same time removing blockages that separate the unified reintegration of these centers and the increased flow of this vital energy force, schizophrenic behavior is likely. For example, smoking may increase mind power and consciousness in the head and arouse Eros in the belly, but because of the retention of physical blockages around the waist or neck regions, erratic and maladjusted behavior is likely to result.

Damages may result also from the uneven stimulation and development of these centers. For instance, to develop one's mind to the highest level where one can see clairvoyantly without being grounded in one's feet in real bioenergetic terms, can easily produce paranoia, fear, and a tendency of flight in the person.

There is also the possibility of prematurely awakening Kundali—the fire power—before one's will or mind is strong enough to control this force so as to focus it at whatever level he requires, upwards or downwards, depending on command, in which case the person becomes a prisoner to this baser earth force.

Specifically Vera Adler (in *The Finding of the Third Eye*) sounded the warning concerning the dangers of disturbing inner consciousness, particularly at the root level of Kundali. It is possible, she stated, that

> ...the body has not had time for all its vibrations to become purified and raised to a higher tempo, and the brain is still full of the dregs of worldly and impure thoughts. When, therefore, by a forcing process, the Kundali serpent of fire is prematurely driven up the spine, burning away all dross as it does, and it arrives within a brain unfitted to use it, parts of the brain cannot stand this bath of fire and perish with the sudden burning of the dross they still contain, and various forms of derangement ensue.

Another notable scholar of occult powers also reminds us of this:
> One very common effect of rousing it prematurely is that it rushes downwards in the body instead of upwards and thus excites the most undesirable passions—excites and intensifies their effects to such a degree that it becomes impossible for the man to resist them. Such men become satyrs, monsters of depravity, because they are in the grasp of a force which is out of all proportion to the ordinary human power of resistance.
> (C.W. Leadbeater, *The Chakras*, p. 82)

Fascists come easily to mind here, as their sex crimes were astounding. But so are those that are going on around us all the time.

It should also be pointed out that only a strong body can endure the strain involved in the process of training the mind to control these forces.

For these reasons it is clear that the power is too great to be controlled by the will-power of a child, or the mind of the immature, and can be dangerous and more alienating than unifying in both cases.

The premature unfolding of the higher aspects of Kundali intensifies everything in the person's nature. Several scholars have warned of the terrible dangers of awakening these tremendous forces without an expert teacher, or guide, for in the words of one, "It gives liberation to yogis but bondage to fools." When Christ said to Thomas in this riddle, "Blessed is the Lion which the man eats and the Lion shall become man. And accursed is the man whom the Lion eats—and the man shall become Lion" (Gospel according to Thomas), he was here making symbolic reference to the ultimate danger to a man when the Kundali Lion Force becomes too overpowering. Likewise, one folk song warned us long ago: "When the lion is asleep, don't you try to wake him, for you might get hurt." The lion is the Kundali-serpent, and the folk is warning of the unpredictable dangers that are entailed in arousing it.

Chapter 8
WEST INDIAN CULTURE THROUGH RASTA EYES

I was born in the ghetto
Grew up in the ghetto
Learned that the cow jumped over de moon
That de dish ran away with the spoon
Where is I culture, where is I culture?
De Chineyman him come from China
De Indian belong to India
De white man come from Europe
But I Ethiopian blood, me deh ya
Where is I culture?
          (Song by the "Ethiopians," for Decultured Ethiopians)

Dennis Forsythe

THE IMPORTANCE OF CULTURE

The above song by the "Ethiopians" introduces us to the central issue of "self identity" and "culture" which have become central concerns to peoples of the world today, and particularly to Rastafarians.

The self-identity of a person or a people is most important to their lives. It affects how others perceive and act toward them; it affects their own energy level and their own behavior and attitude towards others, and how much they get from life. It has an all-important bearing on the direction and decisions we make as individuals and as a people. For instance, the extraordinary survival and achievements of European Jews stem from this: from their conviction that God (Yahweh) loved them and that through them he will make his will known and bring healing to the nations of the world.

Self-identity thus relates to the meaning of the particular "I" or "Me," i.e., Who am I? What am I? For what purpose (if any) am I alive? What have I become? What are our weaknesses and strengths as individuals and as a nation? What is special and unique to us as a people, and what do we have in common with others? There are many diverse answers to these questions.

Most commonly, people adopt a special name, develop a philosophy (or ideology) and use other symbols (flags, totems) as outer signs telling of how they resolve these identity questions and how they choose to live.

While the issue of one's identity is not usually forefront in the minds of the masses these days, it is most imperative that our leaders make this issue uppermost and resolve it in a manner that is most fitting for all people. For the nation's ultimate fate—as well as for the individual's own happiness—rests on this. Our leaders must work towards a harmonious collective self-concept that can unify its people, more especially as the choices become more confusing every day.

The author of *The Plural Society in the British West Indies*, M.G.

Smith, noted in this book that the problem of cultural identity is unusually acute for West Indians:

> West Indians may intuitively sense something distinctive about themselves and their culture without being able to define either satisfactorily. Especially because of their political implications, such definitions are unlikely to win a general consensus. West Indians also recognize the cultural identity within their own and neighbouring territories, without being clear on how these differences fit into the larger schemes of national or cultural unity and distinctiveness.

This issue of identity takes us quickly to the subject of culture, for it is here, lodged in the cultural realm, that we find the commonly accepted answer to this question of self-identity. Culture is a general mode of social response to a social situation which becomes reflected in the personality of its people. *Culture is in fact the people.* It connotes the total body of learned and transmitted behavior that characterizes a particular population and distinguishes it from others.

The starting point of any serious concern with social progress and social change should therefore be a look at that specific culture as this refers to the total functioning of a total people within the total system within a particular environment. An understanding of the nature and significance of culture is thus crucial for conceptualizing and dealing with the problems of society at all of its levels—individual as well as collective. Our present social, economic and political instabilities and confusion in the society can and should therefore be squarely placed within the holistic context of our society's total cultural heritage. Only at this level of a total cultural analysis can we comprehend the most general effects which our common background of slavery and colonialism has left for us as a heritage, and which is now our starting point. It also enables us to delve into our past that predated slavery, from which we can derive wholesome cultural models.

My aim in this chapter is to discuss the subject of culture in a way that can shed some light on its importance from the point of view of change and progress—as an instrument of policy—within the particular situation of Jamaica, with implications for the Caribbean and the Third World as a whole.

It seems to be agreed generally by most Third World countries that culture is important enough to be given its own portfolio. It is as if the cultural beat is more alive in these regions, demanding some greater-than-average emphasis. In Jamaica, both Michael Manley's recent P.N.P. government, as well as the present J.L.P. government of Mr. Edward Seaga, give special prominence to their respective "Ministry of Culture" and to its minister. Both parties envision culture as an organ of social mobilization. It is important to note that this cultural approach has not been yet fully applied to the task of building our nation.

The meaning and application of culture varies much in its conceptualization, and carries over into how people treat and apply what is thus conceived as "culture." *A Marxist definition* of culture sees it as secondary to economic factors, a view which ends up de-emphasizing the spiritual needs of people, and the Marxist thus ends up not only being overly-materialistic but also totalitarian. The elites, on the other hand, define culture as the "high culture," the elite European way of life, which serves as a model for the masses to ape. *Roots culture*, from this elitist point of view, is dismissed or devalued as superstitious, wild, and backward. The *Rastafarian meaning* and application of culture is a third view of culture, from bottom up, that of the folk. "Two thousand years of history—Black history—could not be wiped so easily," sings Bob Marley, "for our hands were made strong by the

Hand of the Almighty." This Rastafarian roots view is the most democratic view. One that is also total (holistic) in that it is not only a *description* of culture, but also a critical appraisal of this reality in terms of the highest possibilities and ideals, as derived from historical, oral and Biblical studies of our ancient traditions. The Rastafarian view of culture is also closer to the meaning of culture as this has been defined by sociologists and anthropologists who have made the subject of culture their most important single contribution to man's understanding of himself and his society.

CULTURE DEFINED

Culture refers to the effect of an environment and of the society upon the people who live there, predisposing them to be and to behave in one way as opposed to another.

This "culture system" includes all the ready-made solutions (or non-solutions) to the general problem of living encountered by the group. It includes all the accepted and patterned ways of behavior of a given people, the total organizational arrangement of all the group's ways of thinking, feeling and acting. In effect the culture and the people are one. To define a people we must therefore define its culture, for it is this culture which gives a people their identity and their collective and individual images of self.

This culture is embodied in its art, music, dance, song and story—all of which attest to the kind of people they are. But it goes beyond these to include everything that is socially significant. As one notable anthropologist puts it:

> Our culture is our routine of sleeping, bathing, dressing, eating and getting to work. It is our household chores and the actions we perform on the job; the way we buy goods and services, write and mail a letter,

> take a taxi or board a bus, make a telephone call, go to the movie, or attend church.
>
> It is the way we greet friends or address a stranger, the admonitions we give our children and the way they respond, what we consider good and bad manners and even to a large extent what we consider right and wrong. All these and thousands of other ways of thinking, feeling and acting that seem to natural and right that we may even wonder how else one could do it.
>
> (Ina Brown, *Understanding Other Cultures*)

The noted anthropologist Tylor likewise defined a culture as "that complex whole which includes knowledge, beliefs, arts, morals, laws, customs and any other capabilities and habits acquired by man as a member of society."

Each people, society, or class has a culture or a patterned way of behaving and believing, but there are usually important cultural differences within a given society between the subgroups of the specific contents of their culture.

Basically, the culture of a group constitutes an adaptive system, one in which the various elements constitute a more or less *integrated whole*. As such, it is a *pattern of survival*. There is a degree of order and consistency within each culture, and it is the overall effect on the practitioners of a particular culture which gives a people their characteristic style. It is also the cumulative and traditional nature of a culture which makes it appear "right" and natural. Those who share a common set of symbols and understandings constitute a "people."

Culture becomes visible in the behavior of the socialized individuals as they engage in their day to day behavior. The practitioners of a culture are most often unaware of the *patterned character* of their actions. Yet it is the very patterned wholeness of a culture—not its separate individual traits—which gives it its greater importance, though each element of a culture is important and is a force in its own right.

Defined as such, a cultural analysis is all-encompassing, and provides us with an important prism for those people wanting *to know themselves individually and collectively* and wanting to "seize the times" and themselves. To know a people one has to penetrate its culture, for it is through culture that man represents and symbolizes himself. One legend of the Sumer people takes the form of this most profound question relating to a people's culture, and which is most relevant to the Black world of today:

> "What became of the Black people of Sumer?" the traveler asked the old man, "for ancient records show that the people of Sumer were Black. What happened to them?" "Ah," the old man sighed, "They lost their History, so they died."

THE CONTEMPORARY SIGNIFICANCE OF RASTA

The special factor best explaining the heightened emphasis on culture in Jamaica in recent years is undoubtedly the mushrooming success of the native-born Rastafarian movement, climaxing a long, strong, and brave tradition of African revivalism and spiritualism in Jamaica. This should not be surprising, for as one most noted anthropologist observed:

> Even under the compulsion of the dominant culture of the whites, Negroes have retained African religious beliefs and practices far more than they have retained economic patterns...Supernatural sanctions figure far

> more in the total life of the people than does any other single fact of the culture, such as those matters having to do with making a living, or family structure or political institutions...But [religious] retentions will of necessity be manifested in syncretisms and reinterpretations.
>
> (M.J. Herskovits, *The Myth of the Negro Past*, p. 352)

The folk belief in spirits is the root component in African thought. The spirits of the dead are ever-present, and constantly interacting with the living and have to be wooed by the living. Amongst Jamaican Africans these spiritual forces were usually perceived by the folk as falling into three types who were constantly affecting the affairs of mortals:

1. Heavenly spirits—God, the archangels, angels and spirits.
2. Earth-bound spirits—fallen angels, Bible prophets and apostles.
3. Ground spirits—usually referred to as ghosts or duppies.

It is believed by the folk that three days after "breath leaves the body," the soul is resurrected from the grave, going up to heaven if one's pilgrimage on Earth was good, and a duppy spirit which wanders around the Earth if it was bad in life as punishment for such wrongs. Such beliefs play an important part not only in Obeah and in all the many African sects, but it spills over in its importance on how the folk lives, works, eats, sleeps, breathes and even votes; in all these areas, he is ever aware of the spirit realm and its moral importance.

This background of African Fundamentalists beliefs is the larger spring out of which Rasta flows. It has brought back this question of African spiritualism and has raised its meaning and level up to a higher pitch by making its meaning, they say, more relevant to the realities of their present lives.

The revival of the African influence in the form of Rastafari needs to be stated and examined, particularly if the cultural perspective and cultural potential which it has elevated and revived is to have its maximum effect, for only then can the traditional roots (Bible) meaning of culture be understood and take its effect. It is in this ancient roots meaning and implications of culture (as used by Rastafarians) that the power of Third World culture lies.

The significance of Rastafari, it is here maintained, lies in the alternative and opposing African definition it gives of the dominant Jamaican culture to which it is a reaction, and of an alternative vision of life and how life should be lived.

Rastafari is indeed the first mass (grassroots) movement among West Indians pre-eminently preoccupied with the task of looking into themselves and consciously *asking* and *answering* the fundamental cultural and human question, Who am I? or What am I? As such, this movement reflects the same spirit of Garveyism at the grassroots level, and it is flourishing in all those areas where black West Indians are concentrated today. It is a desperate call for an alternative culture more suitable to the needs of African peoples in these times.

That there is such a spiritual need and that it is important to the West Indian in search of himself is attested to by a notable Jamaican anthropologist and author of a most impressive book on the subject called *The Sun and the Drum (African Roots in Jamaican Folk Tradition)*. He describes himself as a person of "mixed racial and cultural heritage" who developed the need to define himself. His resolution:

> It was the African ingredients in me that freed my being. I therefore decided to identify myself with my African heritage, setting loose the rhythm that I felt throbbing in me. The conflict resolved I was free to embrace all the members of my family, of whatever hue

> and began to smile at those who were unable to reciprocate because of their European bondage. To this day, the conflict of identity is a social prison which claims thousands of Jamaicans as inmates. (p. 14)

Rastafarians likewise make it clear by their words and by their own changed lifestyles that culture is most important by virtue of its effects upon their lives. It affects their unconscious (biological) energy level, as well as their conscious energy level, particularly their levels of self-awareness, self-knowledge and self-understanding. They assert that this quest for an appropriate self-image and self-knowledge is the key to enduring progress and real growth—both individual and collective—and that this is a more appropriate cornerstone for achieving social stability and order, and life itself. It is not just an end in itself and one of the highest of social values, but also a means in itself, necessary for the attainment of other worthwhile social values. They place great emphasis on self-knowledge.

Knowing-the-self means, for them, knowing one's roots and being connected with them; it means being aware of one's potentials, one's weaknesses and strengths and being aware of the personal effects of history and of society upon our natures.

Their mode for understanding the self, they say, is empirically derived from their own lives and experiences, and from the wisdom, glory and power of their ancient ancestors. Such a theory is of course not unique, says the Rastaman, as it can find support in the social sciences, demonstrated repeatedly in history and enshrined in the Bible, as well as in many other sacred texts and traditions.

As it is here defined, the Movement provides the only roots source from which the intellectual, cultural and emotional guidelines for an alternative and independent Third World perspective can develop. It offers itself as the model-example of an "elite" from the oppressed mass of the base of the international race-class pyramid, exemplifying staying power, wisdom-through-suffering, and an intense spiritual reawakening at the subjective level, so much so that they have come to see and believe firmly that they are the elect of Jah (God) and thus the fulfillment of ancient Biblical prophecy. They see themselves as the modern Israelites, and Africans as God's original people spoken about in the Bible. The Rastafarian is thus the collective Christ, reincarnated, and symbolized by the personage of His Imperial Majesty, Haile Selassie. Surfacing in every sleeping African who rediscovers himself by healing himself, and rediscovering life afresh. It has a message for the world.

One does not have to identify one's self as a Rastafarian nor smoke ganja in order to share the perspective and "truth" of this model. In this sense their definitions parallel and rival other sociological models and perspectives. It can be used as a prism through which one can look at self and society, depending on its validity, of course. In the distillation of Rastafarian images and creative outpourings (by intellectuals from within their own ranks) lie, I believe, the missing and important ingredients for the healing of the self and of our nation. That it contains such a necessary intellectual and cultural corrective has now become my firm conviction as a sociologist.

It is in the process of growing up, looking at ourselves, through the cultural prism, that Rastafari offers a model of itself and of the environing culture, as this culture was, how it now is, and of how it has to, will be and should be in the future. It is in this "looking-glass" cultural, non-partisan and holistic sense that Rastafari is most significant. It offers itself as a dynamic counterculture from which we can derive a theoretical perspective or frame-of-reference which can be used by non-Rastas to look at themselves and the world.

Rastafarian definitions could thus well force us inwards, to look at ourselves and our society, and can endow us with the critical kind of self-consciousness which can prod us forward to a higher and larger and more wholesome (holistic) definition of ourselves. At that level it is possible to have greater peace, greater love and more social harmony. At that level the people can achieve miracles. Rastafari is forcing us to realize that humanity's problems—like yours and mine—are spiritual in nature, and that a purely materialistic approach cannot understand or solve them.

A cultural analysis, grounded and enriched by Rastafarian definitions and an understanding of Rasta can, I believe, enable us to better understand, withstand and deal with some of the fundamental antagonisms and crises faced by our particular people and society at this time. For within and by the movement, many of the deep-rooted antagonisms and alienation endemic to our society are being quietly resolved, and by this very transcending process they point to a way out. And if the society is intelligent enough, adaptable enough, and quick enough, they can benefit from this experience of Jah Rastafari.

The Latin American scholar Frank Tannenbaum once penned a comment about the tremendous impact which Gilberto Freyres' book, *The Masters and the Slaves* (1933), had on Brazilian society. By analogy this commentary mirrors a similar kind of unfolding impact which the Rastafarian movement is having on the Caribbean, and for this reason I make reference to this author. Tannenbaum noted that before the publication of Freyres' book, Brazilian intellectuals were preoccupied with European themes and paid little attention to their own country or to their own problems. However,

> Since the publication of *The Masters and the Slaves*, a flood of volumes have appeared on Brazilian subjects. The great merit of this remarkable book is that it caused Brazilians to discover themselves. Instead of running away from race admixture as a scandal and a shame, they find that their literature, music, art and architecture has

been given vitality and richness through the fusion of races and cultures. They consider Brazil a model for the World and follow Brazilian culture as a uniquely rich contribution to civilization. *The Masters and the Slaves* has the special merit of having changed Brazil's image of itself in one generation.

(F. Tannenbaum, *Ten Keys to Latin America,* p. 125)

Rastafari, by all indications, is generating a similar kind of effect on Jamaican society and on the societies where large groups of African youths are congregated today. It is no passing cultural fad but an evolutionary/revolutionary resolution of the intense racial, economic and color struggles growing out of our collective past. It is both a mirror and a model to Jamaica. It offers a model of bringing about evolutionary/revolutionary changes by starting with self. Rasta is an answer to the questions of the black man's redemption and his repatriation back into the cradle of his blackness—his Africanness and his original power. It is a return to the roots, a search of the self (the "Me" or "Little I") for something else besides what we were taught was there.

As the Rastaman finds himself he becomes, in effect, like the Sun (or the Son of Man) and like Bob Marley, Marcus Garvey, His Imperial Majesty and many other exceptional men who were real leaders, luminaries. One worthy book, *The Gospel According to Thomas*, reminds us that "Within a man of Light there is Light, and he illumes the World," and that "If a blind man leads a blind man, both of them fall into a pit."

Rasta offers itself as a model movement of change, giving us a unique focus—its own perspective, concepts and definitions which might well be more representative of the experiences of Africans who make up 90% of the total population.

Through the transformation attained through Rasta-rebirth, a real encompassing grassroots revolution is indeed taking place—as more and more of the alienated souls on ice are coming in from the cold. This movement is democratically self-directed and as such cannot be stopped from the outside, nor from within itself. It is a revolution that is evolutionary, from within.

For in a population where there is such a high cultural tendency towards aping, mimicking and borrowing, the surest guarantee for change is to nurture and institutionalize sound, sure and appropriate models in positions where they can impart maximum effect. Independence gives us the right and offers us the opportunity to re-examine our heroes and models, and to create new ones if need be.

Within the movement the basic problems of color and class are still present but are being transcended by a heartical (spiritual) definition of man which takes him beyond racism; from this spiritual level, our internal differences become the very source of our newfound collective power: "One Heart, One Love, One Universal Spirit." In fact, it has been found that any man who truly knows himself in the fullest meaning of this universal imperative is indeed the man who is so secure within himself that he does not need to look big or feel big by standing on others. The man or group without this knowledge of self and the self-satisfying spiritual power which this bestows must otherwise seek this power externally, in the form of power over others (ego-power). Moreover, those of us who have light in themselves (like the sun) will not revolve as mere satellites to another; they will be able to stand on their own feet and think for themselves, as grounded individuals invariably do. And through this grounded basis, true equality and respect can ensue. Such larger problems like the meaning of *life* and *hope* and *justice* and *health* are also resolved by the Movement of Jah People.

The real message and significance of the movement is, however, still far from being sympathetically understood by the majority. Even among the vast majority of Rastafarians themselves, the meaning of the overall movement which many have is still piecemeal and is necessarily limited by the fact that each Rastaman is at a different stage in the overall movement towards the unfolding definition of Self. They are all at different stages in moving on towards a more universal consciousness. The Rastafarians need to ponder on this issue as much as others, for the degree of clarity in the Rastaman's own understanding of who he is and what he is all about, will sparkle the Rasta aura in the eyes of himself and of others, and will shift the focus of Jamaican politics towards "Truth and Rights" and away from politricks.

In spite of organizational and individual differences within the Rastafarian movement, a common social theory (a common social criticism) has emerged—one which politicians, sociologists, psychologists and those in quest of "things of the spirit" will be impelled to examine as the material world of today cries out for a solution from another plane.

WEST INDIAN CULTURE?
The Caribbean as a geographical and historical region is not hard to define. Socially, however, the area is diverse, with a great range of internal regional, racial, ethnic, religious and class differences.

Given these variations, is there a common cultural pattern and a common value system which pervades the entire region? If so, what is it? Can this be defined? As a people, who are we? What have we become?

Concern with this issue of West Indian identity has been a prominent concern among a certain group of West Indian intellectuals and writers such as: Orlando Patterson's *An Absence of Ruins*, Vidia

Naipaul's *A House for Mr. Biswas* and *Mimic Man,* Neville Dawe's *The Last Enchantment,* Andrew Salkey's *Escape to an Autumn Pavement,* George Lamming's *The Immigrants* and Samuel Selvon's *The Lonely Londoners* and *Turn Again Tiger,* and Claude McKay's *Banna Bottom.* This theme was also the underlying issue of my own doctoral dissertation submitted to the Sociology Department of McGill University and entitled, "West Indian Immigrants Abroad." It was shown in this study how the process of migration does bring the West Indian migrant face to face, for the first time, with the question of his identity. It was also argued in this study of West Indians abroad that "you can take a people out of a country but not a country out of a people"—not completely.

Who are West Indians? Or rather, what are West Indians? West Indian scholars have attempted to answer this question in terms of two notions or descriptive terms, and "Rastafari" and the "Movement," through my own works and through others, have added a third which we see as a more accurate term signifying what is most common to us as a people. The first of two concepts, produced by liberal middle-class intellectuals, are *Pluralism* and *Creolism*; the third produced by the Rasta folk intellectuals is *Anancism.*

PLURALISM

When we ask most West Indian scholars to please define for us, and discuss the nature of West Indian culture, their minds turn quickly to the concept of pluralism. Our culture is pluralistic, in contrast to one that is homogenous, they quickly say. This "Liberal-democratic" definition is identified with H.G. Smith, and his mentor, Furnivall. H.G. Smith wrote:

> In a culturally homogenous society, such institutions as marriage, the family, religion, property, and the like,

are common to the total population. Where cultural plurality obtains, different sections of the total population practice different forms of these common institutions; and…in their internal social organization their institutional activities and their system of belief and value. (H.G. Smith, *The Plural Society in the British West Indies*, p. 14)

It is, however, quite clear that Furnivall, who first used this concept of pluralism in this particular manner, used it to describe the *form and nature of the colonial Far Eastern society* and not to delineate the substance of its associated culture. To quote Furnivall himself:

In Burma, as in Java, probably the first thing that strikes the visitor is the medley of peoples—European, Chinese, Indian and native. It is in the strictest sense a medley, for they mix but do not combine. Each group holds by its own religion, its own culture and language, its own ideas and ways. As individuals they meet, but only in the market place, in buying and selling. There is a plural society, with different sections of the community living side by side, but separately, within the same political unit. Even in the economic sphere, there is a division of labour among racial lines.

Furnivall might have given the vague impression here that society and culture are one and the same thing. Society and culture are indeed related, but they are not the same thing—so say the sociologists whose main function nowadays is building and refining social concepts, sometimes to absurd limits. In this case, however, the point being made by this (conceptual) distinction by sociologists is sensible and realistic: A society consists of the groups and individuals mutually and diversely affecting each other in their social interaction. These groups are the racial, economic (class) and religious groupings that make up society.

The term culture, on the other hand, refers to the product and outgrowth of such group interaction. The meanings and content of such a culture are lodged in the shared symbols and definitions of its interacting groups and are inculcated in each individual through social interaction. As they become lodged in the mind of each member of a society, they constitute the social heritage of the society—its culture. Distinguished anthropologist Raymond Firth made it quite clear that the two should be separated in our analysis. As he stated:

> The terms represent different facets of components in basic human situations. If, for instance, society is taken to mean an organized set of individuals with a given way of life, culture is that way of life. If society is taken to be an aggregate of social relations, culture is the content of those relations. Society emphasizes the human component, the aggregate of people and relations between them. Culture emphasizes the component of accumulated resource—material as well as non-material—which the people inherit, employ, add to, and transmit.

The essential question to be asked, then, is: *What kind of culture does a plural form of society, such as Burma, Java, or the Caribbean, etc. produce?* To answer—as so many have done—that such a culture is correspondingly "plural" is really to avoid the meat of the question. This plural view of culture is not conceptualized to pinpoint the common effect of a common environment upon its people, and as such this plural view fails to deal with the emergent commonalities between these competing and conflicting groups. Pluralism tells us that West Indians live in separate worlds but fails to highlight any of the common patterns operating to unite as well as divide them. While our peoples have not amalgamated themselves to conform to our nationalist ideal—"Out of Many, One People"—it cannot be denied that some synthesizing and "melting" has occurred between them, though not enough to eradicate racial identities.

Pluralism does not answer the question of what these separate, fragmented peoples have become by virtue of their historical interaction, and yet it is this "who am I" dimension of the cultural expression which is the most important. Even worse, the pluralist view of culture does not prompt a view of culture that leads to self-criticism and self-focus, and as such leads nowhere. In fact, the real truth of the matter is that though many of these sociologists are bedecked with many titles and all the honors denoting the highest intellectual attainment, their levels of consciousness have not yet reached that of men noted also for their high intellectual attainments, but who, like Alvin Gouldner, believe that:

> To be a Social Theorist is not simply to seek out the world that is; it is also to reach for a world that might be...not simply to describe and analyze, but also to pronounce judgment on it...To be a social theorist is to be the oedipal heir to shamans and priests and to the conjurers of philosopher-kings. It is to be a maker and shaker of worlds that are and worlds that might be...All reflect a vision, however dim and indistinct, a world that is more desirable than the one that the theorist knows.
>
> *(Enter Plato)*

CREOLE CULTURE

This concept is also used by some to depict West Indian culture. M.G. Smith also falls in this camp, a fact which shows a lack of fixity and certainty about the nature of our culture in the minds of our liberal middle class intellectual cadre. M.G. Smith wrote of Creole culture:

> The Creole complex has its historical base in slavery, plantation systems and colonialism...The ideal forms of institutional life are of European derivation...But in their Creole contexts, these institutional forms diverge from their metropolitan models in greater or lesser degree to fit local conditions. This local adaptation produces a Creole institutional complex which differs from the metropolitan model...This combination of European and African traditions is the most important feature of Creole life.

Noted anthropologists like Prof. Frances Henry of York University and many others have followed M.G. Smith in using this term to describe West Indian culture, which does have more of a total "roots" connotation to it, than the concept of pluralism. It is an advance on the plural concept, for while acknowledging social and cultural subdiversities, the concept of a Creole culture acknowledges the predominance of European forms and values by sheer force of racism. The European forms predominate at an "ideal level," but in reality other forms often develop and predominate at times. Summarizing West Indian culture in terms of this model, Prof. Frances Henry stated:

> ...the Creole cultural patterning is a lifestyle which is characterized by a colour distribution, by class distribution and by a mixture of European and African elements with Indians mostly outside this culture.

However, the specific nature of a person reared in a Creole culture is hardly even dealt with in any systematic way. Prof. Henry, however, has suggested: "The Creole outlook on life is one of optimistic fatalism...a rather superficial, harmonious cheerfulness which is almost a deliberate mechanism which people use in order to cope with the inescapable, harsh realities of their day-to-day existence." (Frances Henry in *Resource Development in the Caribbean*, McGill Univ. 1972)

It seems clear that this Creole image of the Caribbean is particularly attractive to the colored and educated middle classes who traditionally and by nature see themselves as the "first amongst unequals" and as a buffer group between the whites at the top and the African mass below.

ANANCY CULTURE

Through Rastafarian self-awakening, the folk concept of Anancism has emerged as a more powerful and potent descriptive term telling of our true relationship between God and man, of ourselves and of our society—a more holistic appreciation of ourselves.

While the concept of Anancism does not say all there is to say about the totality of West Indian culture, it does go a long way in symbolizing the fundamental web-like nature of our culture and of our people, showing up both our weaknesses and our strengths. It also allows us to critically look at ourselves rather than taking ourselves for granted and blaming others.

The concept of Anancism cannot be left out of any discussion of our culture owing to its omnipotence. Yet this is not to say that we should be individually called Anancy by others—only by ourselves. Moreover, not all Jamaicans follow the model of Anancy to the point of becoming human Anancis. And as always, there are other competing models to emulate in any social situation.

Anancism is a folk-model or concept, an intellectual framework in its own right, which serves as a measuring rod against which any people can be measured.

A model is a common reference point, a set of ideas or images systematically interrelated to constitute a distinctive point of view. The merit of such a social model lies in its usefulness in directing its people (its creators) towards asking questions relevant to solving their problems. The fact that I speak of Jamaica in this regard is because it is the area of my particular concern. I call Jamaican culture by this name as a sociological deduction, which I found reasonable to make as a result of my intimate associations with it. More important, this concept has provided me with a relevant intellectual and moral framework for understanding Jamaican society in the years 1977-81, in terms of this local folk conception. This was the four year period of my return to Jamaica after spending the previous 16 years living abroad—and growing up there.

I returned to Jamaica only to find that Rastafarian definitions (of Jamaica, and of self, etc.) were at a level and at a rate of vibration more in keeping with how I had grown to see and understand myself, life, struggle, and God. They were more "conscious" than the Jamaican population as a whole, and were far more grounded and rounded than our Marxist intellectuals. Some of the missing and gaping caveats in my understanding of life were filled in by Rastafarian knowledge of reality.

The Anancy concept is a folk concept, incorporated with other Rastafarian concepts, to form a view of our society from the bottom up. It provided me with a most valid framework for understanding otherwise unexplainable aspects of interpersonal life in Jamaica during this period, from a self-critical point of view. It is the major framework which helped me to understand and make sense of my day-to-day experiences (trials and tribulations), at all levels of society, night and day, and even on Sundays! The culture of Anancism confronted me at every turn and corner in this society and tested my own strength and adaptability. There was no rest from it. And it drained my energy often to the point of desperation and bewilderment, ending in an almost complete loss of faith.

In those last days of the People's National Party administration (and lasting down even to this day), an epidemic of racketeering of all sorts emerged in response to the severe economic and political problems. People increasingly developed rackets and "lines" of all sorts in order to survive. This intensified kind of hustling gave rise to a new class of people called "touts" and "wises." These were just new names for "samfie men" and con artists who now emerged to blur the hard-and-fast distinction between the legal and the illegal, as it appeared that more and more people were becoming wises, as racketeering became the new way of life.

This cultural experience occurred to me in the form of a shock, the same kind of shock and loss of faith which I saw expressed by Jah Rastafarians. I suddenly woke up to the reality of the meaning of Jamaica, a reality that I had long forgotten and almost purged from my mind, except as an intellectual idea. This new dissatisfaction acquired by the awakened and returning West Indian migrant is similar to that uprising being experienced by the Rastamen who remain "a yard," who nevertheless have come under the stirring influence of Rastafari—or the mystic journey.

In the remainder of this essay we will therefore summarize the Rastafarian view of Jamaican society and of Jamaican culture. It constitutes a theory in its own right, one that has been tested and tried—by the Folk—and is embodied in Rastafarian movements.

The Rastaman (as folk) tells who he is (or what he aspires to be) through his symbolic forms of representation, such as his art works, his songs, his religious symbols, his animal stories and animal totems. Animal symbolism is particularly an ancient form of representation passed down through the ages, a kind of picture-writing (hieroglyphics), having its own particular meanings to the people who use it. The failings and virtues of their collective experiences are woven into a tapestry of animal fantasies. These symbols thus objectively reflect the internal (subjective) vibrations and aspirations of the people themselves who construct them, so that they become the outer expressions to much deeper meanings and to the mysterious spirits within. It is their way of commenting on the conditions of their lives, both inner and outer.

Rastafarians are not the only persons using this art of symbolic communication. It is one important feature of all traditional peoples, particularly of Africans. *To this day, the consciousness of West Indian Africans is still dominated by animal symbolism, even by those foreign to the West Indian environment.* All animal stories familiar to Africans were transferred with them to the New World along with their creative imagination and the power to symbolize. As a way of instilling morals, children are still educated at home and at school into African folklore which deals with the names, ways and actions of animals. This is reflected in the annual Jamaican National Pantomimes.

The black Jamaican peasant folklore refers to animals and insects of every kind, including those not even found in Jamaica, notably tigers and lions. By far the largest number of references are to animals of lowest or commonest status—to crabs, fowl, "peel-head" john crows, cows, dogs, pigs, horses, donkeys, puss (cats), rats and monkeys. The big animals like tigers, bulls and horses are given greater respect and are characterized by less of the negative stereotyping associated with the more common animals.

Organizations and industrial enterprises here and abroad exploit many of these as advertising totems to sell products: "Dragon Stout," "Greyhound Bus," "Panther Condom," "Put a tiger in your tank" (Esso), "Lions Club," etc. People are also called by totemic names in our culture. Its usage is all-round: to joke is to "skylark," to dodge a blow is to "duck." Black dances are often named after the movements and styles of animals: the fox-trot, the cat walk, the dragon dance, the turtle, the donkey, the bebop, the funky chicken, and now the lion dance among the Rastas, called the "skank." Amongst Jamaican folks, animals are also used as cuss words, that is, as "negative power," as they are intended to hurt. To call a person in Jamaica a dog, a sly mongoose, a pig, a john crow, or a flea is the strongest rebuff, but to call a person lion or tiger carries very positive vibrations. In my boyhood, the greatest insult one could throw at a classmate would be to refer to him or her as a "black hog." In fact, to be black and poor was—and still is—the basis of being compared and incessantly castigated as the lowest of animals.

In terms of this folk scheme of animal representations and symbol-association, Rastafarians consciously totemize the lion; Jamaican society, they declare, has unconsciously *deified Brer Anancy, the spider-trickster ("Baldhead") who has become the central character-type in our mass folk culture. Anancy is our folk hero.* This fact may be deducted from an analysis of Jamaican cultural folk representations against that of the emergent Rastafarian movement.

THE NATURE OF "BREDDA" ANANCY: OUR FOLK-HERO

For Africans, the world outside became terribly awesome and towering. Anancy was the response, a symbol of black survival and of staying power in such a world. Anancy is thus part of the mental fantasy legacy of Africans told in the form of animal stories, with the same kinds of impossible happenings that we find in European fairy tales. But he is also more than a fantasy, as ideas and fantasies do become flesh at times.

Anancy is the smart spider-man whose popularity is such that he dominates Jamaican folk-tales, dwarfing all other animals, both by the frequency of his appearance and by the centrality of his characterization. "Anancy Story" has even come to include riddles and proverbs as well, forming part of the same character type.

Every existing custom is said to be started by Anancy and he is made the prime cause of most things around. Leonard Barrett writes:

> Regardless of his treachery and cunning, Ananci has those components which make him a folk-hero part excellence, for elusive and nimble of spirit and witty of tongue, he is representative of techniques of survival at their best. (Barrett, *The Sun and Drum*, p. 35)

Anancy is both hero and villain, according to African folk consciousness. He represents the ego-projection of the underdog who finds satisfaction in the decomfiture of the larger beasts and the breaking of sacred taboos. But his vanities, lies, deceits, and cunning make his survival possible in a dehumanizing world.

Sometimes our own strengths and powers as a people, however, blind us to the much-needed criticism of self. Particularly because Anancy, under many differing situations, manifests remarkable qualities and is responsible for our historical survival, no doubt we must start with these positives.

I was once instructed by an old lady: "Look at Anancy...It is tireless in its efforts. Even if it falls to the bottom of its web it will pick itself up, again and again."

Anancism as a cultural form is not without its strengths, the qualities which justify its heroic status, particularly in the past, and particularly at a time when the world treated us as children and we are forced by our powerlessness ("littleness") to play the part.

Besides his notorious weakness and shortcomings, Anancy does have his strong points: a hidden resourcefulness, more like the cat reputed to have nine lives. This comes out in the rugged determination of our people to keep on pushing, even when the going gets tough. Our adaptability and toughness are remarkable. Under pressure we will do almost anything and move in any direction, even to the point of switching sex roles. It comes out in the most ingenious schemes of Jamaicans to beat the American immigration restrictions and prohibitions; it comes out in the steadfast and stubborn determination of the several waves of Jamaican people who have left the shores of rural Jamaica to become the acclaimed achievers and leaders in metropolitan capitals abroad. They often achieve these feats with remarkable grace and finesse. It expresses itself in the capacity of Jamaicans to cope and contain myriad stresses while displaying gaiety, style and laughter, even on top of the most trying and agonizing experiences. It comes out in our adaptability to the changing shortages and scarcities characteristic of the Third World. It comes out, even in times like this, when the people seem quite determined not to abandon hope in spite of the inherent desperation of our situation. As a people we are notoriously ambitious, determined, resourceful, aggressive, headstrong, and vociferous for our rights. Our resourcefulness includes our ability to turn negatives into positives, of making a little go a long way, our capacity for recycling things, including ourselves. It explains the extraordinary cultural feat whereby our scholars have expertly mastered the Englishman's language, or the way in which our sportsmen have mastered such English games as cricket, and have made them ours by virtue of their excellence in such forms. All of which suggests and points back to some ancient epoch when we must have been a great people—giants. And the records show this.

Louise Bennett's recent collection of some 31 Anancy stories—*Ananci and Miss Lou*—gives us the opportunity to analyze the character of our folk-hero. In none of these stories, however, is Anancy portrayed as a really virtuous man. Miss Lou, and the other storytellers, usually recognize Anancy's villainy but excuse him, as well as themselves, from any blame, as each story ends "Jack Mandora, me noh choose none," meaning (as we are told by Miss Lou) "I take no responsibility for the story I have told." But who does take responsibility for the effects of such stories?

Through these stories the behavior of Anancy is evidently most deplorable. "As Anancy all ovah," we are told, "him couldn't behave rightful"...He was "fast as usual"... "As Anancy all ovah, he wanted the lion's share." The irony is that although Anancy disobeys all ten of the Lord's commandments, he suffers no remorse or tinge of conscience, and is heroized and applauded for his behavior—even by professed Christians!

It is clear from these stories that Anancy is seen as a very selfish, greedy, lying, thieving, ruthless and malicious jester and bluffer—a loafer who often works but prefers "freeniss," always bawling or squealing and exaggerating. He survives mainly through jinalship and the workings of his "big brains" which compensate for his small size—his relative powerlessness, in a world dominated by others more powerful than he. He is the mischievous busybody who ruthlessly exploits all situations and uses others selfishly, including his own wife and children, old women, animals, and the "wite planter." In these stories he went about "mashing up" the lives of others out of covetousness, grudgefulness, spite, and to save face. He was the ruthless and conniving actor who would use any means whatsoever to mash up others; he started the trouble between Puss and Rat just because they were in "Storybook" and he was not; he spread the lie that Brer Tiger was his daddy's riding horse so as to belittle Tiger in the eyes of Miss Quashiba whom he also liked; he mashed up Brer Wasp's life out of covetousness for Wasp's former pretty teeth; he "beat" a woman—Sister Nanny Goat—into accepting blame for his thievery of plantains; he flatters and plays upon the egos, vanities, weaknesses, and strengths of others; he is notoriously greedy, even to the extent of ruining his voice from the eating of too much sugar cane, and then he even passed on his own long mouth (resulting from his greed) to the innocent Brer Pig; and in self-righteous indignation he chastises and condemns Fire Dragon for stealing from him what he had just scuffled from others.

Bredda Anancy has a forked tongue; he reassures Brer Cockroach that he would not steal from him but all along is plotting to do just that. He makes out always that he was very honest and trustful, even to the extent (as he told his prospective employer) that he had been "workin wid a barbaman fi ten years an nevah even teck a free shave!" Anancy is not just two-faced, but many-faced. In fact, he is such a good actor and disguise artist that he can make appearance in any form, and will abuse you, then comfort you. Such is the character of Anancy.

OUR ANANCY CULTURE

When we feast our children on the exploits of Anancy-the-Hero, we are indeed telling them to be like Anancy, and if conditions allow, they will indeed become Anancies. The end result is most likely a culture in which Anancism becomes a way of life and people become transformed into real human Anancy. People become molded in the character of the totem-insect which symbolized their day-to-day strategy for survival. The Jamaican-born sociologist, Leonard Barrett, remarked:

> So intricately woven is Anancism in Jamaican life that his cunning has become part of the Jamaican personality stereotype.
>
> (*The Sun and the Drum*, p. 32)

Prof. Rex Nettleford, as sociologist and Jamaica's leading artist, agrees that Brer Anancy represents much of the Jamaican character type. Brer Anancy, he said:

> ...expresses much of the Jamaican spirit in his ostentatious professions of love, in his wrong and strong, brave but cowardly postures of bluffs, in his love for leisure and corresponding dislike for work, and in his lovable rascality.

This folk hero was most vividly displayed for us by "Ringo Star" in the Jamaican stage production and movie, "Smile Orange." As an Anancy waiter working in a North Coast hotel, Ringo Star (played eloquently by Carl Bradshaw) hustles on his job as a way of getting a little bit more from the system. He perfected his art of scuffling so well that he was able to teach this survival technique to the newly-employed country boy who proceeded to use it against the tourists after learning the subtleties of the art.

Most of the Jamaican/West Indian plays staged in Jamaica over the past few years featured Anancy as a major—or as *the* major—character type. Songs of the period more and more all talk of this ubiquitous creature, Anancy. But by this time they began warning against him.

Stafford Harrison, a dreadlocked Rastafarian, staged a production of his play, *Anansi and Unsung Heroes Out West*, at Ward Theatre, Kingston, in October 1978. This play was a critical masterpiece analysis of Anancism in our society, a character-type which Harrison found to be particularly relevant to our period. As Harrison explained:

> The trickster aspect of the Jamaican psyche immortalized in the folk character is a defensive mechanism

which developed and was practiced whole scale by the African slaves as a means of survival against brutish, and often-times ignorant, white slave owners. Slavery was abolished but the system remains, administered by black men forced to assume the roles of their white predecessors. Thus, blacks now play their anansi tricks on each other and to their eventual detriment. The warring ghetto street gangs are used by corrupt "godfather" politicians and later infiltrated CIA agents posing as an American. Mankind, through the politicians, is now taking the anansi game a little too far.

In fact, all the leading journalists in Jamaica during this period applied the concept of Anancy to the political and social stage—John Hearne, Evon Blake, Morris Cargill, Wilmott Perkins, Dawn Rich, Dr. Aggrey Brown, Gloria Escoffrey. Mr. Morris Cargill, writing for the *Gleaner,* warned that: "The PNP did not create Anancy—Anancy created the PNP and will create all our governments if we are not careful."

The concept of Anancism became one very important topic in my "Introductory Course in Sociology," taught at the University of the West Indies, Mona 1977-81, so much so that it found its way on several university examination papers—for the first time. But this focus became a serious bone of contention on campus as the Marxist teachers who were responsible for the overall bureaucratic coordination of the sociology course began the self-same Anancy tactics against this folk-concept, so that eventually I was displaced from the teaching of this course and from the university system. This was stated in the Jamaica *Daily Gleaner* of October 18, 1980:

> It is significant that under the concerted and conniving reaction of the organized "Progressive" influence on

Campus the teaching of the Theory of Anancism—which I have developed over the past three years—as a concept crucial for understanding our colonial culture has recently been removed from the Sociology curriculum without anyone at all objecting to this reactionary move.

Apparently this folk concept of Anancism, because of its roots origin has no legitimacy for the understanding of our society and its people. Moreso especially as the foreign education of our elite did not legitimize this local concept, and because the theory of Anancyism points too much in the direction of self-criticism and self-responsibility (and Truth) which would not tally too well with the now PNP strategy of scapegoating outside bogeys over which we frankly have no control. Such is the politics of impotence climaxed by the PNP elite.

Our middle class Marxist teachers, themselves recruited from the brown middle strata, were busy stressing the importance of class factors, ownership and political power, and belittling the significance of culture, which meant that they refused to look at their own selves, as concrete individuals. Particularly they dismissed Anancism as a pattern found only among the lumpenproletariat. They were failing to see it as a general cultural norm of the total society, applicable to themselves, even in their intellectualizing and in their personal relationships and political antics. They were attacking roots culture because of its "cultist" tendency, yet they were practicing an unspoken kind of cultism—an intellectual cultism which says that they were the intellectual elite and equipped to lead, and teach.

But Garvey himself knew otherwise. Garvey was indeed referring to Anancism when he sadly commented that the mass of black Jamaicans have become "like crabs" in a bag, each trying to pull the other down when the other attempts to move. Blacks, he noted, are at war with themselves, and with each other, disrespectful and discourteous to each other, but deferential and respectful to people who have more power than they. Garvey thus preached the need for a "new man." He said:

> Few of us can understand what it takes to make a man—the man who will never say die; the man who will never give up; the man who will never depend on others to do for him what he ought to do for himself; the man who will not blame God, who will not blame Nature, who will not blame fate for his condition, but the man who will go out and make conditions to suit himself.

Garvey himself aspired to live the life of a lion and was referred to in these images and terms even by his trial judge in Atlanta.

The folk tradition in which I was nurtured in my childhood clearly pushed us in the path of Anancy, though we were taught its opposite—the straight and narrow pathway. But because the world was so harsh, this Anancy tradition itself became ascendant and the world of our childhood became one of outward conformity to adult expectations, but inward rebellion and an ensuing array of schemes, intrigues, plots and games against this totalitarian adult world. If we were late for school, we would use certain Anancy "guzu" (tricks) on our way to school so as to tie up our teachers and thus prevent the spanking that would otherwise take place; we would get certain shrubs which we would roll up into a ball and place under a stone after spitting on it and repeating some muddled (magic) words. This, we then solemnly believed, would cause the teachers to accept whatever explanations we cared to give for our lateness. The Obeah practitioners in Jamaica make good usage of many of the antics of Anancy. The Obeah man often incorporates the characteristic traits of Anancy-Spider, who has to use his wit and intelligence against all the forces that be, in all situations.

We were so good at acting as a technique to avoid severe Protestant punishment that we could even make our eyes run water as proof that we were telling the truth, while in fact we were lying. We would even call down lightning and thunder to strike us dead to sanctify lies. One lawyer who practices criminal law in Kingston often comments on how much of this acting continues in the courts of Jamaica even to this day: "Even when the accused are guilty, few will ever be manly enough to confess such guilt; instead they will 'cry tears until thy kingdom come.' Then when the case is finished they will reveal proudly to him that it was a mere 'act.' In English courts, however, there is a far greater tendency for people to plead guilty if they are in fact guilty—to accept the responsibility."

As children we learned the importance of the Anancy art of "mouthing," of throwing words (or "mammaguying" in Trinidad), and Anancy's body language techniques—hissing or sucking the teeth, and of making "monkey faces" and how to pick a fight like Anancy. Anancy picks a fight in his own unique and characteristic style: he might challenge another to a fight by daring him to "say, fe;" or he might dare the person he is seeking the fight with to knock some object from his hand. Another method involves the ambivalent dramatics of teasing some other (weaker) person by a nickname, or by daring the other either to touch a shirt button (or some part of his clothing); or daring another to "tell him of his mamma." If the other is daring enough to take up the challenge in any of these roundabout ways, the Anancy jester will throw himself upon the daring other, while simultaneously entreating any nearby friend—or even a stranger—to hold him back (restrain him) for fear of being provoked into serious trouble, while at the same time still struggling to get at the other person's throat. Ambivalences abound!

In contrast, English school boys would later crowd around us as school boys in England, take off their jackets, and ask more politely if we wanted to fight or not. Our responses to the challenges had to be similarly direct and polite, as we were now in England and had to do what these English "Romans" were doing.

As children, we grew up with a rich sense of humor, but our greatest source of amusement was at the expense of others. The person who slips on a mango peel would be offered a helping hand, but only after we had our full share of laughter. Such is Anancism.

ANANCY INSTITUTIONALISM

Watch ideas and symbols—they do become people. Anancy has become so institutionalized within society that it can be found at every level of society, and across all color, class and ethnic boundaries. Anancy has become the character-personality expressing the adaptive folk character of African slaves turned peasants under slavery and colonialism. But it is a type of adaptation which is employed against any totalitarian system by any people. Like everything else in nature, it has its roots, its causes.

Even when West Indians migrate overseas, they take the image of Anancy with them. In Toronto, the week of April 17-23, 1978 was declared as "Anancy for All People Week," and the white mayor of Toronto officially opened the ceremony in Nathan Phillips Square, with Louise Bennett (queen of Anancy folklore) and the Jamaican Consul General officially promoting Anancism under the guise of fostering a "pleasurable educational experience" for the black community.

Yet our Anancy culture has graduated Anancy politicians, religious ministers ("Sunday jinnals"), Anancy-relationships between neighbors, between people and politicians, teachers and students, between man and nature, and between man and woman. The fundamental relationship of husband and wife seems to be governed by the principles of Anancism, which goes a long way towards explaining the so-called disorganized and denuded nature of West Indian family structures, as any system so affected by Anancism is incapable of generating real mutual fulfillment and genuine communication. The one-parent family, or the family headed by a grandmother or mother; the homosexual upsurgence; the constant theme of alcoholism and the high rate of children born out of wedlock are all significantly related to Anancism between man and woman at home and between workers and employers at the workplace. Underneath our modern family problems is a fundamental disturbance and lack of appropriate self-regulation of libido owing to our lack of culture.

The workings and effects of Anancism are omnipresent in the way we as a people take the bus, how we work and relate to each other; it has even slowed down and corrupted our bureaucracies, as nepotism and racketeerism are all trademarks of Anancy workings and these are the characteristic condition of our bureaucracies. Anancies, for instance, never take their place in a queue, not only the poor Anancies who break lines but also the big-shot Anancies who rely on their influence to break such lines. It even explains why "blacks don't generally do well in business," as this Anancy culture has made the majority of blacks into small-scale hustlers (Anancy capitalists) and has not taught them nor allowed them to hustle the big bureaucratic or capitalist way in a world increasingly dominated by the bigger capitalist hustlers like the multinational corporations.

In this kind of Anancy culture of ours, it is easy for the CIA and other foreign intelligences to exploit the divisions and schisms by using one section or group against another. The extent to which local and foreign women are used (against our native males) as major intelligence-gathering agents is completely overlooked, yet they play a very important role in the American system of imperial control.

Anancism explains why we have so many "naturally" gifted actors, actresses and dramatists among the Jamaican population. Jamaica boasts of having the highest population of actors and actresses in relation to its total population. This is no accident; it is a most telling cultural reality.

PRESENT CULTURAL LEGACY

The end result of this cultural process is a very complex and distorted cultural and personality system, thus making our Third World problems as much a psychological and cultural problem as it is economic. Writers on Caribbean culture have drawn attention to such elements in our culture as our racial self-hatred, our cultural disorientation, our proneness to sycophancy to whites, our proneness to distrust of other black people, our insularity, our hostility to new attitudes regarding African culture, excess individualism, cultural instability, contra-intellectualism, proneness to political paternalism and political messianism. Much of this is simply alienation.

Chronic social and psychological alienation has been and will continue as our most serious national problem, as it eventually leads to deadness of spirit and the immobilization of our energies. Schizophrenia, paranoia, paralysis, and all kinds of personality malfunctioning occurs at the organic level in consequence. Such organic blockages function to block off heartical social communication and hence reduces the total energy level of the society. The level of feelings and understanding are a measure of the total health and organic wholesomeness arising from the unity of self within itself and within the world around. It is the invisible spirit or power arising from unity and organic wholesomeness, and which corresponds to a particular energy level in the people who live that culture.

If you cut out such feelings and vibrations from the human personality, what you have left is the basic ingredient of a fascist on the Right, or a totalitarian baldhead on the Left, as neither has the capacity to feel, to balance, to proportion, and with this the sought after capacity to understand the universal language of love. Neither can feel for his fellow men from his guts. Yet the wealth of one's soul is to be measured by how much it can feel, and its poverty by how little.

The loss of faith induced and sustained by this culture in its people is the major all-round blockage to economic and other productions. It is not the "lack of capital" which our leaders stress so dearly and so conveniently. Is Anancy mek it (cause it), but today the CIA is the leading Anancy.

The movement of Rastafari is an expression of this alienation, and also its resolution. The economic and cultural experiences at the bottom of our race-class pyramid have alienated many and have pushed them towards Jah Rastafari, and have led them to declaring Jamaica and its culture as "Babylonian" in its nature and in its self-destructive tendencies. Coptic Rastas particularly point to such Babylonian aspects in our culture as the widespread occurrence of murder, rape, sodomy, deceit, alcoholism, covetousness, whoredom, false gods and unhealthy foods. Zion fundamentalists, based on similar observations, acknowledge also that the spirit of Lucifer (the devil) now governs our society and the world at large. The Jehovah Witnesses are also hammering home this point.

The sociologists—my colleagues—because of their vacuous or abstract intellectualism and commitment to middle range theorizing, are slow to recognize this larger and more terrifying implications of what has been happening. They cannot see beyond their noses because of their intellectual short-sightedness attested to by this middle range philosophy to which most are committed and which limits their vision.

Jamaica mirrors the world trend, just as Rastafari mirrors one way out. It is because of this fundamental perception of the society that conscious Rastafarians withdraw and move inwards. They have developed their own culture—their own values, definitions, models and dietary habits. And their children are being socialized according to such new cultural standards and definitions. By so doing, they are falling back on self and seeing, as Confucius saw some 500 years before Christ—as did Christ—that:

> If there be righteousness in the heart
> there will be beauty in the character
> If there be beauty in the character
> there will be harmony in the home
> If there by harmony in the home
> there will be order in the nation
> If there be order in the nation
> there will be peace in the world.

Thus by their total reactions, Rastafarians are telling us what is bugging them, what is the basis of their newly declared uprising, and are answering questions such as: What is our problem? Is it a class problem? Who is responsible: them or us? Who is this us and them? By the symbolic meanings veiled in their lore, the Rasta movement has shown that both race and class factors have been combined by way of a cultural legacy which functions to keep the masses disoriented, as it is the totality of the cultural system (including its economic functioning) which robs them of life, eats away at their spirit, and alienates them from themselves and their original species—nature. The erosion of faith which results makes it impossible for a collective conscience to develop.

The Rastafarian uprising is thus living testimony of the impotence of cultural and individual alienation and feelings of purposelessness from bottom up, leaving the big gaping national problem of how to bridge the gaps in and amongst all the inhabitants of the land so as to reintroduce national purpose. By representing the reality of African alienation here in Jamaica, the Rastaman is doing homage to his imprisoned African spirit. By this very assertion of internal meanings, of livity, vibrations, creativity, and the mysteries of the imagination and the mystery of Jah, he is declaring his Africanity and humanity. This African spirit still lives and is our saving grace as a people. Jamaica can only prosper if and when this African spirit rests in peace. Right now it is in agony.

PRESENT POLITICAL LEGACY

The impact of Anancism is most rampant in the political field—"politricks"—not only in the sense of political corruption, but also in the simple sense of that we have allowed ourselves to become trapped into the political mimicry of First World politics.

By education, the basic orientation is for our teachers and leaders to mechanically assume that Third World development must necessarily take place *either* under the paternalistic framework and inspiration of the liberal capitalist American model, *or* alternatively under the totalitarian communist model. Because of our general background of colonial authoritarianism, our leaders easily become the intellectual prisoners of what should be mere *prisms*, and these prisms in turn seriously handicap them in the range of their choices, combinations, alliances and energy level in general. Such is the essential nature of the intellectual *crisis* facing the Third World as a whole. Conservatives and radicals alike continue the very colonial tradition of aping, mimicking, and borrowing the intellectual models, constructs and categories of their big superpower education.

They thereby abandon the responsibility they have of re-evaluating everything through the prism of our own people-based experiences, starting with the experiences of the humblest folk.

In that historic Jamaican general election of October 30, 1980, which significantly altered the balance of world power in favor of Americanism, the Jamaican electorate had a choice between only the J.L.P., who defended and promoted the *American capitalist perspective and world order,* and the P.N.P., who promoted the *Russian perspective and world order.* There was no third party offering an alternative Jamaican Third World orientation to the problem of nation-building, which for us has to be something akin to an uprising of some sort as no one *genuinely* believes in the other two anymore. We are all trapped. It is ironic that although Jamaica's prime minister at the time was leader of the Non-Alignment Movement and the most articulate voice of the Third World, neither base provided Michael Manley with an independent framework from which to deal with specific problems successfully. His failure mounted with time, as it will also be with the other side. Lacking any genuine independent Third World choice, we the Jamaican people chose by an overwhelming majority the American model, as this was more in keeping with our everyday level of consciousness and more in line with our specific social and cultural realities and ties, as well as much more in line with our pragmatic orientation to life. But that was all it was.

The Jamaican people en masse thus voted for the Jamaican Labour Party, under Mr. Edward Seaga. Michael Manley and the P.N.P. were thus booted out of office by the same public who gave him their overwhelming mandate for Democratic Socialism only four years earlier. Manley's massive defeat and failure were, however, more of a warning to Mr. Seaga, as Manley failed precisely because he had become trapped by a model which reinforced our cultural tendency to always look outward and upward, but never inward. Not enough grounding was done by the elite into the real problems affecting the total lives of people. Thus the P.N.P. ignored such human factors as the very nature of the P.N.P. elite itself and the peculiar nature of our plantation culture (of which we are all products) and the alienating impact which this has had on us as a people and as individuals.

The people of Jamaica have taken up the enthusiastic offer which the J.L.P. has made of applying the classic American solution to solving Jamaica's classic Third World problems, and they are now expecting the miracle of economic growth and social development. This was the essence of the "Deliverance" package offered by the J.L.P. to a desperate public in an increasingly desperate world, which would have grabbed at any alternative other than the prospect of another five years of material and cultural decline under P.N.P. bossism that was poised to degenerate more into bald-headed totalitarianism under the impetus of the Marxist model. I am sure that Mr. Manley and his progressive supporters really believed that with the aid of this model the miracle of transformation would have taken place under their rule, had they had more time.

THE ROOTS OF ANANCISM: EXPLANATION

Anancism and the schizophrenia of the soul which it produces is a cultural effect—it occurs as a result of something else: learning—and is not a part of the racial nature of any people. It is the patterned result of cultural conditions in the struggle for survival under the particular conditions of poverty, scarcities, insecurities, inequalities, racism and differing degrees of power between competing groups, and a general departure from and knowledge of the laws of Jah.

Some of the characteristic styles and traits associated with Anancism are attributed by some sociologists to what they have called the "Culture of Poverty," which characterizes marginal people all over the world who are subjected to generations of persistent poverty, within a context of relative affluence for the few. In these situations, the poor have developed a cultural apparatus bearing striking resemblance to Anancism, a culture of poverty or an impoverished culture.

In the Caribbean, Anancism took on quite a respectable image and became very ingrained because of the specific history and social structure of the society, determined by the structure of its economy and its demographic structure, which fostered this as the general, cultural adaptation. West Indian society, based as it was on a plantation economy, gave rise to a corresponding plantation culture—the culture of the yard, a mass culture that locked away any standards and which often fostered mediocrity.

Slavery conditions (like all other totalitarian conditions) were ideally conducive to the growth of Anancism as a survival technique, for both masters and slaves. Blacks were imprisoned in a system in which the most powerful animal was the white planter ("Big Massa" or "Old Backra") who was also far away from home. Africans were thus forced to survive like the partly invisible Anancy who survived by wit but at the cost of denying the African self its full growth and expression. As the black American historian Lerone Bennett wrote:

> The attempt of whites to deny blacks even a minimum of social life involved both slave and masters in a web of espionage, a web of waiting and watching, of measuring and spying and maneuvering. In this web it was every slave against every white man, and every triumph over the master, no matter how petty, was recognized as a triumph for the cause.

White planters themselves encouraged this image of blacks—as the cunning and deceitful creature who scampers off to hide in the ceiling when he has done something to be ashamed of and has been found out. The image of blacks as grown-up but backward children fit in with their scheme for denying blacks their full manhood so that they could be more easily used like beasts of burden without suffering any tinge in their white "Christian" consciences.

This Anancy pattern of cultural adaptation developing with slavery ran the whole length and breadth of social relationships, between field-slave and house-slave, house-slave and white master, field-slave to white master, black to mulatto, mulatto to white master, freed slave to slave, and freed slave to master, man to woman, black to white.

The social structure left behind by slavery and colonialism continues to support and foster the perpetuation of Anancy. It is a social structure strongly influenced both by race and class factors, and as a cultural-personality pattern it tends also to perpetuate itself once it has been established.

The *social structure* is a race-class pyramid, the base of which is constituted mainly by poor Africans, with mulatto (mixed elements) in the middle, and a small white elite on top. The Jamaican sociologist Henriques noted: "This whole colour system is dependent upon the almost complete acceptance by each group of the superiority of white, and the inferiority of black." For certain, that was how it was in the West Indies, no less than anywhere else in the Western world, then as now.

Over the years, biological admixture as well as other economic and social changes, have blurred the solidity of the caste-like boundaries between the stratified groups in the society. Thus, instead of solid dividing brick walls as barriers, we now have barbed wire fences separating the strata. But the color-class hierarchy (ranking-system) remains very much intact to this day, and the biases it gives rise to operate at all levels of the pyramid. Even among the lower segments of this hierarchy there will be shade discrimination and often a pathological preference for things white and foreign. There is also the continued emphasis placed on the outer person—on his phenotype, his looks, his color, his form—with little value placed on spiritual or inner qualities.

In this hierarchical plural society, there is as yet little cosmic or cultural unity, though the potential for this is enormous. Each group had its own distinct perspective on the world, and each manifests divergent interests, styles, approaches and values. Nothing is settled. It is as if confusion reigns supreme. The major common meeting point between these groups is our particular style of operational adaptation towards each other, termed Anancism by the folk. This is the major common pragmatic West Indian cultural adaptation to each other and to their common environment. Chinese, Indians, Syrians, Jews and Africans in Jamaica have largely remained ethnically distinct, but *they have all become Jamaicanized to the extent that they have learned to adapt to each others' relative power and have learned how to get the most out of the interaction with each other by learning the art of Anancism, based on how much relative power each has.*

From the start of their common interaction during slavery, each segment had good (objective) reasons to follow the Brer Anancy model. Each group had a certain degree of relative veto power, but not total power. Whites had superior economic, technical and entrepreneurial skills, but were so outnumbered by the African masses that they had to develop a subtle and shrewd kind of paternalism. Africans, on the other hand, had numerical power and a generic adaptability that can be lauded as "divine," but they were partly overawed by superior white power and confused/disoriented by alien language and religious and other cultural symbols which became the official symbols of the society. They have been confused, but not broken. Only now they are becoming broken.

It is this African majority presence—their numerical superiority — which gives a good many black West Indians their overwhelming sense of confidence and the feeling that they are in control. The colored or mixed elements had the advantage of superior education, their European culture, and their mixed ancestry, but nevertheless they suffered most from severe feelings of cultural marginality at the individual level.

Since each group had some relative advantages alongside their particular disadvantages, *West Indian society became a competitive arena in which each group acted like Brer Anancy towards each other, with each subtly trying to outdo and outsmart the other, both as individuals and as members of their respective groups.* It is in this sense that West Indian society can be described as "competitive pluralism" in the way Schumpeter (*Socialism, Capitalism and Democracy*) used this term of pluralism to denote a theory of checks and balances operating in a competitive market-like situation and fashion. The end result is a weak kind of nationalism

A NOTE ABOUT THE AUTHOR

Dennis Forsythe was born in Islington, Jamaica in 1946. At the age of fifteen he emigrated to England. In 1968 he graduated from the London School of Economics with a degree in Economics and Sociology. In 1969 Dr. Forsythe completed a Masters Degree in Sociology at McGill University in Montreal, Canada. Three years later he earned a Ph.D. at the same institution. Dr. Forsythe returned to Jamaica in 1977. After three years in Jamaica he resigned from the field of academic sociology. In 1990 the author graduated from the University of the West Indies, Norman Manley Law School, as an Attorney-at-Law. He is the author of several books and academic papers, all aimed at transforming society through knowledge.

ONE DROP BOOKS

One Drop Books is proud to present *Rastafari—For the Healing of the Nation* by Dennis Forsythe, Ph.D. Along with this important title, One Drop offers a wide selection of other books on Rastafari, Ethiopia, Haile Selassie I, Jamaica and Reggae Music for retail sale.

Send for your free catalog today.

ONE DROP BOOKS

Post Office Box 20392
New York, New York 10017-0004
www.onedropbooks.com